About the Author

Christopher Davies spent twenty years with the *Daily Telegraph* before becoming freelance in 2007. He spent two years visiting Crown Courts in England and Wales listening to various trials. He lives in Bromley (Kent).

To,
Tony

Hope you don't know anyone featured in here!

Enjoy!

E.P.   Nov 2021

You Decide
Guilty or Not Guilty?

Christopher Davies

You Decide
Guilty or Not Guilty?

Olympia Publishers
London

www.olympiapublishers.com
OLYMPIA PAPERBACK EDITION

A CIP catalogue record for this title is
available from the British Library.

ISBN: 978-1-78830-925-7

First Published in 2021

Olympia Publishers
Tallis House
2 Tallis Street
London
EC4Y 0AB

Printed in Great Britain

Dedication

To Eileen and Tim, the best parents anyone could wish for.

Acknowledgements

CROWN COURTS are places of privacy, secrecy and hushed whispers. Barristers want to give nothing away, no one to hear what they may be saying to their clients. The legal walls can have ears.

Yet I found court life friendly, enjoyable, challenging, rewarding and a huge learning curve (not all of it good) with many people, from barristers, court staff, police and prison officers, security — in fact everybody — cooperating in different ways. Without their various types of help and friendship writing *You Decide* would have been far more difficult.

Seeing first-hand how prosecutors, defence advocates and judges operate gave me an insight into a side of life I knew little about initially. I hope much of that has been passed on to you.

Because of the need to protect those who assisted me, many off-the-record, I cannot reveal their full names, but they all know who they are. My thanks to, in alphabetical order with a few nicknames: Ad, Alison, Claudia, DT, Ed, Heather, Hugo, James, JD, John, Josalina, Kerry, Lee, Linda, Mick, Mike, Natalie, Nina, Ola, Robert, Saoirse, Sarge, Stela, Slinger and Tony.

A particular thank you to Steve Clarke — he knows why — and Laura-Louise Delaney for her work with research, transcribing my handwriting and many hours typing.

A special thank you to James Houghton, Kristina Smith and all at Olympia Publishers for deciding to publish the book.

A CROWN COURT trial in England and Wales is nothing like you see in the movies or on television. There, the courtroom action is fast and entertaining. No dull bits because viewers quickly become bored. The actors playing the defendants, claimants, witnesses, barristers and judges are usually familiar faces.

In contrast, those involved in real Crown Court trials are mostly unknown, seen only on their particular legal stage. No Julia Roberts, Richard Gere, Jodie Foster, George Clooney, Robert De Niro or Joe Pesci. Crown Court defendants tend to reside in HMP Belmarsh rather than Beverley Hills.

Inevitably many believe what they watch about the judicial system, particularly in slick American television series, is how it is on the other side of the pond too. Wrong. In Crown Courts in England and Wales you will never see a judge's gavel — in fact, despite public perception they have never been used in criminal courts here. Barristers, who wear wigs and gowns rather than Hugo Boss suits with any grey hair apparently banned, will not interrupt one another by saying "objection" (known as pre-emptory challenges in the USA) and therefore the judge will not reply "overruled" or "sustained." You will never hear "strike that from the record."

A Crown Court judge will never ask the advocates to approach the bench and say: "My chambers — now." Adult defendants do not sit next to their legal team. In England and Wales, they are always in a secure dock with high walls made of thick shatterproof glass to ensure there is no way out. They also have a defence barrister rather than a defense attorney. US courts allow television cameras into courtrooms and criminal trials are often broadcast live which has never happened in England and Wales.

The most anonymous, but in many ways the most important people involved in a Crown Court trial are the twelve jurors who cannot be named and are banned by law from explaining to anybody how they reached their verdict. If they have a question for the judge, it is written down (unsigned) and passed on by the clerk of the court. The only words any member of a jury says as a verdict is announced are by the foreman — "guilty," or "not guilty."

You Decide gives you the chance to consider, on the evidence the jury heard, whether you think the defendant was found guilty or not guilty.

DURING any given day a Crown Court trial can be frustratingly slow, with mind-numbingly tedious legal arguments (which jurors and, therefore, readers of this book are spared) followed by a nail-biting, unpredictable climax with cross-examinations building up to a nerve-tingling finale as barristers go head-to-head with defendants and claimants.

The calm before the legal storm.

You will wonder why some defendants pleaded not guilty when all the evidence against them pointed to a guilty verdict. Perhaps taking the case all the way to court is an act of belated revenge by the accused against the claimant who put them in the dock, a final chance to control the victim. Or perhaps they just think they should roll the dice with a jury. After all, some not guilty gambles can pay off, though for reasons that can never explained by the twelve jurors who reach the verdict.

Crown Court trials can also leave you baffled how the Crown Prosecution Service believed that with the evidence available there would be a realistic chance of a conviction. As Crown Court trials can cost around £12,000 per day that's a lot of money from the public purse.

If the outcome of some chapters is not too difficult to predict, they have been included for this purpose — to make readers aware of how weak the evidence against some defendants can be, yet the case still made it to a Crown Court.

I spent two years visiting different Crown Courts in England and Wales to hear a variety of trials, from actual bodily harm to arson, rape, revenge porn, grievous bodily harm with intent, attempted murder and murder. While a magistrates' court, where the maximum sentence for an offence is twenty-six weeks (or up to twelve months in total for more offences than one) deals with matters such as theft, driving charges and particularly domestic violence, Crown Courts are where some truly evil defendants appear.

Even so, once they plead not guilty, thus giving up a possible one third reduction on their sentence for an early confession, they are entitled to as vigilant a defence as the claimant's prosecution. The legal system in England and Wales is based on the idea that there's a barrister on each side, the jury looks at the case from both angles and makes up its mind on the evidence it hears.

No defendant has to prove their innocence. The burden of proof is on the prosecution to convince the jury of the defendant's guilt, yet there is always a presumption of innocence. The prosecution brings the case and the prosecution has to prove the case. The bar is set high for the Crown which must satisfy the jury it is sure the accused is guilty. Not probably or almost certainly — it has to be sure, otherwise it must acquit.

There is no room for error as the prosecution goes to work.

I HOPE *You Decide* can prepare would-be jurors for the testing and challenging experience ahead, while taking you into the world of the courtroom. You will discover what goes on in a place of which relatively few have inside knowledge and learn some of the intricacies of law and how a Crown Court trial proceeds from start to finish.

Perhaps more than anything, the degree of intimate questioning with sexual cases is likely to shock you as you will read evidence that does not appear in newspapers. Inevitably, the language is explicit and I have reported the evidence as it was heard by the jury. A Crown Court trial is not a place for the faint-hearted, but it is crucial to present a realistic picture of precisely what was heard by the jury as you try to guess the verdict.

If the book contains what you might think is a disproportionate number of rape or sexual assault trials, they account for the majority of cases at many Crown Courts. *You Decide* merely represents this.

Witnesses have to say the actual words used during the incident. The F- or C-words must be repeated in full by claimants if used when making their initial police statement after the incident. There is something surreal about a barrister with a cut glass accent asking a witness: "So, after he called you a fucking cunt, how did you feel?"

A Crown Court deals with facts and trying to predict the outcome of trials is rarely straightforward. You will learn how prosecution and defence barristers cross-examine those in the witness box, searching for a way to discredit them in the interest of their respective clients. They will challenge the accuracy and truthfulness of their evidence, the defence advocate making a claimant feel like they are on trial.

The barristers representing both sides are human lie detectors, experts at forensically checking statements made to the police, usually given soon after the incident, to see if there are any contradictions or differences in what is said in court under cross-examination.

A barrister told me: "I cannot understand why more people don't come and sit in the public gallery of Crown Courts. It's the best free entertainment in the country."

That is true to a certain extent and there can be moments of comedy even in the most serious of scenarios. For instance…

Prosecutor: "Can you describe the car?"

Witness: "Parked."

Or denials such as the guy caught on CCTV at a railway station punching someone sitting next to him in the face. "I was yawning," he said stretching his arms out to illustrate the point that it was not really assault. Oh yes it was.

The worst evidence for denying the theft of a vehicle — maybe the worst denial ever — was, according to the defendant, that whoever actually stole the car had dumped it outside his girlfriend's house where he was staying. An incredible coincidence, the defendant agreed. And total rubbish.

Some defendants make it easy for juries. One, among a gang who broke into a house demanding the elderly couple tell them where the safe was (it was the wrong house) was kind enough to leave his balaclava on the stairs. Police checked it for DNA and to no one's surprise the owner was in the system. Even so, he still pleaded not guilty. He claimed: "I make balaclavas in my spare time. Whoever I sold it to must have been in the house. It had my DNA on it because I made it." Or perhaps, made it all up, which is what the jury decided.

One day, as I was leaving court, a man approached me to ask where Court Six was. "It's closed now," I said. "Oh… do you know the outcome of the Wallace Wright trial?"

"Yes, I do. And you are?"

"His brother."

For reasons I cannot explain I asked him what he thought the verdict was. "Well, guilty — he did it."

"Not guilty," I said and a happy brother clicked his fingers and bid me farewell with: "Brilliant jury." The guy who was shot may not agree.

A defendant accused of murder — and I promise this is true — told the jury he was not guilty as he was not at the scene at the time. So, where was he? "I was driving along and saw a girl on a bridge and her mood concerned me. I stopped and chatted to her. I managed to talk her out of committing suicide. She was so grateful we went to my car and she gave me a blow job."

At which point the judge said: "Enough of this."

One prosecutor had a magnificent upper-class accent which made this even funnier. He said to this witness: "You say, 'I love you LOL' — who is LOL?" When it was explained, he replied: "There is still much about the English language I have to learn."

A court was trying to fix a date for a homeless defendant's trial. His lawyer turned to his client and asked: "Do you have any holidays planned?"

At times Crown Court cross-examinations can be a lesson in pedantry, but one defence barrister took this to a new level. The male claimant said the female defendant put a heated iron on his leg "for two to three seconds." The defence barrister retorted: "I put it to you it was no more than one to two seconds."

One Crown Court advocate inadvertently turned to Shakespeare when addressing the judge during a sentencing. "It is a question of whether you include the charge 2B," and after a pause continued "Or not 2B." That indeed was the question.

A police officer asked someone who had enjoyed one or six too many what his name was.

"Donald Duck."

"What's your name?"

"Mickey Mouse."

"You have one more chance."

"Michelangelo."

The officer was hardly dancing on the ceiling as he arrested the would-be Sistine Chapel painter. The drunk's ID showed his name to be Michael John Angelo.

Defendants should be careful what they Google because whatever they may have deleted can be recovered by the police techno wizards. The guy charged with perjury should not really have Googled: "What happens if I lie in court?" He found out when he was sentenced.

Similarly, the car thief charged with stealing a green Range Rover probably never realised at the time that Googling "how to break into a green Range Rover" would come back to haunt him. Yes, even the colour.

One money-launderer texted his partner in crime: "Delete all messages on your blower." Too late. The message about deleting messages was recovered by the police and read out in court.

A claimant admitted she was not sure the defendant had taken Class A drug, so kept her options open. "He went to the kitchen to snort a line of coke," she said. "Well, I assume it was coke. It went up his nose anyway."

There was a claimant living in a caravan on the front drive of her daughter's house who accused her ex-partner of setting fire to her "home." However, the claimant had got her dates wrong. "The defendant was in custody at the time," said the judge. "Apart from being dead, that seems a pretty good alibi." As good as it gets, really.

The so-called entertainment is a rare break from the reality of realising how cruel, vindictive and unimaginably vicious some people can be, often to those nearest and supposedly dearest to them.

TWELVE random strangers chosen from the electoral register decide the verdict that can change a person's life, a process that has been in place for almost 1,000 years. In England and Wales there is a 35 per cent chance of being called up for jury service and around half of those selected make it to the courtroom.

The jurors' main qualification is that they have lived in Britain for five years since the age of thirteen and are between eighteen and seventy-five. While having a criminal record does not necessarily disqualify you from jury service, it would if you were convicted by a court in the United Kingdom, the Channel Islands or the Isle of Man and sentenced to five years or more in prison.

Many see the jury system as a contradiction, with highly qualified barristers in charge of cross-examinations and judges deciding the law representing the professionals with twelve people who almost certainly have no legal training responsible for the verdict. The jurors will know nothing about the defendants apart from their name and the charge(s) they face, so it is only fair the legal bar is set very high. The jury must be sure the defendant is guilty. It used to be "beyond all reasonable doubt" but some jurors were confused what this meant so, now "sure" is the accepted yardstick. Whatever misgivings there may be of being tried by twelve of your peers, most surveys show that claimants, defendants and even judges are generally positive about the juries deciding the outcome rather than, for example, a single judge.

The average length of a trial is four or five days, though jurors are initially told they will be needed for at least a fortnight. Some trials can take weeks, even months — a time scale that must be experienced to appreciate the pressures involved and the effect it has on jurors' lives. Imagine, for six months, you come home, your partner asks how your day was and you can say little more than "interesting" as jurors are banned from speaking about the trial to anyone who is not on the jury (and then only when all twelve are together). More seriously, some jurors are so traumatised by the evidence they hear, they need counselling.

At court, the jury process starts with the selection of the panel, as it is often called. Sixteen people selected for jury service will make their way from the jury room to the courtroom hoping they will be one of the chosen twelve.

The clerk of the court is constantly shuffling the cards on which the would-be jurors' names are written. These are read out and one by one the twelve selected jurors identify themselves, taking their place in the jury box and repeating the oath holding the holy book of their choice: "I swear by Almighty God that I will give a true verdict according to the evidence" — or affirmation: "I solemnly and sincerely declare and affirm that I will give a true verdict according to the evidence."

A jury could consist of twelve males or twelve females of the same colour (whatever it may be). It might comprise twelve people of the same religion; twelve under the age of thirty or twelve over the age of sixty. The selection process is entirely random.

In 1988 the defence's right to challenge jurors without cause was abolished. The prosecution's right to do so was, however, retained. This means that the prosecution can object to a potential juror without giving any reason, but in essence the use of this right is limited to those cases which involve national security or terrorism.

The jurors would be told the names of the main witnesses in the case for both the prosecution and defence, together with any relevant locations. The purpose of this is to ensure that the jury has no prior knowledge of anyone involved in the trial. If a member of the panel has any connection with the witnesses the judge will usually excuse them and a juror-in-waiting will take their place; hence one of the reasons for an initial panel of more than twelve.

The jury selection process complete, the unlucky four almost-jurors return to the jury room hoping for better luck next time. The judge will instruct the designated dozen that they must not talk about the case with any friends or relatives, or go on the internet to discover details of the defendant or the case. If a juror is found to have breached this order imprisonment is possible.

The jury will be told by the judge: "You must reach a verdict only on the evidence you have heard in court. My job is to decide law and you, the jurors, must follow my directions. The facts are your responsibility. It is your judgement alone that counts.

"The burden of proof is with the prosecution to prove guilt. The defendant does not have to prove anything. How does the Crown succeed? By making you sure, nothing less will do.

"You will reach your verdict by deciding whose evidence is the most accurate, detailed, reliable, credible, consistent, dependable, plausible and believable. You must be fully satisfied of the guilt of the accused person and should not find a verdict against them unless you feel sure."

Of course, there are facts and then there is the truth. For the jurors it will be one of the most important decisions they will make. And being sure of something when you are not present is a tall order for the prosecution. If a defendant is found not guilty, it is not necessarily because the jury did not believe the claimant — simply that the evidence it heard could not make it sure to convict.

The clerk of the court reads out the indictment(s) against the defendant(s) — I have kept it to one, though there could be multiple defendants — sat in the dock. This is the first time the jury knows what the accused is charged with.

The prosecutor outlines details of the case to the jury and the trial is up and running. By the end of the prosecution's opening speech the jury should have a good idea of what the trial is about.

Prosecution witnesses are called first, usually starting with the claimant (no one is a victim until there is a guilty verdict). It is important that the jury hears the witness's account and not one that could be moulded by the cross-examining prosecutor. For this reason, the prosecution cannot lead a claimant through their evidence, asking questions constructed in a way to prompt or suggest the answer the Crown wants.

After the claimant has been cross-examined by the prosecutor — in effect, their barrister who they meet for the first time on the opening day of the trial — the defence advocate challenges the witness's evidence. Their job is to put whatever the defendant has told them to the claimant. It is this cross-examination that can go a long way to influencing the jury's verdict.

The defence will want to demonstrate to the jury that the evidence the claimant gave during the prosecution's cross-examination cannot be relied upon. The barrister for the defendant will be particularly keen to highlight any discrepancies or inconsistencies given by the claimant in their police statement and what was said in court.

After the claimant has completed their evidence, any other prosecution witnesses are cross-examined. When the Crown has finished its case, the defendant and any witnesses for the defence are cross-examined, though defendants are not obliged to say anything at any stage. They very rarely refuse to give evidence in court because the jury needs to hear the defendant's side of the story.

The defence barrister will ask their client what will be considered the easier questions as the defendant puts their case to the jury. The prosecution's cross-examination is to try to make the defendant's evidence unreliable. A familiar exchange you will read is: "You answered 'no comment' to every question at the police station when arrested. Why?"

"I followed the advice of my solicitor."

"Yes, but ultimately it was your decision."

Advice does not have to be taken and it will be difficult for a juror not to wonder why, if the person who has been arrested is as innocent as they claim, they would not want the chance to explain to the police why they did not commit the alleged crime. The emphasis jurors place on what amounts to silence is up to them.

The cross-examination from both sides completed, the Crown then begins its summing-up with the hope of making the jury sure the Crown has proved its case and urges the jury to find the defendant guilty. The defence is the last to be heard and as such the speech by the barrister acting for the accused can be said to have an advantage.

The judge then sums up the main points of the trial and directs the jury on law before it retires to consider the verdict(s).

The jury will be told to select one of its number to act as the foreman (male or female) who will not only deliver the verdict(s) in court, but can chair the discussions in the jury room.

After being sworn in, the court bailiff — the usher — leads the jury to its deliberation room, collecting mobile phones to the horror of many jurors. Once in their room, which has toilet facilities, the jurors are not allowed out. They have to bring their own food; water is provided. The jury is in retirement from 10.00 until 16.00 or thereabouts and is under no pressure of time.

The jury will be told only a unanimous verdict can be received on each count and jurors should put any thoughts of a majority verdict out of their minds unless and until they receive a further direction from the judge.

Usually, this will be if a unanimous verdict has not been reached after a second day's deliberations; then the judge is likely to tell the jury he or she will accept a majority verdict: 11-1 or 10-2. While a majority verdict of 10-2 is acceptable, it means that a different outcome is only one juror's opinion anyway. Fine margins, indeed.

Should a majority verdict prove impossible and there is a hung jury, the Crown Prosecution Service decides whether there will be a retrial with a new jury after consulting the claimant.

If a different jury is unable to agree a verdict following a second trial, the convention is for the prosecution not to seek a third trial and to offer no evidence, which effectively results in a not guilty verdict.

Should a defendant be found not guilty at an initial or even second trial, it is not necessarily because the jury did not believe the claimant. Rather, simply the evidence it heard could not make it sure to convict. It is not so much whether the jury reached the correct (or perceived correct) verdict, but whether its verdict was reasonable in light of the evidence presented by the prosecution and the law.

A not guilty verdict does not mean the claimant was lying, though of course some do. Or the defendant did not commit the crime. Just that the jury has to be sure of the defendant's guilt with the evidence it heard. While Crown Courts are open to the public to ensure transparency, how and why a jury reaches its verdict remains a secret. The Juries Act states: "It is an offence for a person intentionally to disclose information about statements made, opinions expressed, arguments advanced or votes cast by members of a jury in the course of their deliberations in proceedings before a court, or to solicit or obtain such information." This carries a maximum sentence of two years.

It could hardly be more different than in the United States where a television show called *The Jury Speaks* reunites jurors and asks them to vote on their verdict again.

WHAT YOU read in *You Decide* are not scripts written for a TV series or a movie. They are real trials involving real defendants, real claimants, real witnesses, real barristers, real judges and real evidence plus a real jury.

Inevitably, there are real liars. This is how it really is.

But can you correctly guess if those who were accused were found guilty or not guilty? Whether the jury was sure the prosecution had proved its case? Or if the evidence presented by the Crown was insufficient for the jury to be sure the defendant committed the crime and a guilty verdict could be reached?

You decide.

Some names have been changed for legal reasons. All trials covered before the Covid-19 pandemic.

1

NISHITH BATRA: sexual assault on a child under 13

BLOWING A RASPBERRY GAVE JURY FOOD FOR THOUGHT

NISHITH BATRA was tried twice for the offence of sexual assault on a child under thirteen after the original jury could not agree on a majority verdict.

Nishith and Karin, his soon-to-be ex-wife, were clearly a million miles from their original wedding vows. How much of an influence this had on her evidence and particularly what the claimant said was something for the jury to ponder.

When Child D told her Auntie Karin that Uncle Nishith had touched her "mini" it ended with Batra being charged with intentionally sexually assaulting a child under the age of thirteen… touching her in a sexual way.

What had initially appeared a relatively straightforward trial was to have some unexpected twists and turns, giving the jury — or juries, as it transpired — something of a roller-coaster ride as details unfurled.

Child D was ten by the time she gave evidence — a year after the alleged incident — but still too young to take an oath so the judge merely reminded her of the need to tell the truth as she was cross-examined via video link.

THE DEFENCE barrister started by asking Child D about Auntie Karin and Uncle Nishith after the video of her police interview had been shown to the jury.

"Did they have a bit of a falling out when you stayed with them?"

"Can't remember."

"How did she describe him?"

"Horrible and obnoxious."

"You said [in the police interview] he was miserable and grumpy. Was that what Auntie Karin had said about him?"

"Yes."

"A lot of the time Auntie Karin shouted at him."

"Yes."

"Did he shout back?"

"No."

"Do you think Auntie Karin liked Uncle Nishith?"

"No."

"On the day of the alleged incident did they argue?"

"Can't remember."

Child D and Child B, the latter Karin and Nishith's daughter, were in the kitchen with him after dinner.

"He started to massage his daughter."

"Yes, but she said she wasn't interested and went upstairs."

"He began to massage your shoulders."

"Yes. I moved forward, but he pulled me back."

"You asked him to stop and he did."

"Yes."

"You had a shower and went to bed."

"Yes."

"When Nishith came into your bedroom he went to Child B first."

"Yes."

"This woke you up."

"Yes, but only a little bit."

"He came over to your bed and you pretended to be asleep."

"Yes."

"There was a duvet on the bed."

"Yes."

"Up over you."

"Yes."

"You told the police he put his hand under the duvet."

"I can't remember."

"Your eyes were closed throughout all this."

"I think so."

"You opened them at the end when he left."

23

"Yes."

"What happened?"

"He pulled my [pyjama] trousers down and tickled my tummy. I pulled them up again."

"You told the police he put something in your hand. Was that wet as well?"

"No. The only wetness was on my tummy."

"When did you notice that?"

"After he left."

"Why, in your second interview with the police, did you say there was wetness on your mini?"

"Don't know."

"And all that time the duvet was up."

"Yes."

"When you felt the wet on your tummy, was that when his hands were on you?"

"No."

"Was it before or after?"

"Can't remember."

"Do you think it could have been Child U [Karin's eleven-year-old son in the next bedroom] who could have been playing a trick?"

"No."

"You are sure it was Nishith who came in?"

"I don't know, but I'm sure it was him. There was no one else there."

After the alleged incident Child D went to Karin's bedroom across the landing to tell her what had happened.

"What was her reaction?"

"She asked me if I was sure and kept repeating 'are you sure'?"

"Is it possible Nishith blew raspberries on your stomach?"

"It could of…"

IN THE initial trial Karin was cross-examined by the defence via video link. For the second trial she attended court.

"After dinner, what was Nishith doing?"

Karin replied: "Drinking whisky and playing on his phone, the same as usual when he wasn't working. He hardly ever worked and used child benefits to pay the car insurance."

"Is it fair to say you were not happy to be with him?"

"I'd had him thrown out a year ago, but we were trying to make it work. I didn't like his drinking, but I was not unhappy with the marriage overall. Every couple has their ups and downs."

"When you had arguments, I suggest you'd shout and he would say nothing."

"Not at all."

"So he was the aggressor?"

"Yes."

"Was he lazy?"

"Yes. He had to be pushed to do anything, even shower."

"Did you call him miserable and grumpy in front of Child D?"

"Not directly. She may have heard me speaking to my mother."

"Your children both suffer from hyper-mobility."

"They are double-jointed and can bruise easily. It does not require massage, only hot baths."

"I suggest massage was a regular thing."

"Not regular, only when, say, I was applying sun lotion."

When Child D had gone into Karin's bedroom following the alleged incident, Karin said her niece was "petrified... she was shaking... physically shaking."

"Did she say why she had come in?" asked the defence.

"She said she had been woken up and someone had been pulling her trousers. I asked if she had seen who it was and she said she saw a black head."

"Did you ask if it was your son or husband?"

"No. She just said she saw a black head."

The defence asked Karin: "You called the police. Was Child D with you?"

"No. I was outside having a cigarette."

"You told the police you thought it was Nishith who had done it."

"There is no way my son could have done it. He was on medication and was asleep."

"Did the police ask you to stop talking on the phone?"

"Yes. They didn't want me speaking in front of Child D, though I was only repeating what she had said."

NISHITH BATRA, whose first language is Punjabi, denied he was an alcoholic. "I occasionally drink, but I am a minicab driver. I cannot afford to drink and drive," he told the jury.

In his police statement Batra said he had "finished" a bottle of whisky. When asked to explain this more fully to the jury, the defendant said what he had meant was that he'd had a couple of whisky and Cokes and then put the bottle of whisky away because he had finished with it.

The prosecution put it to him: "When you were asked if you'd finished the bottle you said 'yes'."

"I was not asked the question in the way, not directly. I meant I'd finished drinking from the bottle."

"I'm suggesting you're lying."

"Not lying."

Batra claimed massaging was in his culture and he massaged the calves of his daughter and the complainant.

"Did you think it was appropriate to touch her, a nine-year-old girl?"

"She asked me to do it."

"I suggest you just started."

"No. She asked me."

When Batra went to the girls' bedroom he kissed his daughter on the forehead and tucked her up. He went to Child D and kissed her on the forehead.

"I saw nothing wrong in this. I didn't want her to feel left out."

The jury was told he was unsure whether Child D was asleep.

The defence asked: "Why didn't you ask her… whisper it?"

"Don't know."

Before putting the duvet over her Batra blew a raspberry on her tummy.

"Why did you do this?"

"Sometimes people just do things. There was nothing sexual in it. It was only to see whether she was awake. If she laughed then she was not sleeping. I never touched her with my hands."

"Did you put anything in the claimant's hand?"

"No."

"She said you did. She said you moved her hand and put something in it. What do you think she was talking about?"

26

"I never put anything in her hand."

"I suggest you put your penis in her hand."

"I never did. I put her hand back in the bed."

"You pulled her pyjama bottoms down."

"I never touched them."

"What was the wetness on her tummy and mini?"

"No idea."

"She said it trickled down her tummy."

"I have no clue."

"Did you get her hand to masturbate you for a short while?"

"No."

"Are you going to say she had a nightmare and this is what it is all about?"

"No."

"I suggest it was the last night she was staying with you, you'd been drinking alcohol and it was all planned."

"No."

"All for sexual gratification."

"No."

When the police arrived at the house, they took swabs from Child D's hand and stomach area, but no male DNA was found. There were no traces of semen on her pyjama bottoms or top.

IN ITS summing up, the prosecution said: "Nishith Batra went into the bedroom and touched her [the claimant]. He thought he could get away with it because she was asleep, but she wasn't.

"Child D's vocabulary is less developed, but because she is a child it does not mean she is any less trustworthy. She was consistent and credible and you can rely on her as factual and truthful. She knew what was going on was wrong which was why she pretended to be asleep.

"The defence says her account was tainted and corrupted, that Karin put words into her niece's mouth. Why would she want the shame on the family if it was not true? Karin wanted out of the marriage, but where is the evidence to show, she would go to such lengths to get Nishith out of the house? She just repeated the evidence her niece gave her.

"Why did he blow a raspberry on her tummy? To make the child laugh? Fun? It was suggested that was what made her tummy wet. How much spittle would it take to make her tummy and mini as wet as she described?"

THE DEFENCE highlighted the lack of any male DNA on the claimant to the jury. "If his penis had been in her hand and if the wet came from Nishith Batra why was no DNA found? You might find it extraordinary.

"There was no suggestion from the police the defendant was suffering from the effect of drink or was hungover. I am not suggesting Karin deliberately told the claimant what to say, but it is important to realise the context in which the allegation was made. When the claimant went to her auntie, she never said the name 'Nishith', only that she saw a black head. By the time [after the incident] the police were called it was Nishith even though Child D had never said this.

"We don't know what was said between Karin and her niece. When the police arrived, Karin was blabbing on the phone to someone and the claimant heard all this. Can you be sure these inferences did not come into play?"

THE JUDGE told the jury the defendant was a man of good character, without a caution or conviction. "That in itself does not provide a defence against a criminal act, but it is evidence you must take in when considering your verdict. A person of good character may mean he is less likely to commit an offence. It is for you to decide how much weight you put on this."

1

NISHITH BATRA: sexual assault on a child under 13

THE JURY was unaware this was in fact the third trial of Nishith Batra for the same charge. It knew the original jury had been unable to reach a majority verdict. What it did not know was that during a second trial the judge had dismissed the jury after Karin had told the jury: "He was accused of something similar six years ago. No charges were ever brought and I never believed it."

Crown Court judges instruct jurors not to use social media to find anything about the defendant as nothing should prejudice their verdict and this, the defence argued, would have the same effect.

The judge told the jury that hearing about the previous sexual accusation, while unfounded, would have a prejudicial effect. He said: "Nothing I say could eliminate the prejudicial effect and ensure a fair trial. I do not think any direction I give you would be able to put this out of your minds and not play a role in your decision-making."

During the aborted trial Karin had said she was so afraid to even be in the same building as her husband with fears of reprisals from his family, she wanted to give evidence via a video link rather than in court, even behind screens. The judge ruled that her evidence would be diminished by fear if she was in court so he granted the application for a video link. In the final trial Karin was in court and gave evidence to the jury in person.

Just about the only thing Karin and Nishith had in common was their opinion of each other.

The jury had to decide whether to believe the Crown's case that Batra intentionally touched Child D sexually… whether events happened as the claimant said or if her evidence was not credible then what happened was harmless fun.

We shall never know in which way the second jury's verdict would have gone, but the impression was to any 12 reasonable people Child D's evidence would have been barely credible — no fault of her own given her tender years — while Batra's wife clearly had an agenda against him, which is putting it mildly.

The prosecution was left with the task of putting a third trial together in a belated hope of proving the case against Batra. Four months after the aborted trial, the defendant was back in court for a third time. Following one hung jury and one dismissed jury it was third time lucky for the Crown as Batra was found guilty.

I was staggered at the jury's decision. Had I been able to bet on the verdict I would be sleeping on a park bench as I would have put my house on an acquittal. I could see no reason how the jury was sure Batra was guilty of the charge. In fact, I was amazed the initial jury could not reach a not guilty verdict. Or even that the Crown Prosecution Service believed the case against the defendant was strong enough to have a good chance of a conviction.

Yes, Batra was ill advised to blow a raspberry on his niece's stomach, but that was not what he was on trial for.

The case against Batra was based on the uncertain evidence of a nine-year-old and a wife who had a very large axe to grind. The lack of any DNA evidence was a serious weakness against a man of good character. Without that I saw no way the defendant could be found guilty.

Despite no DNA evidence, the jury still believed Batra had masturbated with a little assistance from his niece's hand and then ejaculated on her stomach. Remember, his daughter was also in the bedroom which should make any impropriety far less likely.

Presumably, the jury did not consider the lack of semen relevant when reaching its guilty verdict, believing the rather less than convincing evidence of a young girl and a woman who had to be reminded by the judge how to behave in the public gallery when she had completed giving evidence.

THE TRIAL underlined the need for those who do not have English as their first language to use an interpreter. Nishith Batra had been in England for 20 years, but his misunderstanding over "finishing drink" highlighted the small margins that can be pounced upon in a Crown

Court. A word or phrase that the jury can misinterpret can be crucial; the other advantage is that using a translator gives a witness extra thinking time.

However convoluted Batra's English may have been, I will never know how the jury's deliberations ended with a belated guilty verdict and I am certain an innocent man was sent to jail for four years, a term at the lower range for an offence which carries a maximum of fourteen years.

2

BERRICK DEVEAUX: Two counts of attempted murder; one count of possession of a firearm with intent to endanger life; two counts of possession of a prohibited weapon

DUANE PETERSON: Two counts of attempted murder

JUST 'LARKING ABOUT' WITH A SHOTGUN

GANG WARFARE is alive and kicking, not to mention thumping, stabbing and shooting in south-east London.

The TN1 (Trust No One) and the GAS (Guns And Shanks) gangs are sworn enemies. Revenge attacks are rife and a way of life, occasionally death, with innocent members of the public paying a heavy price for being in the wrong place at the wrong time.

In July 2010, a fifteen-year-old who cannot be named for legal reasons was stabbed to death by members of the GAS gang as part of a revenge ambush. A month earlier a member of the GAS gang had been stabbed by TN1 and the teenager was present during the stabbing.

As he came out of school, the teenager was chased by members of the GAS gang — Kyle Kinghorn, eighteen, and four others, including a sixteen-year-old getaway driver.

The fifteen-year-old was stabbed in the heart, neck and buttock by the GAS gang members. It was considered a joint-enterprise, regardless of who administered the fatal blow and the infamous five received a combined jail time of seventy-six years. Also stabbed, though sustaining only superficial wounds, was Child P, aged fourteen at the time, who became a member of TN1 soon after the incident. His scar was considered a badge of honour in gangland.

This is the shadow under which law-abiding people have to live on the mean streets of Brixton and Stockwell. Meanwhile, gang affiliation is mandatory among those involved in unlawful activity — there are no neutrals if you are part of the power struggle in south-east London.

When Berrick Deveaux was seventeen, he and Duane Peterson were accused of two counts of attempted murder. Deveaux was further accused of one count of possession of a firearm [a revolver] with intent to endanger life and two counts of possession of a prohibited weapon [a sawn-off shotgun].

There were no witnesses to either shooting, no conclusive CCTV evidence. The prosecution hoped it had enough circumstantial evidence to prove the charges.

POLICE were called following reports of a teenager having been shot in Brixton. He was not involved with any gang and was an innocent bystander who proved to be the wrong target. The seventeen-year-old was blinded as pellets from the sawn-off shotgun splattered into his face.

Berrick Deveaux was arrested in connection with the incident three days later. Police searched his home and recovered a loaded revolver and a sawn-off shotgun.

The prosecution alleged that Deveaux and Duane Peterson drove to the scene on a silver moped — CCTV did not identify the number plates — both wearing helmets. The judge told the jury in such circumstances it did not matter which pulled the trigger, both would be equally guilty.

A second incident saw two males drive up on a silver moped and shoot George Green, whose injuries were serious, but not life-threatening. He was shot in the face which resulted in him being blinded in one eye.

CCTV showed the route of two males on a silver moped, but its number plate could not be identified.

A witness for the first shooting, who cannot be named, said: "I saw two guys on a bike pull up. They were black, wearing helmets. The passenger pulled a shotgun out of a JD Sports bag which was on his back. When I saw the gun, I ran off."

Three weeks later Deveaux was stopped in the car he was driving. Police found two motorbike helmets and gloves in the boot. Deveaux was the registered owner of the vehicle while he also owned a silver moped.

Deveaux claimed his TN1 seniors had ordered him to look after a revolver and shotgun. As a younger member of the TN1 gang, he was called a "tiny" and claimed senior members would ask [i.e., tell] him to store drugs or firearms. He put the revolver in his father's house and the shotgun at his mother's.

"I couldn't say no. My mum was cleaning my room and she found it [the shotgun]," said Deveaux. "She phoned my dad and he took it. He wasn't happy and told me I could get seven years for this."

Deveaux's fingerprints were found on the shotgun, but he claimed this was because he was "just larking about with it" as he danced to a rap video. Gunshot residue was found on one of the gloves in Deveaux's car.

Both Deveaux and Peterson had alibis for the incidents, claiming they were with friends nearby at the times of the attempted murders.

Mobile tracking data can prove where a mobile phone that is switched on was used at the start and finish of a journey, but not in the middle. An expert told the court that data from the phone network provider of Deveaux's mobile showed that there was evidence "consistent with" the phone being in the area of the two incidents, but not conclusive.

Was there enough circumstantial evidence to convict the pair? Was it too much of a coincidence that Deveaux owned a silver moped, identified as the type used by the gunmen seen very close to the shootings? How credible was the mobile tracking data that put Deveaux "in the area" of the two shootings? Was Deveaux's alibi about the firearm and sawn-off shotgun credible?

You decide whether you think the defendants were found guilty of any or all of the charges... or none.

2

BERRICK DEVEAUX: Two counts of attempted murder; one count of possession of a firearm with intent to endanger life; two counts of possession of a prohibited weapon

DUANE PETERSON: Two counts of attempted murder

THE POLICE hoped it had enough circumstantial evidence, also known as indirect evidence, to secure guilty verdicts against the defendants.

Circumstantial evidence relates to a series of facts other than the particular fact sought to be proved. The party offering circumstantial evidence argues that this series of facts, by reason and experience, is so closely associated with the fact to be proved that the fact to be proved may be inferred simply from the existence of the circumstantial evidence (that is the legal explanation — not mine). On this occasion it was not enough to completely convince the jury which had deliberated for five and a half days before returning with its verdicts.

It found Berrick Deveaux and Duane Peterson not guilty of attempted murder. Deveaux was found guilty of one count of possession of a firearm with intent to endanger life, namely a revolver; and two counts of possession of a prohibited weapon, namely a sawn-off shotgun.

A combination of disappointment and relief greeted the jury foreman's announcement of the not guilty verdicts for the attempted murder charges. The police, who had worked on the case for two years, had been confident that there was sufficient circumstantial evidence to convict and were naturally frustrated the most serious charges had not been proved.

Peterson left court with his family to celebrate, phoning a friend to tell them: "I got off."

Which, of course, is very different from being found not guilty.

For Deveaux it was a mixture of good news and bad news. The good news — for him — was that he was found not guilty of attempted murder; the bad news was that he was sentenced to eight years for possession of a firearm with intent to endanger life and two counts of possession of a prohibited weapon.

While there were no witnesses to either shooting, listening to the cross-examinations I shared the police view that the Crown had enough circumstantial evidence to prove the attempted murder charges.

Perhaps the crucial point for the jury was that the mobile phone data did not conclusively show the pair were at the scenes of the crimes, only "probably" which is not sufficient to return a guilty verdict where the threshold is "sure".

The suspicion was that in football terms Peterson definitely had a result. Deveaux would serve four years before he was eligible for parole.

However, the seventeen-year-old shot in error has a life sentence of blindness.

STATISTICS show convicted defendants are more likely to re-offend than not. Prison sentences are not a deterrent for most of those found guilty in a Crown Court of a serious offence to stay on the straight and narrow. Almost half of all prisoners re-offend within a year of release and this cycle costs up to £13 billion a year from the public purse.

Around 90 per cent of those sentenced in England and Wales have offended before and almost a half had committed or were linked to fifteen or more crimes.

3

JASON PHILLIPS: possession of a mobile phone in prison

WAS INMATE THREATENED TO TAKE CELL PHONE?

JASON PHILLIPS was sharing a prison cell with two other inmates. Suddenly the Dedicated Search Team came in, acting on intelligence: there was a mobile phone within.

The prisoners were searched and a mobile phone was found on Phillips. Section 40D (3A) of the Prison Act 1952 makes possession, without authorisation, of a device capable of transmitting or receiving images, sounds or information by electronic communications (including a mobile telephone) inside a prison an offence.

However, Phillips pleaded not guilty on grounds of duress. The jury had to decide whether or not the defendant was compelled to act as he did because, on the basis of the circumstances as he honestly believed them to be, he thought his life was in immediate danger.

BRIAN PYE of the Dedicated Search Team was cross-examined by the prosecution about the incident which had taken 11 months to come to court.

"You were acting on intelligence."

"Yes, for a particular cell. It was an intelligence-led search because there could be something they [the prisoners] should not have."

"What did you do?"

"We went to the cell, opened the door and told the prisoners to show us their hands."

"How many of you were there?"

"Usually, five or six initially. Then, after risk assessment, in this instance two of us."

"How many were in the cell?"

"Two or three. I cannot remember exactly."

"What did you do?"

"The search went ahead. The defendant was fully compliant throughout."

"How did you search him?"

"His mouth, his ears, he took his top off and the top of his body was searched. Then he took off his bottoms and boxer shorts. Inside the shorts was a mobile phone."

"Did he say anything?"

"No."

"You?"

"No. They were put in a holding cell while their cell was searched."

"Anything else found?"

"No."

"It was a small mobile phone."

"Yes. They are very popular, easy to hide or secrete."

"Did the prisoners know about the search?"

"No."

THE JURY was told the agreed facts between the prosecution and defence. Jonathan N'Gogo was a cell mate. No data was found on the phone linking it to either Jason Phillips or N'Gogo. The latter said he did not wish to make a statement when asked. N'Gogo is 6ft 5ins tall.

JASON PHILLIPS was cross-examined by the defence.

"How come you were in possession of the phone?"

"I was forced to hold it by Mr N'Gogo."

"How?"

"He made threats on my well-being. That if I didn't [hide it] I'd be hurt."

"Did you know him?"

"I knew him from previous prisons. I get shipped around a lot."

"Describe him."

"He's a giant. He has to bow his head when he comes in the cell. I had one option — to do what he said."

"When did he threaten you?"

"Just before the search."

"How real were the threats?"

"People die every day in prison, there's a lot of violence. They make weapons out of razor blades. Even ice picks, you know."

"Did he have a weapon?"

"Not sure, but I just complied."

"Why did you not tell a prison officer?"

"It's not something you do. You don't tell on people."

"Had you used the phone?"

"No."

"Did you tell anyone afterwards what happened?"

"There were three of us in the cell. We keep information from the officers, but everyone on the wing knows what's going on."

"Who was the other prisoner?"

"Christopher Todd. He'd had hold of it [the phone] as well. Just happened this day it was me."

"Why is Mr Todd not here?"

"He broke his back and is in a wheelchair. His doctor advised against it."

"If you had told someone immediately this would not have happened."

"If I hadn't [taken it] he [N'Gogo] would have attacked me and I'd have to defend myself. I didn't know he was going to put it on me."

THE PROSECUTION cross-examined Jason Phillips about the threats Jonathan N'Gogo made.

Phillips said: "He said there would be consequences. That I would feel pain. He would hurt me. I'm not an angel, but he is massive. A regular participant in the gym. You have no idea what might happen in this place when you are asleep. Boiling water and worse. Prison is a very violent place."

"You could have told an officer and been moved to another cell."

"If I'm moved and he gets done… he's not stupid… two plus two equals four."

"Solitary confinement?"

"Stuck 24 hours a day deep in some dungeon? No one wants that."

"The fact is he did not make any threats."

"He did."

"He has not assaulted you before."

"Is that a question?"

"Has he assaulted you before?"

"No."

"You can look after yourself."

"He's a giant."

"I suggest you were never threatened."

"Sorry. You asking?"

"Yes."

"I was."

"He never put you under duress."

"I was."

IN ITS summing up, the prosecution told the jury: "Mr Phillips gives evidence to say about threats. Yet there is no evidence of any problems with Mr N'Gogo before and we saw no evidence or clues today."

The defence countered: "You must be sure Mr Phillips was not under duress. The reality is that in prison if you tell on another person you can end up in hospital. This depends on whether you think what Mr Phillips said was a pack of lies."

THE JUDGE reminded the jury that the burden of proof lies with the prosecution. Duress arises if the defendant has been induced to do something because he reasonably felt for his safety… sustaining serious injury. Could the defendant have had no choice? How would an ordinary person react?

The jury went away to deliberate about the illegal cell phone and whether the defendant was justified in being in possession of it.

3

JASON PHILLIPS: possession of a mobile phone in prison

THE JURY did not know that Jason Phillips was serving an 18-year stretch for aggravated burglary. While Jonathan N'Gogo may have been "a giant" the defendant was capable of looking after himself. He was not a shy retiring rose.

Whether knowledge of the offence and for how long Phillips was in jail for would have had any bearing on the jury's verdict we shall never know, but it was understandable — just — it could not be sure the defendant was not acting under duress.

Around 15,000 mobile phones and SIM cards were recovered in prisons in England and Wales in 2019. However, where there is a will, there is always a way with mobile phones in prisons.

The offence carries a maximum sentence of two years and it is likely, had Phillips been found guilty, that any custodial period would have run concurrently with his existing term rather than consecutively. The main effect would have been on the subsequent parole board hearing which decides whether a defendant is eligible to be released on licence.

What does not help the detection of illegal phones is that they are now - legally - manufactured in all plastic with no metal and are smaller than a credit card. Some even have inbuilt tasers.

4

DONNIE DiMARCO: Possession of a firearm and ammunition with intent

A LOADED GUN, BUT WHAT DID DEFENDANT INTEND?

WHEN the police stopped Donnie DiMarco's car they found he was in possession of a revolver and ammunition. He had a British Bulldog with five modified cartridges. A forensic scientist told the jury two could cause "serious" injury and a third was capable of a "trivial" injury. The other cartridges were damaged.

DiMarco pleaded guilty to possessing a firearm and ammunition without a firearms certificate, but denied intent to endanger life.

When the defendant was interviewed by the police he answered "no comment" to every question, as is his right. He declined to be cross-examined in court which, while also his right, leaves many questions unanswered for the jury. What does a defendant who refuses to give evidence have to hide?

However, maybe early opinion was misplaced. DNA analysis of the firearm found on DiMarco showed evidence of at least four people, but none attributable to the defendant. A forensic scientist told the jury: "The absence of his DNA may be because he had no direct contact, though he could have handled it. Scientific findings do not indicate whether he had contact with the gun."

So, was DiMarco effectively in possession of a firearm, where there was no conclusive proof he had handled it?

DC JAMES KING of Trident, which specialises in gang crime, told the jury when Donnie DiMarco was stopped and searched the gun and ammunition were found in a safe bag by ballistics.

"The gun was wrapped in a yellow duster," the prosecution put to

DC King.

"Yes."

"The gun was loaded."

"Yes."

THE DEFENCE continued the cross-examination of DC King: "Prior to the car being stopped were there any reports of a commotion?"

"Not that I was aware of."

"No threats."

"No."

"The first time you came in contact [with the defendant] was in the car."

"Yes."

"There were two women in the car, too."

"Yes."

"They were arrested."

"Yes."

"Same charges?"

"Yes."

"All three were taken to a police station."

"Yes."

"The defendant was charged and the other two released without action."

"Yes."

"The defendant had three mobile phones. Were they examined?"

"Yes."

"No evidence of threats was found."

"Correct."

AS THE defendant chose not to be cross-examined, it was left to the Crown to sum up its case because, in effect, that was the end of the prosecution's evidence. The prosecutor said: "The Crown's case is that a gun was found in the defendant's trousers. We say he had it ready to use. Even if he had hidden it under a bed at home, it would still have been ready to use. He has not given evidence. It is up to the jury to decide whether the case deserved an explanation. Then ask yourselves, what is he concerned about? Who gave the gun to him? Where was he going with it?

"It would have been much safer if the ammunition was carried separately. We say his answers would not stand up to cross-examination. What sort of intention could there have been other than endangering life?"

The jury was made aware that Donnie DiMarco had two previous convictions: he was found guilty of affray in 2014 and he had pleaded guilty to GBH in 2016 when a 20-year-old male was stabbed four times, though the defendant "only" punched the victim.

THE DEFENCE told the jury: "You know he has committed a criminal offence — it's easy to say he must be guilty of everything. Everyone is innocent until proven guilty so your starting point must be he did not have the intention of endangering life. Has the Crown shown anything above possession? The Crown says he knew what he had in his possession. If he knew what he had could not endanger lives, how could he have endangered life? There is nothing more to show than simple possession."

THE JUDGE told the jury it must "decide what inferences you draw on hearing no evidence from the defendant." He continued: "Do not speculate or guess. You must decide what his intention was of being in possession of a gun and ammunition. The Crown says he intended to endanger lives. What was in his mind?"

The judge concluded: "You cannot use his bad character as a propensity of being in possession of a firearm with intent. His previous convictions relate to different reprehensible behaviour."

It was a straightforward yes-or-no decision for the jury: did the defendant intend to endanger life with the "loaded" gun? Or was he, perhaps, delivering it to somebody else? How significant was the lack of DNA evidence linking the defendant directly to the firearm?

4

DONNIE DiMARCO: Possession of a firearm and ammunition with intent

THE JUDGE had told the jury to decide "what was in his mind" when Donnie DiMarco was stopped by the police and found to have a revolver and modified ammunition in his trousers.

In reality, it is impossible to guess precisely what anyone plans to do, but it was no surprise when it took the jury just one hour to conclude DiMarco's intention was, despite his denial, to endanger life. If you are in possession of a loaded gun, even without real bullets, what else could a person reasonably be intending to do?

It like saying he had a toothbrush with toothpaste on it, but he did not intend to clean his teeth.

Refusing to answer any questions during his police interview and not taking to the witness box to be cross-examined was damaging to the defendant's credibility which did not start from a particularly high point. While choosing to be silent is a legal right, it will hardly work in the defendant's favour with the jury. DiMarco's previous convictions, albeit not for firearms offences, showed a propensity towards violence. With this in mind, being caught with a revolver and ammunition appeared to make the jury's deliberations easy and unsurprisingly the defendant was found guilty.

WHEN Donnie DiMarco was due to be sentenced for the firearm offence after probation reports, a very different — horrifying — picture emerged of a five-handed attack on a person in which the defendant was involved.

DiMarco was one of five involved in a sustained attack on Kevin Kennedy who was punched, kicked and stabbed in a pre-planned attack. The five in the dock for the sentencing looked a motley crew and were

45

warned by the judge about their smirking and aggressive body language.

The defence barristers set about their task of trying to ensure the most lenient sentences for their clients, but in many ways King Canute had an easier job.

Tyrone Martindale, 19, was "in a relationship" and the couple were "expecting their first child next month." Anthony Brown, 20, was "a caring father" according to his barrister. "It is heart-breaking that his daughter will have to be taken to prison to see him and he will miss her formative years," his advocate told the judge.

It was surely far more heart-breaking that an innocent man should have suffered from a premeditated attack which included the so-called caring father and the father-to-be. Perhaps the pair of perps should have thought of their families before inflicting grievous bodily harm on Kennedy.

On the night in question two defendants — Brown and Martindale — arrived on foot. The other three were in a car and the early arrivals' job was to keep the victim until the knife-men arrived. Kennedy sustained multiple injuries including a 4cm stab wound to his ribs, a fractured rib, cuts to his hands and fingers so bad that seven months later he could not move them normally. He had been unable to work since the attack and suffered from flashbacks.

Two years previously Brown was in a car when it was struck by the victim's vehicle. "Goodness knows how long a grudge you would hold if someone did something serious to you," said the judge.

He had been convicted of a previous similar assault so vicious that Brown's accomplice jumped from a first-floor window to get away. "You were one of the knife-men in the attack [on Kennedy]," said the judge. "You pass the dangerousness test and the public must be protected from you."

He was sentenced to 13 years for GBH with intent. "You will serve at least two-thirds of your sentence in custody when the Parole Board will decide if it is safe for you to be released," said the judge. "You will be on licence for three years extra." The three-year sentence for possession of a bladed object would run concurrently.

In 2013, when he was 16, Martindale was found guilty of being in possession of a bladed object. On two separate occasions he was convicted of being in possession of Class A drugs with intent to supply. Martindale had written a letter to the judge saying Kennedy had lied about him, which did not impress Her Honour who said: "You played a significant role and you kicked and punched the victim while he was being stabbed." Martindale was sentenced to 12 years and had to serve at least of half of this before being eligible for release.

Jason Hewie was the driver on the night. "You said you did not know him so what was in it for you?" said the judge. Hewie was found guilty of his first offence when he was 13, though he was only 12 at the time of the robbery being committed. He had three separate offences of possession of a bladed object including a 15-inch bread knife. There were also offences of possession of cannabis and two of possessing Class A drugs with an intent to supply.

When he was arrested for the last offence Hewie swallowed 13.48g of crack cocaine. He collapsed and was taken to hospital by police. Probation reports on Hewie had been encouraging and the judge said: "You are intelligent, but the two sides of your personality are hard to reconcile." Hewie was sentenced to a total of seven years and nine months for GBH and the last drugs offence.

Mohammad Wahibi had conspired with Hewie to supply Class A drugs. He was 17 when found guilty of the drugs offence and GBH though delays in the joint-sentencing meant he was 18 when he appeared with his four partners in crime. Sentencing guidelines are different for a 17-year-old and the judge decided the delay was not Wahibi's fault so he was given a lighter sentence plus a discount for a guilty plea to the drugs offence. Wahibi was sentenced to a total of 27 months.

Last, but by no means least, Donnie DiMarco was jailed for 12 years for possessing a firearm, 10 years for possessing ammunition and five years for possessing the prohibited weapon [knife]. All these sentences will run concurrently.

A sentence of three years and three months' imprisonment, to be served consecutively, was imposed in relation to the charge of GBH with intent — a total of 15 years and three months.

5

PATRICK O'MALLEY: Indecent assault of a child under 13; gross indecency; rape

HOLLYOAKS PROMPTED RAPE ALLEGATION

PATRICK O'MALLEY sat expressionless in the dock as the accusations against him were read out. There were eight counts of sexual charges involving his stepdaughter from the age of four or five to 12. The indictments included: indecent assault on a child under the age of 13, occasioning putting his hand down her knickers; gross indecency, occasioning making her hold and stroke his penis; the rape of a child under 13, penetrating her vagina with his penis and the rape of a child under 13, penetrating her mouth with his penis.

Outlining the case, the prosecution told the jury Miss L went to the police with the allegations when she was 16. Though hesitant, she was taken to a private room by a female police officer who described the claimant as "shaken and visibly upset" but feeling she needed to tell the police what had happened.

The Crown said: "Having plucked up the courage, she said that when she was four or five years old, after her mother left the house, the defendant would touch her vagina, grab her hand, wrap it round his penis and masturbate him by moving it up and down.

"It got worse as she got older. The substance and nature of the abuse would escalate. He vaginally raped her, made her perform oral sex on him and he performed oral sex on her. He would ejaculate on her vagina rather than inside.

"He gave her money, he gave her sweets, which she began to understand was money for her to keep quiet. When she was 10 she began to understand that what was happening was wrong and she wanted to tell someone, but feared nobody would believe her."

When the allegations came to light O'Malley was arrested and interviewed by the police on two occasions, "Suffice to say he denied them [the allegations] all." The Crown said there was no forensic evidence because of the time of the attacks which was long before the complainant went to the police.

"There were no witnesses, but there hardly ever is in cases of sexual abuse. The defence will say because she was not getting her own way, she was blackmailing her mother and [step]father and this is her payback, her revenge. That she was a troubled teenager, badly behaved making wild accusations.

"Or were her behavioural issues and anger the result of the sexual abuse she experienced? Either the account she gave to the police is fantastic lies, wicked lies or, and I just want to you ask yourselves — is she a consummate liar, is she an accomplished actress?

"In fact, is the truth really much more straightforward? Who is telling the truth and who is not?"

THE JURY was shown a video of Miss L's police interview.

She was asked: "Tell us in your own words what happened."

"When I was a lot younger, my stepdad started off touching my mini and making me touch him. It got to a point when I was older, he would rape me and make me perform oral sex on him. I was quite young. It was a secret I didn't want to keep to myself any more. I wanted help.

"My cousin got raped by her stepdad. It came out last year, but I didn't want anyone to think I was just copying her."

The family lived in a three-bedroom semi-detached house with her mother, her sister, a half-brother and half-sister [by O'Malley]. Miss L was six when O'Malley married Kathy. Miss L and her sister have had no contact with their respective biological fathers.

"When was the first time he touched you?"

"In the flat [before they moved to the house]. He would just touch me in my private parts and make me touch him, sort of thing."

"Explain to me what would happen after he touched you."

"He portrayed to mum that he was perfectly normal, but when we were alone, he would touch us. It was not full-on rape until I was eight or nine."

"You said touch 'us'."

"I don't know 100 per cent if he touched my sister, but I'm sure he did. He thought it was all right."

"So what would he do?"

"I'd sit with him and he would slide his hand inside my knickers, only if we were alone. He would touch me inappropriately. He would touch me, not finger me, just touch me. I didn't know if it was right or wrong. I'd never had a dad before that. I didn't know if it happened to everyone or just me. I didn't know any different. It could have happened to everyone and was normal. It happened on a daily basis, whenever he had the chance. When mum was out it was his perfect opportunity."

"Did you tell anyone?"

"We were not like a close family. My sister had another dad. We didn't talk like a normal family or eat at the same time. When I think of a normal family I think of mum, dad, children and they're happy. We were different to everyone. I used to play with dolls and imagined they were my family. I imagined they were my mum and dad, brothers and sisters, and we were happy and we all went out. My childhood was ripped out. I never had the childhood of a normal kid. I became very independent. I can't even understand it myself, so I can't expect anyone else to understand it. Then mum got cancer [when Miss L was 12] and it stopped."

"Did he get you to touch him?"

"He would take my hand and put it down his trousers. He'd put it round his penis and hold my hand, guiding my hand up and down. At this stage it was just touching, he'd touch me and I'd touch him."

"Do you know the word?"

"We'd call it tossing off."

"Any other names, maybe you heard at school?"

"I heard on telly, a hand job."

"You mentioned when you were older."

"Sometimes it was the same stuff, but he also thought it was OK to have sexual intercourse with me. He'd pull my trousers off, get on top of me and rape me. Sometimes he'd say, 'you like it, you're enjoying it.' I can't remember how old I was... eight, maybe nine."

"When did this happen?"

50

"It would just happen any time he was alone with me, any time he could. I remember being in a lot of pain, crying cos it really hurt. I didn't really understand what was going on. When I was 10, maybe a bit older, I realised what was going on. I wanted to tell someone, but was scared and didn't know how to put it into words. I used to have dreams that I'd tell people and they'd believe me."

"When did it stop?"

"It stopped when I was in year seven, when I was 12 or 13."

"What is sexual intercourse?"

"Like, when someone's penis enters someone's vagina and at the end he ejaculates."

"What do you remember?"

"He would just kiss me, I'd kiss him. He'd be on top of me and breathe quite heavily. Other times I'd be on my side and he'd say 'you like it.' Stuff like that. His breathing was very heavy and I remember his bad breath cos he smoked. Sometimes he gave me money for sweets, to keep me quiet, I guess. I knew it was wrong, but did not know how to stop it. I was really scared."

"Did he ejaculate?"

"I remember on more than one occasion and his sperm would be in my knickers."

"How did it get there?"

"He used to, like, when he had cum his sperm… ejaculate… I cannot remember him ejaculating inside me, only on me if that makes sense. His sperm would be on my vagina, not in it. When I went to the toilet it'd be in my knickers."

"Why didn't you tell anyone?"

"I thought I'd be made out to be a liar. I wanted someone to listen, but it was hard, like. I didn't know what to say. I didn't want to think about it cos it weren't normal. It held me back a lot in life, it made me angry. I'd scream in someone's face and make threats so they'd feel as I did. I did it so they would understand how it hurt me… how I felt. It was, like, my way of telling them. I thought about telling someone, but everyone would think, like, he's taken on two other children. Yeah, he did that and portrayed he was normal, all happy. This stopped me cos no one would believe me. I thought my mum would hate me cos I wasn't his flesh and blood."

"Why report it all now?"

"I needed to move on with my life, go to college, to end the confusion. He ripped my childhood away and I can never get that back. I thought once I told someone this pain and worry would go away and I'd feel half-normal. The hardest thing was mum didn't believe me. I wanted her to give me a hug and hear her tell me she was there for me. It makes me sick she thinks I could lie about something like this. When she said I was lying, my heart dropped into my stomach. If she didn't believe me, how could I expect anyone else to? I felt like a dirty prostitute. I felt broken. It was like, you're supposed to be my mum and you don't believe me. It's literally his word against mine and my own mum don't believe me."

The police officer, needing more details of the assaults, took Miss L back to the allegations about oral sex.

"It happened once, maybe twice. He would grab my head and, like, put his penis in my mouth and move my head for me. It wasn't as regular as everything else. I remember just feeling scared because I didn't know what was going on. At that age I didn't even know it was possible. It all made me feel so sick, so ashamed. I felt like a dirty tramp. When I think back, it's the reason why I am like I am. I do not know how to show I love someone or hate them properly. I get confused. Then there were days I remember feeling his stubble on my private parts. I was on his bed and was lying on my back. I felt his tongue and stubble on my private parts."

"Did he ever wear protection?"

"A condom? No, he didn't."

Miss L said she was motivated to go to the police after seeing an episode of Hollyoaks where a character had nearly been raped.

The police officer ended by asking: "What you've said today is the truth?"

"One hundred per cent the truth."

IN COURT Miss L gave evidence from behind screens, as is usual in sexual assault cases, hidden from the public gallery and the defendant.

The defence said: "Mr O'Malley's case is that he never touched you sexually at all."

"No."

"He has done his best to love and care for you."

"No."

"The accusations are lies."

"No."

"You were unhappy at home when you made the allegations."

"I've been unhappy for a time."

"You had a particularly difficult relationship with your mother."

"Not always very well."

"In your police interview you said it started when you were four."

"It started when I was young."

"Sex started when you were eight or nine."

"About that."

"Did Mr O'Malley say 'not to tell anyone'?"

"Not too sure."

"You don't remember him saying 'don't tell'?"

"No."

"You said he put his penis inside you and you did not understand what it was all about. Was there any blood?"

"I can't be too sure."

"Any reason why you didn't tell mum or a teacher you didn't like what daddy is doing?"

"I didn't have a close relationship with mum."

"Your cousin, who's roughly the same age as you, told you she'd been raped by her stepfather."

"Yes."

"That it happened when she was between 11 and 15."

"I think so."

"You told the police you had been told [about your cousin] when you were 13."

"When we were walking in a wood."

"So on one occasion you were with your cousin and your best friend, Jessica, who was also part of the conversation."

"Yes."

"What your cousin told you was very similar to what happened to you."

"Yes. He was raping her."

"Why initially did you not believe her?"

"It was so shocking to me."

"It was the same. Why could you not believe her?"

"I didn't feel comfortable."

"When you were 10 you realised, you'd been raped and wanted to tell someone."

"Yes."

"Here you are, aged 13, with your cousin and best friend — why not say what happened to you?"

"Just felt uncomfortable."

"When your cousin was 15, she sat down with a police officer to tell of a crime of a sexual nature. Why not say this was what happened to you?"

"Cos I felt dirty. I felt like a tramp and wouldn't be believed. With my cousin and my friend, I just wanted to have fun and not talk of such things."

"When you were 14, you, your cousin and your friend were at your friend's nan's house around the time of Tia Sharp [a schoolgirl who, in August 2012, was murdered by a former boyfriend of Tia's grandmother… he had been sexually interested in Tia, sexually assaulted her and photographed the child's body in a sexual pose]. Your nan told you details of what he did. I am going to suggest you said words to the effect that Patrick [O'Malley] would never do anything like that to you."

"I don't remember that."

"When interviewed by the police you said you thought your sister was also being abused."

"Yes, I did."

"But he would not abuse his own blood children?"

"Can't be too sure, but less likely."

"Did you not feel you should say something to protect your sister?"

"I probably should have, but I was scared."

"In the weeks leading up to going to the police you had a series of arguments with your mum and stepdad."

"Me and mum argued every day."

"There was a row about a bedroom. You said you had a plan if you did not get your own way you would go to Social Services."

"To tell them about the state of the house, it was not clean. They'd tell her not to be dirty, how to keep it clean."

"You wanted your own accommodation."

"At that moment I just wanted a clean home."

"You said some terrible things to your mum. You threatened to stab her and hoped she'd die of cancer."

"I can't remember what I said."

"You hated her."

"I had hate for her."

"If you didn't get your own way, she'd regret it."

"Not remember."

"You'd been smoking cannabis at times."

"Yes. But not when I got pregnant."

"You wanted money from your mother to buy drugs."

"Yes."

"You had a bitter argument with her the day before you went to the police."

"She was going away for the weekend and I'd need money."

THE JURY was read an exchange of texts between Miss L and her mother.

Miss L's single bedroom was a converted back-room downstairs, behind the lounge. Her sister and half-sister shared a double bedroom upstairs while her half-brother shared the bedroom of her mother and stepfather. Miss L wanted the bigger room shared by the other two girls with them moving to her smaller room.

Miss L: "I want my own room."

Mother: "Let's speak about it later."

Miss L: "No don't leave it, I want it now or I'm taking you to court."

Mother: "Don't talk stupid."

Miss L: "I'm being serious, watch."

Mother: "Watch what?"

Miss L: "I hate you so much. When you get back from Brighton you won't have to worry where I am. Social Services will agree with me not having a suitable room."

Mother: "I told you I'd speak to your sister and dad later."

Miss L: "Go fuck yourself. Obviously, you don't care."

Mother: "You know I care."

Miss L: "All I want is £50 for a pair of Nike boots."

Mother: "I can't give you what I don't have."

Miss L: "I'll go ahead with my plan. Fuck you."

Then Miss L went to the police station.

THE DEFENCE continued: "Those texts, a matter of hours before you made the allegations, illustrate the relationship with your mother was very poor."

"I always argued with mum."

"They were hurtful."

"At the time I did hate her."

"You were trying to manipulate her to get your own way, trying to persuade her to give you money and a big bedroom, trying to make her feel bad… to rubbish your mum."

"The way I saw it she was a rubbish mum."

"You threatened to stab your mum."

"I wouldn't have done it."

"You decided on a plan to stop her."

"No. Only Social Services. The fact I went to the police station had nothing to do with earlier plans."

"You had a lot of opportunities to speak to people in a similar situation and people who could investigate it, but you say something on Hollyoaks made you go to the police station. That's a lie."

"No."

"The only difference between Hollyoaks and you is that theirs was true."

"Mine is completely true."

THE JUDGE told the jury there was no evidence that the defendant had done anything untoward to Miss L's sister. He also reminded the jury that the claimant had never said her sister had told her anything about the defendant, it was mere speculation. The jury was told the defendant had no convictions or cautions and was a man of good character.

THE DEFENCE asked Patrick O'Malley about his stepdaughter.

"At 13… 14… she changed. She started smoking cannabis at 13. She started kicking off. She wouldn't get up [to go to school], she said she did not get on with the teachers. She treated her mum horribly. She

56

was scared of her daughter. I could see her shaking sometimes when she kicked off about money."

"In the week leading up to her going to the police station, what happened?"

"She would argue all the time about the bedroom. She wanted the big bedroom upstairs with a double bed. She was paranoid someone was in the garden looking at her [in her current room]. She kept saying 'there's someone in the back garden.' There wasn't. Me and her mum even spoke about letting her have our bedroom."

"Why?"

"She was our daughter, we loved her."

"How did things continue?"

"Terrible. She started smashing up the house, wanted her mum to die of cancer and threatened to stab her."

THE PROSECUTION began its cross-examination of Patrick O'Malley.

"Someone's lying."

"Yes."

"You or your stepdaughter?"

"[says her name]"

"Is it unlike her?"

"No."

"She has told other lies?"

"She said I assaulted other children."

"Give me another example of lies."

"She denied smoking weed when asked."

"OK, give me a big manufactured lie she's told."

"She got caught nicking from Primark. She had told us she got the clothes from friends."

"Any other fantasy she's created?"

"No."

"So the only completely made up lies in total detail are the allegations against you."

"Yes."

"What is her reason for all this then?"

"She wanted to destroy her mum."

"But she accused you."

"The last thing she said to me when she left the house was 'love you'."

"So she is prepared to sacrifice you to get to her mother?"

"Yes."

"That's vicious."

"Yes."

"We can agree [the claimant] became unhappy at 12 or 13, the age when you stopped abusing her."

"I never abused her."

"So all her revelations are made up?"

"Yes."

"How it started, hands down her knickers."

"I never touched her."

"Your stubble when you licked her vagina."

"I never done that."

"Wrapped her hand round your penis. It was very detailed."

"She'd done it to her boyfriend. I heard her telling a friend about it."

"Did you say anything to her?"

"Yes. I told her I did not want to hear this."

"It's nearly two years since she made the allegations and she's done it because of an argument about a bedroom."

"Yes. She hates her mum so much. I heard her say 'I'll destroy you [her mother]'."

"She has had a baby since, so no reason to lie."

"Yes. To destroy her mother."

THE JURY had heard some harrowing details of Miss L's allegations. Would the claimant really make up such accusations against her stepfather to destroy her mother? Was Patrick O'Malley, a man of good character, hiding a dark secret? There was much in the evidence it had heard for the jury to deliberate before it reached its verdicts.

5

PATRICK O'MALLEY: Indecent assault of a child under 13; gross indecency; rape

IT WAS strange that a street-wise 18-year-old mother would struggle to find a word or phrase for masturbation. It seemed ludicrous that an episode of Hollyoaks would be the springboard for her to tell the police about a childhood of sexual abuse.

Most of all, it was impossible to understand how Miss L could fabricate allegations against her stepfather as part of the continuing vendetta with her mother which could have seen an innocent man receive a double-digit prison sentence.

The jury did not take long to come to the view that Miss L was, to use the prosecution's words "a consummate liar... .an accomplished actress" — though maybe not the latter — as Patrick O'Malley was found not guilty of all charges.

Altogether, O'Malley was cleared of seven charges, including sexual assault, rape, indecent assault, gross indecency with a child and causing a child under 13 to engage in sexual activity.

THE POLICE have a duty to take every claim of sexual assault seriously. They are responsible for investigating allegations of rape and for gathering the evidence. When a police decision-maker considers there is sufficient evidence to charge the offence of rape, the case must be referred to a Crown prosecutor who will make the final decision whether to charge.

The Crown Prosecution Service must be satisfied first of all that there is enough evidence to provide a realistic prospect of a conviction against a defendant on each charge. This means that a jury, properly directed by a judge in accordance with the law, is more likely than not to convict the defendant of the alleged offence.

If the case does not pass the evidential stage, it must not go ahead, no matter how important or serious it may be. In the instance of Patrick O'Malley, it was staggering how the CPS believed, on the evidence it had, there was a good chance of a conviction to any of the charges.

6

PAUL CARNEY: Attempted murder/grievous bodily harm with intent/not guilty by reasons of insanity

AWAKENED BY HIS BEST PAL STABBING HIM

THERE WAS no dispute that Paul Carney had stabbed his close friend Garry Davis 11 times, causing him life-threatening injuries. Davis had to have a kidney and his gallbladder removed after the attack at his home one Saturday afternoon.

The jury had to decide whether Carney was sane or insane at the time. If it concluded he was sane, would it then find him guilty of attempted murder or grievous bodily harm with intent? Or would it conclude that Carney was not guilty by reason of insanity?

Davis, who had known Carney for about 14 years, received a call from the defendant asking if he could stay with him and his family for a few days. Carney had done this previously "so it was nothing out of the ordinary," said Davis.

Asked by the police about Carney, Davis said: "We'd never had an argument or fallen out. We'd always got on. Thinking back, he had suggested he wanted to stab someone, but I never thought he would do it. I just put it down to him being a bit mouthy.

"I went to primary school with him. He's always been a bit of a mad one, a bit crazy, but as mates he's been all right. He got on with the kids."

THE CROWN asked Garry Davis if he knew anything of Paul Carney's mental health issues.

He said: "His mum rang me once and said he'd been running through gardens and hit a bloke over the head with something."

The day before the incident Carney was found walking along

railway tracks in what was described as "a paranoid state." He was assessed under the Mental Health Act, but was said to be "alert and coherent" when examined and was released.

Davis was asked about Carney's marijuana smoking. "Would you describe him as an abuser?"

"No. He just did a bit of weed now and again."

"He seemed OK that morning."

"Yes."

"What did you talk about?"

"Nothing in depth. Just chit-chat."

"What happened next?"

"He had a shower. We had a few glasses of cider. My partner had returned from food shopping and I went upstairs to take a little sleep on the bed."

"What time was this?"

"About half past one."

"I'm just trying to work out the catalyst for this."

"No idea."

"How did he get the knives?"

"Don't know. There was a knife block in the kitchen."

"How many knives did he have?"

"Two. A big fat one and I think the other might have been a bread knife."

"This was not after an argument."

"No."

Davis told the jury what happened when he was awakened by Carney.

"I opened my eyes and he was sitting on the bed with knives on his lap. I sat up, but he said: 'Stay down, I'm in charge'."

"Did you think he was serious?"

"I thought he was messing about, but I saw his face. When he did [stab] my leg I knew [he was serious]."

Davis's mother had been alerted to something going on and went upstairs. He said: "She told him to get off me. He was, like, stabbing me. My girlfriend came upstairs and asked him: 'What are you doing?'

"He told her: 'They've come for me. Get out or I'll stab you'."

By then Davis's brother, who lived nearby, had been told what was going on.

"What happened when he came in?"

"Paul said to him: 'I'll stab you.' I told him: 'Don't come in, he'll kill you.' I didn't want to say too much, just calm him down. My brother threw a hammer at Paul who was shouting 'Allah... Allah'."

THE DEFENCE cross-examined Garry Davis.

"This was obviously a hugely distressing incident. You made it clear it was not justified and he was a very good mate."

"Yes."

"He'd stayed at your house before."

"Yes."

"Not had any rows."

"No."

"How much did he drink that day?"

"Just a couple."

"Cannabis?"

"One."

"He did not seem intoxicated."

"No."

"Paranoid?"

"No."

"How long did the incident last?"

"From the moment I woke up to when I managed to leave, 45 to 50 minutes. I can't say to be sure, but 45 to 50. It was a long time."

"Apparently you took your trousers off and he said it was just a graze, so he didn't seem to realise what he'd done to you."

"Dunno."

THE FIRST police officer arrived around 18.00 with back-up minutes later. By then, a heavily bleeding Garry Davis was laying on a grass verge near the property. By luck, a paramedic who lived nearby was on his way to work and treated the seriously injured Davis.

The WPC told the jury: "When I entered the house, I heard a man shouting and objects being thrown around. I did not enter the bedroom as the door was barricaded. I withdrew my CS spray for precautionary reasons in a low-profile position by my leg. There was a male standing on the bed armed with a hammer."

The prosecution asked her: "What did you say?"

"I asked him to put the hammer down."

"Did he?"

"Yes. There was also a male shouting over me. I wanted to separate the parties. It was difficult to build up a rapport with someone with so much shouting going on."

"Did he still have the hammer?"

"Yes. I said: 'Leave it and show me your hands'."

"What did he say?"

"He said: 'I'm not going to hurt you… I'm not going to hurt you'."

"What was his demeanour?"

"There were times when he was talking normally. Then he started to speak about the devil and talk to himself. He told me the devil was coming to save him and he'd save me, too. He said they had brought him here to kill him. I asked who, but he did not reply. As much as anything my main aim was to keep him focused on me. He was disturbed by people on the stairs and the shouting outside."

"The second officer was in possession of a taser."

"Yes."

"How did he [the defendant] react?"

"It seemed to excite him. He said: 'Taser me, I'll take my chance'."

"How was he?"

"Agitated, muttering about the devil. He veered between calm and animated, not saying normal things. His behaviour was up and down… unpredictable."

Three other officers arrived and managed to handcuff Carney who was informed that he was being arrested for attempted murder and cautioned. One of the other female officers told the jury: "His head was covered in sweat. He said if I didn't save him, he'd rape me, but I didn't take the remark seriously. He also said if we killed him then he would kill us, but if he lived then we would live."

AFTER being taken to a police station, Paul Carney was driven to a nearby hospital for treatment to some wounds. The senior medical examiner reported Carney's thought process was "quick and alert."

When interviewed back at the police station Carney replied "no comment" to every question.

Garry Davis sustained 11 injuries to both arms and legs and his torso. The worst was one stab wound in the middle of his abdomen which was 20cm in depth, just one or two centimetres away from a main artery. His gallbladder and a kidney were removed.

THE TRIAL was on hold for a week before the psychiatric experts could be brought to court. Two represented the defence, one the prosecution. Unsurprisingly different pictures were painted of Paul Carney's state of mind.

First in the witness box was Dr Phillip Oliver for the defence who had given evidence in many violent criminal trials. He had seen Carney on two occasions.

The defence said: "Tell us about the day before the incident when the defendant was sectioned."

"He agreed to come to the mental health unit so he was not sectioned, though he would have been [had he not volunteered]. He'd been detached from reality for some weeks."

"What happened before he went to the unit?"

"He had been found walking along a railway track. There are accounts of him almost being hit on two occasions. He was so deluded and paranoid he believed a gang of travellers were going to kill him."

Carney was assessed by the mental health service and released.

Doctor Oliver was asked by the defence to tell the jury the symptoms of insanity.

"Psychosis is a change in someone where you lose touch with reality, you become deluded. Hallucination is where people can hear or see sensations that are 100 per cent real to them, but do not happen."

"Living in their own world."

"Certainly not able to understand reality."

"A paranoid schizophrenic."

"Yes. Not able to think or talk clearly."

"Was what happened drug-induced psychosis? There was a positive test for cannabis and cocaine."

"In this case not necessarily. His symptoms continued long after the incident. He said the prison staff were out to get him and he barricaded himself in."

"Did he say it was because he was mentally ill?"

"No. A characteristic of being schizoid is a lack of insight into what has been done."

"Was he playing the mental health card?"

"My job is to assess people and some do [play the mental health card], but at no stage did I assess him to be doing this. He did not know the nature of his act."

"He repeatedly stabbed an old friend. What drove him to do that?"

"There is no other explanation than he was motivated by delusional beliefs. I don't believe he knew what he was doing was wrong. He thought there were people outside wanting to kill him. Of course, there were not any travellers outside, but he had a delusional belief that he was about to be killed. That meant he felt he was satisfied in defending himself. I see no motive other than a deluded self-defence brought on by paranoid schizophrenia."

The prosecution continued the cross-examination of Dr Phillip Oliver.

"When he was required to give an account of what happened on the day he gave a pretty consistent account, in fairness to him."

"His account is clouded by the fact he does not believe he is mentally ill."

"He said: 'If you come in, I'm going to kill you' which suggests there is an understanding that he knew what he could do."

"He was so disturbed, alternating between talking about he was god and then the devil. It is difficult to imagine he was thinking clearly and that at any stage he knew right from wrong. In his mind he thought he was under threat, the delusion about the travellers who were out to get him."

"You say there was no motive other than deluded paranoia."

"He thought everyone was in league against him."

DR JOHN LEONARD of the Royal College of Psychiatrists for the defence was next in the witness box.

The defence barrister asked: "Did the defendant know what he was doing was wrong?"

"He told me he felt people from a travellers' community were out to get him and the claimant was locked into the community. He thought Mr

Davis's family were colluding with him."

"He never said he had any awareness of what he did was wrong."

"Correct. In his mind he thought he was a god… divine."

"He is seriously mentally ill."

"Yes."

"How was he with you?"

"Very guarded. He did not want to be seen as mentally ill. He'd prefer a prison sentence as you know how long that will be. At a secure unit it is not the same. For me, the risk he carries can only be managed in a hospital."

"From the public's viewpoint he needs to be kept away."

"Yes. He needs to be monitored. He was very dismissive of a strong family history of mental illness. His father and grandfather were schizoid."

"So it's in his DNA."

"Yes, a strong factor."

DR BRIAN MESSENGER, a consultant psychologist, was the final witness, called on behalf of the prosecution.

The Crown began: "Everyone agrees he suffers from paranoid schizophrenia."

"Yes."

"Did he know what he was doing?"

"In his view he did know what he was doing."

"He was extremely unwell."

"Clearly, at the time he was troubled by delusions and psychotic symptoms. Yes, he was unwell. The test is whether he knew and I say 'yes'."

"How?"

"The previous day he believed he was being threatened by a travellers' community. On the journey from the hospital to the house he was relatively calm. During the day he believed Mr Davis was in cahoots with the travellers. When his girlfriend asked him to leave to him it was proof they were working against him."

"How much weight should be attached to his threat 'I'll kill you'?"

"He gave specific details about what would happen if certain events occurred. That he would stab the unarmed Mr Davis. He understood he felt people were out to get him, but knew Mr Davis did not pose a direct threat. He said: 'If you come in, I'll stab him' so he did what he said he would do. I believe he evaluated what was right or wrong and took measures to protect himself."

"As far as 'I am god' is concerned, as a divine being, did he not believe he was above the law?"

"I did not see evidence that he believed he was god. I do not believe religion played a major part in stabbing Mr Davis."

The defence put it to Dr Messenger: "You say he was scared during the stabbing, but still knew what he was doing was wrong."

"Yes."

"So his thought process was he thought Mr Davis was put in a conspiracy that could take him away and kill him."

"He told me he did not think they would kill him, but would give him a good kicking. He did not see Mr Davis as someone who would hurt him, only as part of a conspiracy."

"We are dealing with a deluded fantasist."

"I'm applying law as I see it to sanity and whether he appreciated what he was doing was wrong."

IN ITS closing speech the prosecution told the jury: "There was no motive for the defendant to hurt Mr Davis as he did. Was he, at the time, sane or insane? The Crown says Mr Carney attempted to kill Mr Davis. There is no dispute whether he stabbed him or not. You must decide if what he did was unlawful.

"Ultimately what he said he would do was what he did. The knife was pressed deep with force into Mr Davis's main organs. If this was not to kill him, what was it? People who suffer from schizoid delusions can still decide what is right or wrong. Did he believe what he was doing was wrong?

"Just because he said things does not mean he believed them. God wouldn't be troubled by travellers outside. It's up to you how much weight you place on this."

THE DEFENCE tore into Dr Brian Messenger's evidence, calling him "a worthless witness." It began: "The special verdict is not guilty by reason of insanity. That is not an acquittal. He does not walk out of here. It leaves the judge with considerable power how to deal with a very dangerous man. A hospital order means going somewhere like Broadmoor, a secure unit. It can be years, if ever, that he is released.

"Dr Messenger said he knew what he was doing, but never really explained how he came to this [opinion]. He kept going on about Mr Davis being unarmed, but completely failed to grasp the central issue.

"Paul Carney was suffering from psychotic delusions. The previous day he had been taken to a mental health institution which was an indication of his state of mind at the time. He was, sadly, released. Had he not been released this would not have happened."

HOW much such conflicting statements by experts helped or confused the jury is unknown. It is one thing to decide a defendant's guilt for rape, burglary or arson. This jury was asked to decide whether a defendant who had, in effect, admitted his guilt, was sane or insane when he attacked a close friend rather than simply guilty or not guilty.

If Paul Carney was sane, did he try to kill Garry Davis or simply stab him to injure him? If killing Davis was not considered his motive, was it grievous bodily harm with intent?

Insanity is a defence to criminal charges based on the idea that the defendant was unable to understand what he was doing, or that he was unable to understand that what he was doing was wrong. The defence's case was that the defendant was either suffering from a disease which damaged the functioning of the mind and led to a defect of reason that prevented him from understanding what he was doing, or that he could not tell that what he was doing was wrong.

THE JUDGE told the jury: "All three [doctors] agree the defendant was suffering from schizophrenia. Two doctors said he was so disturbed he could not think rationally about what he was doing. One said he knew what he was doing was wrong."

The jury retired to consider the specifics of the verdict of guilty, but what would it find Paul Carney, a mentally disordered offender to use the legal term, guilty of? Would it be attempted murder or grievous bodily harm with intent? Or not guilty by reason of insanity?

6

PAUL CARNEY: Attempted murder/grievous bodily harm with intent/not guilty by reasons of insanity

THE JURY knew Paul Carney was guilty. It had to decide what the defendant was guilty of. Carney did not get his wish of a custodial sentence as the jury concluded he was not guilty by reasons of insanity

Judges have far-reaching powers for this conclusion. Before they make such an order, they must be satisfied that it is necessary to do so to protect the public from serious harm.

Carney was given a Section 37/41 of the Mental Health Act. It meant that he cannot be discharged from hospital unless the Ministry of Justice or a tribunal says he can leave; he may then be subject to certain conditions. There is no time limit on a Section 37/41.

7

BILL ADAKU: Rape

ALLEGED RAPIST STAYED THE NIGHT

BILL ADAKU and Miss M had been in a relationship for 18 months, though she was becoming increasingly uncomfortable that he was coy about where he lived and whom he lived with.

When she asked him round to discuss their future together it ended with Adaku charged with one count of rape against Miss M — that he intentionally penetrated, with his penis, the vagina of the claimant without her consent.

Miss M, who had met someone else, wanted to end the relationship with Adaku. "It was my intention to break up with him," she said in a police interview, a few days after the alleged incident. "He was so secretive. I was not happy with it."

Her worries increased when she discovered he had been using a false identity during their friendship. "He said he was a plumber who lived in Wembley," said Miss M. "He had two children, but they did not live with their mother. I had never met his family or seen where he lived."

IN COMMON with almost all criminal trials, the legal system seems to favour the defendant, but more so with rape. The accused is allowed to discuss his case with his lawyer before and during the trial. He can build a close relationship with his legal team while awaiting trial. The laws of disclosure also allow him access to all of the prosecution evidence, including the claimant's and other prosecution witness statements, giving his advocate time to plan all angles of questioning that may take place at the trial.

It is not the even playing field which many will think a Crown Court trial should be. The claimant will not have met the prosecutor acting on behalf of the Crown Prosecution Service before the trial and has no right to see any of the other statements apart from their own which they are allowed to read upon arriving at court to refresh their memory.

Claimants will have little idea of the questions they are likely to face or how they should answer them, because they do not know what the defendant has said in their statements. Only the first person Miss M spoke to after the alleged rape happened — in her case her cousin — was allowed to give evidence on her behalf.

ON THE night in question Bill Adaku turned up at Miss M's flat as arranged. She let him in and after a while they had consensual oral sex on the sofa and floor. "Maybe I felt guilty," she said, confirming Adaku did not use a condom and he ejaculated in her mouth.

Afterwards he went upstairs — her two children aged seven and nine were in a shared bedroom. "He was half-naked, the bottom half, and I had a bra and dressing gown on," Miss M said in her videoed police interview which the jury saw.

"He was kneeling on the bed when I told him I was seeing someone else. He asked if I was sleeping with him [the other man] and I said 'yes.' He was calm at that time and asked me to shut the [bedroom] door. He then said 'come here' and grabbed me round the throat and slapped me, calling me his bitch.

"I just went along with it because I was so scared. He told me he was not letting me go and asked if I had gone down on him [the other man]. I said I did and he told me to show him how I did it.

"I licked his penis probably three times. He then put me on my front, put his penis in me and had sex with me from the back. He kept asking: 'Did he do this to you?'

"After he had cum he sat next to me."

Later in the police interview Miss M, who said she had last had sex with the defendant two weeks previously, was asked again about what happened in her bedroom.

"I must have still had my dressing-gown on," she said. "I was lying flat and he put his penis in my vagina. I said I wasn't in the mood and didn't want to do this. He told me to shut up. I was crying. He came again. It lasted probably three minutes."

Adaku stayed the night.

Miss M, who worked as a receptionist in a hospital, said: "I didn't ask him to leave in the morning because I didn't want to escalate things. I was shocked he was acting so normal. That scared me.

"I left and went to work. I phoned a friend to tell him that my boyfriend had forced himself on me. I was on a train and we kept cutting out."

Adaku was arrested a couple of days later.

IN COURT, Miss M's cousin recounted what she was told by the claimant. The cousin said: "We are very close. When she phoned me, she was very upset. She said something had happened with her partner the previous night.

"They ended up in her bedroom. He was still coming on to her. She didn't want to, she was seeing someone else. She said he told her that she would always be his bitch.

"He forced her down on him, slapping her face. He pushed her on her stomach or side and put his penis in from behind."

THE DEFENCE was surprised at how detailed the cousin's account was, not least as she did not give a statement to the police until four months after the incident and she agreed she did not take notes when she initially spoke to the claimant.

"Did Miss M not tell you they initially had consensual [oral] sex downstairs on the sofa?"

"No."

"She told you the only sex they had was upstairs."

"Yes."

UNDER cross-examination by the prosecution, Bill Adaku said he had been in a relationship with the mother of his two children for 11 years. The friendship with Miss M "developed sexually" and explicit Instagram messages, including photos of her naked sent by her to him confirmed this. One message sent a month before the incident was: "That dick of you [sic] felt so good between my legs."

On the night in question Adaku said they had sex downstairs after, he thought, they had sorted out the issues between them. He told the jury: "When I went upstairs, I went to the toilet to wipe myself down. She then said to me: 'I've been lying.' She said she'd had unprotected sex with a

73

guy from Uganda. I wish she had told me that before we had sex downstairs. I was thinking that I had better go to the clinic to get myself tested.

"I never had sex with her upstairs. I never have, because the kids are upstairs. I have never had sex twice in a night. I can't ejaculate twice. My mind switches off."

THERE is no doubt the pair had sex on the night in question. What would the jury make of the evidence by the claimant and her cousin? But most important, would the jury decide whether the alleged sex upstairs was consensual or rape?

7

BILL ADAKU: Rape

MISS M was unreliable and untruthful, lacking any credibility. She wanted to dump Bill Adaku so she accused him of rape. It was little surprise when the jury took just 30 minutes to acquit Adaku. When a jury returns so quickly with a not guilty verdict it can be taken as an indication that the case should never have been brought to court in the first place.

Adaku denied any sexual act took place in Miss M's bedroom and it soon became obvious the evidence of the claimant and her cousin contained many contradictions and anomalies.

For a start, the time scale between Adaku ejaculating in the lounge and again in the bedroom which appears to be no more than 30 minutes. Even Superman would struggle to match that. And why on earth would a girl who had allegedly been raped allow the alleged rapist to stay the night?

When the alleged rape took place, in one statement it was claimed that it was anal sex; another said that it was vaginal sex. According to her cousin, the claimant did not mention the consensual oral sex downstairs.

Miss M said while she was on a train to work, she telephoned her cousin to tell her what had happened. On a train? All I ever hear is "what's for dinner?" or an update on the dog's visit to the vet.

Yes, Adaku was deceiving the mother of his children by playing away, but this is irrelevant. A Crown Court is not a headquarters of moral judgment, only law.

For Adaku being falsely accused of rape will be a tattoo for life and one he does not deserve. He may be less reluctant to cheat on his partner, but the lesson could have been learned in a less costly way .both for him and the taxpayer.

The Crown Prosecution Service maintains that for all offences, not just those involving sexual assault, it will only bring a case to court if "there is a real prospect of conviction."

Bill Adaku, for one, would question this.

8

MATTHEW WALFORD: Child cruelty

EXECUTIONS OR THE
NEWS ON TV?

HOW RELIABLE is the evidence of an eight-year-old boy regarding violent videos?

Child J's father, Matthew Walford, used to be a Rastafarian. When he converted to Islam his ex-partner, Rita, had cut off his dreadlocks.

According to Child J, Walford's commitment to Islam extended to making him watch videos of ISIS beheading enemies of their faith. Police officers who watched four videos retrieved from Walford's computer were alerted by the level of violence they witnessed.

But was Child J's evidence credible or the understandable exaggerations of someone so young? And was he groomed to say such things by his mother in the wake of a bitter separation?

The jury had to decide whether Walford was guilty of child cruelty. Did Child J watch the videos of beheading and did his father encourage him to see images that would shock any reasonable person? Was Child J's evidence the imagination of a young boy who had no doubt seen violence on video games or mainstream television — noticeably the news?

THE INITIAL investigation started when Matthew Walford's ex-partner phoned the police alleging he had assaulted her as they met to discuss a telephone bill. When police officers visited her property Child J told them about the videos he claimed to have seen.

Walford was arrested and charged, his laptop, tablet and computer confiscated by the police.

By video link, Child J told the jury: "He [Walford] showed it about

100 times on different days. He watched it with me. He liked to repeat the bits I don't like. One I kind of liked was the Battle of Buddha."

THE DEFENDANT denied the allegation. Matthew Walford told the jury: "These are malicious lies [by my ex-partner] to get custody of the children [they also had two daughters], putting things in his mind. She gets more benefits then."

Walford admitted that he watched Al Jazeera, the Qatar-based television network, rather than ITV or BBC. "I like to keep in touch with what is happening in the Middle East," he said.

Cross-examining Walford, the prosecution asked whether he had ever seen any beheadings.

"Yes, once. It was Nick Berg, the American journalist who was beheaded in Iraq in 2004. Everyone was talking about it. But the video was edited so you only saw the after effects. I do not like beheading."

"Your son claimed he'd seen a child killed by a crossbow."

"He's never seen that."

"Is he allowed to watch videos of men who have their heads chopped off?"

"No. It's never happened."

"Have you ever bought him a toy gun?"

"Only a water pistol."

"You watched Omar [a series based on the senior disciple of the prophet Muhammad which comprised 30 episodes]."

"Yes. A woman gets killed, but not beheaded. There are no Army fatigues or uniforms. My son told me he had seen head-less videos like Lord of the Rings, where heads are cut off. Or the Hobbit where there is beheading. He can download them. There is beheading in films about Henry VIII."

"Your son said when he was 10 you told him you would take him to Syria to fight for ISIS."

"I said: 'When you have a one in front of your age, I'll maybe take you to Indonesia' where I have been twice."

"He spoke about fighting for the black flag. Where did he see that?"

"It is the flag ISIS use. It is shown on the news. I cannot watch him 24/7. I only see him three days a week. He could have been talking to friends at school. When he's seen bombings in Syria on TV, he asked me why it was happening. I told him the president of Syria was involved in a war with extremists. He sees it on TV like everyone does. I try to explain, but I have never spoken to him about ISIS. I cannot take my son anywhere. When we split up, his passport was given to a solicitor and we [his ex] both have to give permission for him to be taken anywhere."

"Your ex claimed after you converted to Islam you watched videos of people being beheaded and shot."

"I've never shown her that. It's a lie."

"He said he had had nightmares."

"He's never had them at my house. When he moved, she [his ex] mentioned it one time, but never said anything about videos. He's telling lies. He's angry with me. His mother told him I was married. I'm not. It's almost like he has two minds going on."

"The police recovered four violent videos on your computer."

"They were not downloaded. They were on YouTube from Islamic state news because I wanted to see what was happening. I have never seen them."

"You have never seen them?"

"No."

"Why not?"

"I have a chronic back condition. I take tramadol [a strong painkiller] and need to rest a lot. Also, the police took my computer."

"I am suggesting to you, when your son said he saw beheading on your laptop it had to be those."

"He doesn't have the password for my laptop or computer, so he couldn't have watched them."

WHEN Child J was interviewed at a police station, his mother was not allowed to be present. He subsequently told her he had been strangled by a police officer. His mother said she had "seen the marks" but later retracted the complaint.

She phoned Matthew Walford's mother and told her she didn't think Child J was telling the truth [about the alleged strangling]. A police investigation concluded it was "impossible" for the incident to have taken place as Child J was recorded on CCTV at all times.

Walford's ex-partner made a statement to the police, but in court she claimed that even though she had signed it as being a true version of what she had said, there were 11 mistakes. Among these were that she had told the police Walford wanted to take their son to Syria, claiming she had said Indonesia. "It all happened so quickly," said the defendant's ex-partner. "I'm not really a good reader. They got some things wrong."

The jury had to decide whether her unreliable evidence impacted on the accusations made against her former partner. And whether Child J's "strangled" story at the police station cast doubts on his overall reliability.

8

MATTHEW WALFORD: Child cruelty

MATTHEW WALFORD did himself no favours by answering questions with questions when cross-examined. "Would you do that to your child?" he asked the prosecutor and was told by the judge not to be petulant. In court, barristers ask questions and witnesses answer them.

The main witnesses against Walford, his son and ex-partner, were far from reliable and I did not think that the jury could be sure Child J had been shown ISIS videos by his father. I was wrong.

Walford had spent six months in custody. The jury delivered a unanimous verdict of guilty and he was sentenced to a further 40 weeks in prison.

9

RICHARD JONES: ABH

IT BOILED DOWN TO SELF DEFENCE
WITH A KETTLE

CHRISTMAS is a time for goodwill to all men according to the carol "I Heard the Bells on Christmas Day" written by Henry Longfellow, though goodwill can be in short supply in prison any time.

Richard Jones and Lloyd Young were cell mates for four days, but certainly not soul mates. In fact, they were both violent men with records which prove that for some offenders, jail is far from a deterrent.

Jones was charged with assault occasioning actual bodily harm on Young on December 25 in the cell they shared while at Her Majesty's pleasure. Young claimed Jones threw boiling water over his face and upper body. Jones said he acted in self-defence as Young was about to toss the contents of the kettle over him.

In the previous three years Jones had been convicted for eight counts of assault (five involving police officers), two counts of common assault and 11 counts of battery.

THIS WAS a short trial lasting less than a day. Little did the jury know what it was about to hear as the prosecution began cross-examining Lloyd Young.

"Had you known him [Richard Jones] before?"

"No."

"You were sharing a cell on December 25?"

"Yes, I was."

"Lockdown was at six."

"Yes."

"The defendant was there."

"Yes. Just the two of us."

"What was the mood like between you?"

"Bad."

"Any discussions between you?"

"Technically, I wanted to sit in silence."

"Did he say anything to you?"

"He asked me to get him some drugs."

"Anything else?"

"He told me to call him 'boss' or 'sir'."

"Why?"

"He was the boss of the cell."

"What did you say?"

"I said 'no'."

"What was his reaction?"

"He poured boiling water over me."

"Whose kettle, was it?"

"It belonged to the cell."

"Was the kettle boiled when he asked you to call him 'sir'?"

"Don't know. I thought he was going to make a cup of tea."

"Where were you both when he threw the water?"

"Five metres apart." [Young's spread hands indicated nearer one foot].

"Did it land on you?"

"Yes. On my face and chest."

"What did you do?"

"I had to press the [alarm] buzzer in the cell and one of the officers opened the flap, took me out and I was taken to hospital."

"How long were you in hospital?"

"Until Boxing Day."

"Did you have further treatment?"

"I was moved to the hospital wing."

The jury was shown photographs of Young's injuries.

"How long did the marks take to clear?"

"Two weeks."

THE DEFENCE cross-examined Lloyd Young.

"You said there was a bad atmosphere. You say you refused to get him drugs."

"I didn't want to get involved."

"Or call him 'sir'."

"No."

"I suggest this is not true. I suggest Mr Jones said he wanted the cell to be clean."

"Disagree."

"He cleaned the cell."

"No. He was a cleaner, but not in the cell."

"He wanted it clean and tidy and said you should have a shower."

"I did have a shower."

"He said to you that you should shower more."

"He did say that."

"You were upset and offended."

"Yes, I was."

"Did he tell you that you smelt?"

"He said I stank, which I didn't."

"You didn't like that."

"Not the way he said it."

"That's why there was a bad atmosphere. A second reason is that you were always scrounging tobacco."

"Rubbish."

"I suggest you were constantly pestering him."

"No."

"He has more prison provisions."

"Yes. But I didn't ask him for anything."

"Did you not earn any money?"

"How can anyone have a job when he's disabled? I have epilepsy."

"You smoke?"

"Yes."

"He was fed up with you asking and said he had given you enough tobacco."

"Rubbish, a load of bullshit."

"He put some curtains up in the cell."

"Don't know."

"I suggest you pulled them down."

"I'd never do anything like that. I never touched any curtains. You calling me a liar?"

"Yes, I am."

"Defending a fucking drug addict, are you?"

"You're not to ask me questions. I'm not the one on trial. I suggest you are lying when you say he asked you to get him drugs."

"I suggest he's lying."

"About calling him 'boss' or something. This was on TV. You've invented this."

"No. Can I say something? Well, I won't because it'll be offensive. I'd swear. Well, I'm going to. You are defending a fucking drug addict and you are a fucking cunt."

"Mr Young, you are no angel yourself."

"I do not want to listen." [Young puts his fingers in his ears].

"You were in prison for over three years for grievous bodily harm."

"Wrong."

"That's what the record says."

"Malicious wounding, it was malicious fucking wounding. Get your facts right."

"OK, I'll call it that. You were sentenced to 38 months for malicious wounding."

"Three years and two months."

"I agree. A serious matter."

"Yes."

"Involving a wine bottle."

"I put it over someone's head."

"You have a previous conviction for having a broken bottle. You were given 16 months for possession of an offensive weapon."

"Can't remember."

"You were serving the sentence for this on Christmas Day."

"Yes."

"There's another offence, battery. You were fined £34."

"Not know."

"You had been released the previous June on licence."

"Yes, I went back in."

"Why?"

"Someone hit me across the face with a shoe. I picked up a bottle and the police came."

"You're still in prison now."

"Yes."

"You say: 'How can I defend a drug dealer?' yet you are no angel. You have committed violent offences."

Young did not respond.

"Let's go back to the cell and Christmas Day."

"Get the facts right."

"OK, what I suggest is that Mr Jones went to have a pee and you tore down the curtains."

"Not agree."

"He said: 'What the fuck are you doing'?"

"Bullshit. Fucking bullshit."

"It's the truth."

"No, fucking bullshit."

"He put the kettle on to make some coffee."

"Bullshit, you're a liar."

"I am putting his case. You were getting angry and picked up the kettle."

"I didn't. Fucking bullshit."

"You almost spilt some on yourself."

"A load of fucking bullshit."

"You brought your arm back as if to throw the kettle. He kicked it and it went over you."

"A load of fucking bullshit. You're not telling the truth. The officer opened the flap and saw him throw it at me."

"I suggest you were the author of your own misfortune."

"No."

RICHARD JONES took to the witness box and was cross-examined by the defence.

"Were you pleased to be sharing a cell with anyone?"

"No. I suffer from anxiety and depression. I like my own space."

"How did you get on?"

"At first OK. It was OK being banged up with him."

"You had a prison job."

"Yes. I earned £23 a week and used it to buy tobacco, biscuits and stuff."

"Did Young buy anything?"

"Nothing."

"Did you share?"

"Yes. I offered him some burn [tobacco]."

"In a friendly way."

"Yes. I smoke and wouldn't like someone to have a roll-up without offering me one. I treated him with respect."

"What about him calling you 'boss'?"

"We were watching TV one day, a comedy, and someone said: 'Call me sir.' I said: 'That's what you should call me.' He laughed. It was banter."

"Was it mentioned again?"

"No, it was just a joke."

"He claimed you asked him to get you drugs."

"Incorrect. It's easier to get drugs in prison than in the community so I would not have to ask him."

"Did you ever talk to him about drugs?"

"Only in the context of which ones we'd used."

"How did the incident happen?"

"My burn was running out and I explained that to him."

"How did he react?"

"At first all right. He told me he would sell meals for burn or scrounge around bins."

"You accused him of not showering."

"I said it a couple of times. Even the officers said he should shower. His feet smelled. I told him so on Christmas Day."

"How did he take it?"

"He said I should have respect for him."

"Did he have one [a shower]?"

"No."

"He said you did not clean the cell."

"Lies. We have a shower in the cell. I showered two or three times a day and cleaned up."

"A little obsessive."

"Yes."

"The boiling water, how did it happen?"

"He said he'd sold his dinner for a roll-up. But he kept asking me [for one] every five minutes. It was driving me mad. I eventually gave him some snout after 20 minutes."

"You were locked up at six."

"Yes. He hadn't showered for three days. Same clothes, same socks. I didn't really speak to him. We were on our beds watching telly. I boiled the kettle to make some coffee, went to the toilet. When I came out he was pacing up and down. He'd ripped the curtains down."

"Why did you have curtains?"

"Just to make it a bit more homely. I said: 'Why did you do that?' He said: 'I need a roll-up.' I told him to chill out. I told him not to smash up the cell. The kettle boiled and he picked it up. His hand was shaking. He was epileptic or something. It almost fell on my legs. I jumped up. He pulled back the kettle, like shoulder height, as if to chuck it in my face. It was an instant reaction. I kicked it out of his hand. I feared for my safety. The top came off and water went in his face."

"Are you telling the truth when you say he picked up the kettle?"

"One hundred per cent. He was aggressive and had anger in his eyes."

THE CROWN took over cross-examination.

"Why did you think he picked the kettle up?"

"To make a drink."

"Even though he had no coffee."

"We get a breakfast kit. There's some in there."

"You said the kettle was shoulder height."

"Yes."

"You kicked it out of his hand."

"Yes."

"At shoulder height."

"It wasn't a fly-kick."

"You indicated your foot did not go higher than his hip. How did you manage to kick the kettle?"

"Course I did."

"When you kicked it, the lid came off straight away."

"Yes."

"Any water land on you?"

"A few drops."

"So you managed to have no burns."

"No."

"The water just went on him."

"Yes."

The prosecutor went back to the relationship between the pair.

"You told him 'you stink'."

"If I stunk, I'd want someone to tell me."

"You were being a bully."

"No."

"You said 'call me sir'."

"No."

"You are a violent man."

"I have a slight temper, yes. I have mental health issues."

"You are a bully."

"The one thing I am not is a bully."

"You wanted to make a name for yourself."

"That's the last thing you want to do in prison."

THE JURY had to decide which violent prisoner to believe. Which of the two men, each with a string of convictions, was the more truthful?

Lloyd Young's language would hardly have endeared him to the jury. But could Richard Jones have managed to kick the kettle from Young and the boiling water only have gone over the "victim"?

9

RICHARD JONES: ABH

THE JURY preferred to believe Richard Jones's account of Kettlegate and found him not guilty of occasioning actual bodily harm to Lloyd Young.

The jurors were no doubt left to ponder on Jones's revelation that drugs are easier to get in prison than in the community.

Worryingly, he said it with such conviction — an apt word under the circumstances — which made it one of the more credible statements in an unusual trial.

10

ZENA WALSH: Arson

ARSONIST WAS UNAWARE OF THE DANGER

ZENA WALSH wanted to commit suicide. She decided to set fire to her bedroom, putting a towel under the locked door. Her husband, who slept in a different bedroom, had a heightened sense of smell so, Walsh thought, he would be able to escape on a roof. Walsh had medical and emotional difficulties to the extent an appropriate adult — a friend — sat with her in the dock.

She was charged with two counts of arson. The first, with intent to damage property and endanger the life of another; the second, acting in a reckless manner to damage property and the life of another — i.e., she saw the danger in setting fire to her room, but carried on regardless though not intending any harm to anyone.

The defendant admitted she had drunk a bottle of wine in the afternoon. When Walsh's husband, Craig, returned home early evening she joined him for more alcohol before they went to their separate bedrooms around 21.30. She said she locked her door, placed a towel at the bottom, sprayed her curtains with hairspray and set light to them before going to bed. At around 22.30 Craig was awakened by the smell of burning. He managed to open the door and his wife was rescued.

CRAIG WALSH was cross-examined by the prosecution who asked him what state his wife was in when he returned home.

"She'd had a drink."

"What did you do then?"

"We had a drink, watched some TV and went to bed."

"What did you drink?"

"Two or three bottles of Leffe [Belgian beer]. Zena had more wine and some cider, I think."

"By the time you went to bed, what was your state of inebriation?"

"We were both pretty inebriated. I hadn't had much to eat. Zena went up first, to read, I think. I followed her soon after and went to sleep quickly as I was up early that day."

"What happened next?"

"I was awakened by a strange smell. I thought: 'What is this?' I jumped out of bed. I knew something was not right. There was smoke coming from Zena's door."

"What did you do?"

"I opened the door and I was in a state of massive panic. There was so much black smoke you could almost feel it. I saw a flame on the curtains, but could not see Zena. I decided to get some water, so ran downstairs and filled a bucket. I still couldn't see Zena when I went back up. I could not go in, the smoke was so thick."

"Did you manage to douse the flames?"

"Probably not. I went to get some more water and rang the fire brigade. By then I could see Zena on the floor. She was covered in black smoke, even her teeth and gums. I think the water I tried to throw at the curtains went over her and woke her up. I dragged her on to the landing."

"What state was she in?"

"Semi-conscious, saying: 'Leave me Craig, I just want to die'."

The fire brigade arrived quickly and Zena was given oxygen before she and Craig were taken away in an ambulance as the fire service put out the flames.

"Did she say anything else?"

"In the ambulance she was in quite a manic state. She told one of the paramedics her roots were showing and she should get them done properly."

THE DEFENCE put it to Craig Walsh it was not in dispute that Zena had a history of mental health issues and was an inmate at an acute psychiatric ward.

"It was where we met," said Craig. "I was a senior staff nurse and became her primary carer. After her discharge we became friends socially."

"Was she there because of previous attempts to take her life when she was 18 [she was now 50]?"

"No. Because of a threat to do it."

"Let us go back to the incident. Had she been working hard?"

"Obsessively hard. She worked at a school for children with behavioural problems. She had worked there before, but was asked to go back. They just dumped work on her to get results which were unrealistic. She'd work through the night sometimes."

A PREPARED statement made to the police after her arrest was read out to the jury. Zena Walsh said she had taken more than her usual dosage of medicine plus diazepam bought on the internet. She had also drunk more than a bottle of wine. She said she had been treated by a clinical psychiatrist and had no recollection of incidents that day.

A report by the doctor who had been treating Walsh said she had a history of overdosing since she was a teenager. Walsh said she chose fire [for her suicide] because she had tried overdosing, but it did not work. The doctor believed the stress of her job upon returning to school, problems with her marriage, the effects of having only four hours sleep some nights plus the use of [non-prescription] diazepam helped produce a feeling of worthlessness.

He said: "The only person she wanted to hurt was herself. She did not see how the arson would harm her husband. The arson attempt was to commit suicide."

THE DEFENCE submitted there was no evidence that Zena Walsh had wanted to harm her husband's life. The judge agreed that the first count — intent to damage property and endanger the life of another — should be struck off.

Regarding count two — and this is a joy for language pedants — "reckless" is a term that has caused a lot of difficulty in law. It is such a subjective word. The House of Lords had agreed what constitutes reckless… which is that in circumstances where someone is aware of the risk that exists or will exist… the person must be aware that a risk exists and it was known to the person that they reasonably took a risk. At the same time, there is a recognition that if the balance of mind is disturbed then a rational analysis cannot be made.

The judge ruled Walsh had a case to answer on count two and there was sufficient evidence for the jury to decide whether the defendant was acting in a reckless manner to damage property and the life of another. There was no doubt Walsh had mental and emotional problems, but how far could these extend regarding the one remaining arson charge? Could she have been, in her mind, totally unaware that setting fire to her curtains was reckless and would endanger others?

10

ZENA WALSH: Arson

THE JURY, which had been sent out for numerous legal arguments during the trial, found Zena Walsh not guilty of the one remaining charge of arson: acting in a reckless manner to damage property and the life of another.

The jury believed her state of mind was such that she thought no further than ending her own life.

11

JORGE GONZÁLEZ: Rape

MAN FROM BOLIVIA AND THE
GIRL FROM PERU

THE MOST unexpected trial I attended was that of a Peruvian girl who claimed she had been raped by a Bolivian male in London on Christmas Day. South America came to south London in controversial and hardly seasonal circumstances.

As with virtually all rape cases, there were no other witnesses to the actual incident so the crucial evidence came only from the claimant and the defendant. Jorge González admitted having sex with Miss P, but said it was consensual. She said she was so drunk she didn't know what had happened.

The jury had to decide, on the evidence presented, whether Miss P had drunk so much she was incapable of consenting and González knew she was incapable of consenting.

The claimant, defendant and witnesses all spoke through a Spanish interpreter which ensured a lengthy process for the jury.

THE PARTY was at a house with five bedrooms — two downstairs, two upstairs and an attic conversion. Miss P had moved into a room downstairs, which she shared with Pamela and Nellie, a few days before Christmas; Jorge González had been in the house for a couple of months in the attic room.

Juan, who shared an upstairs room with his wife Vanessa, invited the lodgers — the landlord was on holiday — and a friend Hugo, to the party which started around 5 p.m. after everyone had eaten.

Miss P said in her statement to the police on December 27: "Nellie came to the room and told Pamela about the party. I said 'let's go.' I was chatting to Nellie [at the party] and someone gave me a can of beer. I remember having three cans. I had never met González before. He was slim, taller than me and dark skinned because he's from Bolivia."

When asked by the police if she agreed to have sex with him, she replied: "No."

Miss P continued: "I have drunk three, four, five cans of beer before and been all right. I cannot remember how long it was, a few hours, at least two. My last memory is dancing with Nellie. I've never had a loss of memory like this before."

It was revealed that Miss P had to be helped into the landlord's room by other girls where she was put in the bed and covered with a blanket.

"I was wearing leggings and a red top. I do not wear a bra indoors as I have very big breasts. When I go out it's different. My next memory is waking up about 9 a.m. in a different room [to where I live] with Nellie, next to [the room] where the party took place. When I got up, I looked in the mirror and saw a mark on my chest and asked myself 'what's going on?'

"When I went to wee it hurt. I had never felt like this before. I don't normally have problems. I started to wonder what had gone on. Something must have gone on, but I had no idea what it could be. I went to the police station a couple of hours after I woke up because I wanted someone to tell me what had happened."

UNDER cross-examination by the prosecution, Miss P said: "I drank the beers slowly, about half an hour for each one. They made me feel happy, but not drunk. I've never suffered memory loss before. I think perhaps something was mixed with my drink. It's the only thing I can think of."

NELLIE told the jury: "I did not drink [alcohol], I never do. Miss P was drinking beer. She was drinking fast. She started drinking at 8.30. She was drinking too much, she was drunk. Pamela and Vanessa saw she was drunk and went to put her to bed next door. They came back to the party where the music was still playing.

"González went for a smoke, but didn't come back. After 15 minutes we [Nellie, Pamela and Vanessa] went to the landlord's room. They had shut the door, but not locked it. Now it was locked. We knocked on the door and shouted 'open the door' which González eventually did. Miss P was lying on the bed with no clothes on. I asked González what had happened. He said: 'Nothing because she was too drunk.'

"After she was dressed, I slept with her. She wanted to go back to the party. It was about 11.30. We went to bed."

Vanessa, under cross-examination by the prosecution, said: "Miss P was drinking beer. I don't know if she drank wine, but it was there. She was happy. I didn't think she was drinking fast, but the beer was affecting her behaviour in the way she was dancing. She wanted to change the music [which was played through a computer] but she couldn't. She was drunk.

"I asked Nellie to take her downstairs [to her room] but we were afraid she might fall. She couldn't walk very well. So me, Pamela and Nellie took her to the bedroom next door. She went to the toilet by herself. We helped her lay down, covered her with the bedspread and went back to the party. The door was closed, not locked. We left the door to the party room ajar so we could see if she got up.

"González left the room for a smoke. He was gone about 15 minutes and we said: 'What do we do?' The door wasn't how we left it [not locked] so we thought he must be there. We knocked, there was no reply. We shouted: 'Open the door, you are inside.'

"I went downstairs to the kitchen to get a hammer. By the time I came back the door was open. We walked in and Miss P was naked on the bed. I didn't say anything. It seemed like she had been crying. We picked up her clothes from the floor and dressed her.

"All González said was: 'I haven't done anything, it's not what you are thinking, no.' He went outside by himself. Miss P didn't say anything, she was like… lost. We went back to the party.

"The next day we told Miss P what we had seen and said she should report it to the police."

THE DEFENCE took over cross-examination. Vanessa said: "Miss P was drinking quickly to me, you know, down in one go. She was drunk before anyone else. She was flirting, dancing close… very close and kissing him on the cheek. She was dancing very sexily with all the men."

Juan, Vanessa's husband, told the jury: "Miss P was drinking wine, rum and beer, I think. She was helping herself. She was drinking a lot. She was happy, euphoric."

Linda said Miss P was unaware how drunk she was. "She was drinking a lot of beer. She was happy and amused. At one point she could not stand. We took her to the room to put her to bed. She was wearing leggings and a long-sleeve top, everything was black. We had to help her into bed. I don't think she knew how drunk she was, but when you're drunk you don't. She wanted to go back to the party.

"She was able to go to sleep. We closed the door and left the door to the party open so we could see if she got up. We were concerned she might fall down the stairs. We carried on partying. We thought González had gone to smoke, but were concerned he was taking too long. We looked for him."

A forensic scientist was given a urine sample of Miss P taken on Boxing Day plus blood and urine samples from December 27. His conclusion was that no alcohol or drugs were detected, only caffeine and nicotine. Another specialist examined a vaginal swab taken from Miss P. He said that there were traces of semen on the vulva, indicative of some form of sexual activity, namely penile-vaginal intercourse.

THE LANDLORD told Jorge González to leave the property when he heard what had happened. The defendant was spotted the following April by two police officers who recognised him as someone who was wanted for an offence. Checks proved this was the case and he was charged with rape.

González told the jury: "I had drunk about three cans of beer slowly. I'd say I was three-tenths drunk. Miss P was a bit strange. The way she danced and spoke was very provocative. She moved her body from side to side when we were dancing, she had her hands on my waist...our bodies were touching.

"We were talking about speaking English. I told her I couldn't speak it very well and was going to college to learn. We danced for a couple of songs. She then went to change the music, but couldn't work out how to do it. Juan told her not to touch the computer. She wasn't happy.

"She became sad, there were tears coming from her eyes. I didn't see her leave the party. I had been out to smoke twice. When I came back after the third cigarette, I saw Miss P coming out of the bedroom. I thought it was strange as it was the landlord's room. She looked a bit tired, a bit tearful.

"We both went into the bedroom together. We sat on the bed. The light was off. I asked her if she liked me. She didn't answer. She touched my face and started kissing me. The kissing became very intense. She told me to close the door… to lock it. We kissed again and lay down on the bed. She got on top of me and took off her top. She was wearing nothing underneath. She was very aroused. She took her trousers off down to her feet. I pulled my trousers down to my knees. She was kissing me and in English said: 'Go hard… go hard.'

"We made love… intercourse… it lasted five to seven minutes. I can't remember whether I ejaculated. I stopped because there was a knock on the door. They were knocking for about five minutes. I was waiting for her to get dressed, but she could not find her clothes.

"I could now hear voices. When I unlocked the door Pamela was there, no one else, and she asked me what I was doing. I said: 'It's not what you are thinking' because I guessed she thought I was abusing Miss P. I went to my attic room for a couple of minutes before going downstairs. Pamela was shouting: 'What have you done to my cousin?' I told her I hadn't done anything."

González had previously pleaded guilty to illegally obtaining a Spanish ID card.

WHEN people speak through an interpreter it can be difficult to assess their personality and character, which would not have helped the jury as it went away to decide its verdict.

There was a significant difference of evidence between the female witnesses and Juan about how much and what the claimant had consumed. They said Miss P stayed in the landlord's bedroom while Nellie claimed she slept with her. Juan said Miss P was in the downstairs kitchen at 1 a.m.

Why would a girl who believed she had been raped want to go back to the party? Was it the drink — however much of it — talking?

There was much for the jury to deliberate before it reached its verdict.

11

JORGE GONZÁLEZ: Rape.

THIS SEEMED a relatively easy one for the jury which has to be sure of either verdict — no doubts at all.

Had I been a juror I would have asked myself how much alcohol Miss P had consumed and how much she would reasonably have needed to drink to become so [allegedly] drunk. She claimed to have had three cans of beer. I was surprised none of the police, prosecution or defence barrister asked the strength of the alcohol. Three beers would probably not have made her legless, even though individuals have different alcohol tolerance levels.

There was no evidence of her drinks being spiked with anything, though Juan claimed she had consumed beer, wine and rum. To be so drunk that you could not walk without assistance and have sex without being able to remember would surely take more than three cans of beer.

Nobody becomes drunk suddenly and it was unusual that none of her friends seemed to spot Miss P's downward spiral and tried to stop her.

I found it strange that the other girls began worrying about Jorge González after he had been missing for 15 minutes when he allegedly went for a cigarette. It was Christmas Day and it would be understandable for somebody to be on the phone while having a cigarette. Why were they so concerned?

Some girls, who have consensual sex when tipsy, but not drunk, regret it in the cold light of day and can react in different ways.

After two days of deliberation González was found guilty by a 10-2 majority verdict and was sentenced to six years for rape plus eight months for the fake Spanish ID. I have re-read the evidence and I remain surprised that 10 jurors could be sure of González's guilt.

Perhaps it is wrong to feel sympathy for anyone convicted of rape and only two people really know what went on in that room, but from the evidence I heard, which was the same as the jury of course, I could not be sure — always the key word — it was sufficient to find him guilty.

My hunch is the jurors based their decision solely on whether González knew Miss P, who never once mentioned "rape" in her evidence, was not able to consent to sexual intercourse. The same Miss P who her friends admitted wanted to return to the party after whatever had happened.

*There was almost a premature end to this trial. One juror wanted to go out for a cigarette after five hours of deliberation and permission was granted. The protocol for this should have been all the other 11 jurors going outside with the smoker. However, he was allowed to leave the court with a jury bailiff while the other 11 jurors remained in the deliberation room. Court rules demand that the 12 jurors can only discuss the trial when together, but the other 11 claimed while the smoker was outside, they did not discuss the case. The judge seemed less than convinced, but felt obliged to take their word, not least because of the problems dismissing a jury and ordering a retrial, so allowed the deliberation to continue.

12

HEATHER NORMAN: Revenge porn

A HARD LESSON FOR DUMPING
A 'SCARLET WOMAN'

REVENGE, it is said, is a dish best served cold. For Heather Norman, it was best served erect.

Norman had a three-month affair with a married man who cannot be named for legal reasons after meeting him on a "no strings attached" web site. When he ended their relationship, Norman said she "wanted to hurt him in the same way as he had hurt me" and decided to send his wife six photographs of his erect penis.

She pleaded not guilty to one count of disclosing private sexual photographs with intent to cause distress, which is also known as revenge porn — a specific law that was introduced in April 2015.

"Hell hath no fury like a woman scorned," wrote the English playwright William Congreve in 1697. It is a line the claimant could have been excused for thinking certainly applied to Heather Norman.

THE PROSECUTION outlined its case to the jury.

"Their sexual relationship lasted around five months. Heather Norman did not take that news [of it ending] well. In the days that followed she sent him a number of messages that he found distressing."

The jury was told Norman had accepted a police caution for harassment of the man 10 days after their relationship ended.

Norman had sent an email to a third party, cc'ing the man and, for reasons that were never explained, the customer services department at John Lewis, which discussed their relationship in depth. The defendant was highly critical of the appearance of a friend of the man and complained that he had gone to the police.

The prosecution continued: "A further email, sent in the same way, described a conversation Norman had with her nephew about how the man 'needed to be stopped.' On February 25, the man was at his home address when a recorded delivery addressed to his wife arrived.

"When he checked the return address, he found it was from Norman. In light of what happened before he was concerned that the letter may contain material that would upset his wife so he opened it. The envelope contained a long letter addressed to his wife detailing the affair that he had with the defendant.

"It had attached to it a number of photographs, including six of his erect penis. During the sexual relationship those photographs had been exchanged and now Norman was sending them to his wife. He was, as you would expect, extremely distressed to see the contents of that envelope."

The man reported the letter and the previous emails to the police. A few days later he received an email, this time addressed just to him from Norman "expressing her disgust" that he had gone to the police.

A second email was sent to him in the same way claiming that he had hurt her when he ended their relationship. A second copy of the letter that was posted to his home arrived on March 14 and Norman later admitted to the police she had hand delivered it.

This time, however, the photographs of his penis were not attached. Three days later Norman was arrested and she gave the police a detailed account of how she felt after the relationship had ended.

The prosecution said: "She stated the emails she sent to him were cc'd into his wife by accident. She accepted she had sent the letters to his wife. She told the police that she accepted she shouldn't have sent them, but she wanted his wife to know 'what he was really like' and she was 'concerned about the wife catching a sexually transmitted disease'."

Norman told the police that she did not intend to cause the alleged victim distress when she sent the photographs. However, the prosecution said: "If you send photographs of the penis of a man you have had an affair with to his wife, what could you possibly intend by doing that? The only inference you can draw from that is that she intended to cause distress to the person to whom the penis belonged."

What had really angered Norman was that the man was also having an affair with the wife of a friend of her niece.

CROSS-EXAMINED by the prosecutor, Heather Norman told the jury she had initially informed the claimant she would not date a married man, but he had said he would leave his wife.

Norman said: "For three months he pursued me relentlessly and said he wanted to marry me eventually. He completely led me along and then, like a bombshell, told me 'I've led you up the garden path'."

"How did you feel?"

"I felt betrayed. I wanted to hurt him as he had hurt me. When he said he didn't love me I felt cheap. He treated me abominably. He was cheating on his wife and cheating on me."

"Why did you send the photographs to the man's wife?"

"I had spoken to [a woman] who had told me that she had given oral sex to him and they had been having an affair for a few years. She said that she phoned him in Miami and her friend had a flat and they could use it to have sex. He said he'd think about it, but if her friend agreed to a threesome, he'd definitely think about it. I felt his wife should be informed about his antics because at that time I had a discharge and I didn't know what it was. I didn't want my niece to think I was some scarlet woman who was having an affair with her friend's husband.

"I thought she should know because he'd been having these sexual encounters, also because he was such a complete and utter liar and it was unfair. He was cheating on his wife. He was cheating on me and cheating on other people too."

"Why did you not just write a letter to the man's wife? Wasn't sending photographs vindictive?"

"I am not vindictive. If I wanted to distress him, I would have put them on Facebook, Twitter, the photographs, I could have had them blown up. I sent them by private mail, special delivery only for his wife so that she knew what her husband was and what danger he was putting her in. I could have sent them to his friends on Facebook. I'm not vindictive, I'm not like that."

"There was any number of ways you could have demonstrated the affair to the man's wife."

"The photographs were the best proof because they showed him in his own home. I didn't believe for a moment that he would admit it. He would say 'no that's lies' and 'she was making it up.' Obviously photographic evidence is better than written evidence. You work in law, you know that. He had betrayed a potential relationship with my niece. As much as anything I just wanted him to keep me [as a friend] on his Facebook so my niece would not get suspicious. I said if he did that, he'd never hear from me again."

THE JURY was told it was not against the law of the land to play away from home. A Crown Court is not a place for such emotions to be judged. Revenge porn is the sharing of private, sexual materials, either photos or videos of another person without their consent and with the purpose of causing embarrassment or distress.

The offence, which carries a maximum of two years' imprisonment, criminalised the sharing of private, sexual photographs or films where what is shown would not usually be seen in public. Sexual material not only covers images that show the genitals, but also anything that a reasonable person would consider to be sexual; so this could be a picture of someone who is engaged in sexual behaviour or posing in a sexually provocative way.

Did Heather Norman act to cause the man distress or whether it was simply to inform his wife what her husband was up to?

12

HEATHER NORMAN: Revenge porn

THE JURY had to decide what Heather Norman's motive was for sending her ex-partner's wife photographs of his erect penis. Was it to cause the man who had been having an affair with her distress or simply to tell his wife what her husband had been getting up to?

Inevitably the case had a bit of Fatal Attraction's Bunny Boiler about it. The prosecution had said: "If you send photographs of the penis of a man you have had an affair with to his wife, what could you possibly intend by doing that? The only inference you can draw from that is that she intended to cause distress to the person to whom the penis belonged."

The jury acquitted Norman, deciding she did not intend to cause the man distress.

No, I couldn't understand it, either.

13

KENWYNE JAMESON: Common assault; threats to kill

TOO TIRED FOR SEX AND
A WEE PROBLEM

ACCORDING to Alisha Turner, her ex-partner Kenwyne Jameson urinated in her bedroom waste bin, on the floor of the bathroom and on the hallway carpet. Jameson, allegedly, struck her and threatened to kill her with a knife.

Jameson denied two charges of common assault and threats to kill. He claimed Turner just wanted him for sex and because he refused, this was her revenge.

The jury could not have suspected wee-wee would form a large part of the verdict it had to decide.

ALISHA TURNER told the jury Kenwyne Jameson was "drunk" when he came round one night/morning (depending on which you believe).

She said: "We were arguing and it was getting louder. I went to my bedroom and my two-year-old daughter started crying. I went to pick her up and make a bottle. I was holding her because he was drunk."

The prosecution asked Turner if Jameson was the baby's father.

"Yes."

"What happened next?"

"I was standing by the cupboard and he started shouting 'give me my daughter.' I was holding her and he punched me on the left side of my face, not that hard. Then he slapped my face."

"How many times?"

"About three."

"You were still holding your baby."

"Yes, because I thought that might stop him. I told him to get out. He went to the kitchen and came back with a silver knife."

"What happened?"

"He put part of the knife in my face and said 'stop the noise or I might have to kill you'."

"And then?"

"He slapped me again. Then, I have a brown box where my shoes are and I tripped over it and my daughter banged her head [on the cupboard door]. I called his mum and then my mum, but there was no reply. I dialled 999. He tried to take my phone."

"Where was your daughter?"

"I'd put her on the bed. An ambulance was called because she has some heart problems [unrelated to the incident]."

"She was taken to hospital."

"Yes."

"Any injuries to you?"

"A reddening to my arms."

THE DEFENCE asked Alisha Turner what the relationship was like with Kenwyne Jameson at the time.

"Not very good."

"You were calling him because you wanted a physical relationship."

"No, not true."

"You called him on the day and asked him to come round."

"No."

"You are in a new relationship."

"Yes."

"Is he in court?"

"Yes."

"Is that why you are embarrassed answering about sex?"

"No."

"What help did he [the defendant] give his daughter?"

"Very little support. He bought a few nappies now and again."

"He loves his daughter."

"I don't know."

"So, he came round. I'm going to say he got there about 11 p.m. and the reason he came round is because you had told him his daughter was crying for him."

"I spoke to him in the daytime and I don't remember saying that."

"You don't seem very sure."

"I am."

"You let him in. He had a quick look at his daughter."

"He went straight to the kitchen."

"He got on the sofa and didn't pay you any attention at all."

"He was drunk."

"I suggest he was tired and wanted to sleep."

"He was drunk."

"You went to your room and I suggest it was three or four hours later before anything happened."

"It was 30 minutes."

"You shook him to wake him up."

"Not true."

"He may have wet himself a little bit."

"I did not wake him up. He was sitting up. I know nothing about urine."

"You accused him of urinating in the bedroom."

"He did do it."

"In the hallway on the carpet."

"He did it."

"At no time did he urinate on the bathroom floor."

"He did."

"Eventually the two of you got together and you say he just punched you in the face."

"He spoke to me first."

"He says he didn't do anything of the sort."

"He did."

"You say he held a knife in your face. Why didn't you phone the police first of all?"

"I did and he threatened to kill me."

"You never mentioned a knife being held to your face [to the police]."

"I did."

"After you'd finished arguing the first call you made was to your mother."

"No. His mother."

"Did you tell the police that?"

"Yes."

"In the second call to your mother you left a message saying you were frightened by what had happened to you. So why not call the police?"

"I wanted to call his parents first, see what they could do."

"By the time you phoned the police everything had stopped."

"Not really. We were still arguing."

"There was no physical contact by then."

"No."

"Did you at any time tell them he threatened you with a knife to your face?"

"Not remember the exact words. I was hysterical."

"You did not tell the first police officer who arrived."

"I did."

"You did not tell him your daughter had banged her head."

"I did."

"That you'd been slapped four or five times."

"I told one of the police, yes."

"In your statement, you never said anything about weeing on the bathroom floor."

"I did say it."

"Or the hallway carpet."

"I did."

"Is there any reference in your statement about this?"

"I did tell them."

The claimant's statement to the police was handed to her.

"Do you agree it's not in the statement?"

"Yes."

"Or that he held a knife to your face?"

"Not sure."

"Have a look [at the statement]. Is there anything about a knife being held to your face?"

"No."

"That he threatened to kill you?"

"No."

"You told the jury he said he might kill you."

"I told the police when they arrived."

"That you called his mother?"

"Not see it."

"There was clearly a dispute, but not on the level you have told the jury."

"There was. He was drunk."

"You are exaggerating and it got out of control."

"No."

"Your account is a false account against Mr Jameson."

"No, it's not."

PC SUE DUNN was asked by the prosecution if she inspected the waste bin in the bedroom the defendant was accused of urinating in.

"Not closely."

"Your conclusion?"

"I could not see anything wet in the bin or on the [bedroom] floor."

"What about the hall?"

"I saw nothing. She said she'd cleared it up."

"Did you see any marks of the alleged assault [to the claimant]?"

"Slight reddening of the left arm."

"Did you see the baby?"

"Yes, in her bedroom. She was OK."

A STATEMENT by PC Paul Andrews was read to the jury. "When I arrived, a male was leaving. I told him to stop, but he carried on walking. He put his hands in his pockets. I told him to take them out. He started to get aggressive and smelt strongly of alcohol so he was handcuffed. He was arrested and cautioned before being taken to the police station."

DC PETER CORRIE was asked by the prosecution about the interview with Kenwyne Jameson. The defendant made a prepared statement: "I deny the allegations. I had a couple of bottles of Guinness. She wanted me to go round and said our daughter wanted to see me. At some point when suddenly awakened I may have accidentally urinated then. I did not hit her, grab her or threaten her with a knife. Our daughter remained in her bedroom. She [the claimant] wanted sex and I'd fallen asleep."

Jameson was given the chance to put his side, but answered "no comment" to almost every question. The jury was told the defendant had no previous convictions or cautions.

KENWYNE JAMESON, 22, was cross-examined by the defence. His heavy West Indian accent, street slang and minimalistic answers were an unusual background to the side-show of weeing in a waste bin.

"What was your relationship with the claimant at the time?"

"Arguments."

"So it was coming to an end."

"Yes."

"What happened in the days leading up to the incident?"

"She phoned me. I'd get up in the morning and she'd say: 'Come and visit.' Stressed me out."

"What did she want in particular?"

"Sex. I said 'no,' just see my daughter and that's it."

"On the day of the incident?"

"Same day, right through the day. Had to turn my phones off. When I turned them on, same thing again."

"Did you make arrangements to see her?"

"Yes. I had some food, had some drink. Had two Guinness and walked to her house. I was tired."

"How were you feeling? Drunk?"

"No."

"Affected by alcohol?"

"I was OK, just tired."

"You knocked on the window when you got there."

"Yes. Went in. Not say much. Went to the living room/kitchen, it's all in one like. Watched TV."

"Did you speak?"

"She was tired and went to her room. I went to sleep."

"What time was this?"

"Around 11."

"There came a time when something happened."

"OK, she woke me up about four. I got up, went to the bathroom. My daughter was sleeping. We started arguing."

113

"Did you urinate in the bin?"

"No."

"Hallway?"

"No."

"What did you argue about?"

"I put my jacket on and headed out."

"There was allegation of a slap."

"No, not slap her."

"Punch her?"

"No."

"Get a knife?"

"No."

"Threaten to kill her?"

"No."

"Were you aware she was calling the police?"

"No. I heard her shouting. I thought she was arguing with me and I wasn't answering."

"Did you grab the phone from her hand?"

"No, not see her on the phone."

"Where did you go?"

"Outside. Saw police coming."

"Were you aggressive?"

"No. Just said: 'What have I done'?"

"You were told about the allegations."

"I said I'd done nothing. How is it I'm getting arrested?"

"It was said your eyes were glazed."

"Just woken up."

"There was a fight between you and the claimant."

"No. No fight."

"All this time where was your daughter?"

"Asleep in her room."

"You were interviewed by the police. You made a prepared statement and made no comments to extra questions."

"Advised by solicitor."

THE PROSECUTION took over the cross-examination of Kenwyne Jameson.

"You said she wanted sex. You turned up at 11 and said she was silent. What happened to the sex?"

"She could see I was tired."

"Or completely drunk."

"No."

"So, no sex and you did not see your daughter."

"She was asleep. I opened the door. Not going to wake her up."

"You turned up plastered. You did not give two hoots about your daughter. You have just used the claimant as your baby's mother."

"No."

"Why did you not go over in the day? Do you work?"

"In a restaurant."

"You must have left long before it closed."

"I was near the restaurant."

"You did not arrive at 11."

"I did."

"What do you do at the restaurant?"

"Cook, clean up, serve."

"What time did you leave?"

"Ten."

"No customers after 10?"

"Not the only one there."

"You turned up in the morning absolutely plastered."

"Not true."

"You said she woke you at four and accused you of weeing in her bin. Did you?"

"No."

"Why would she accuse you? It doesn't make sense."

"I don't know. Maybe because I wanted to end the relationship."

"Just the two of you in the bedroom. No one else and she accused you of weeing in the bin. Why were you in the bedroom?"

"Not for sex or anything. At some time, I wanted to wee so went to the toilet."

"You said you may have urinated when you woke up."

"Might have when she woke me."

"A common occurrence, is it? Were you drunk?"

"I just felt I wanted to go to the toilet."

"The police said you smelt of alcohol."

"It was my jacket. I spilt some on it."

"How many Guinness did you have?"

"Three."

"A few shots?"

"No."

"In your statement you said you had two drinks. Now you say three. How many was it?"

"Three."

"You spilt one bottle."

"Yes."

"When asked [by the police] about urinating in the bin, you said 'no comment' but laughed."

"Yes."

"What did you laugh at?"

"The question, innit."

"Did you or did you not accidentally wee yourself?"

"No."

"Sure?"

"Yes."

"I suggest you picked up a knife and threatened her."

"No. Not true. No knife."

"So it's completely made up."

"Yes."

"Why not deny it to the police?"

"Solicitor said no comment."

"Because you did pick it [a knife] up."

"No."

"In your drunken state."

"No."

"You said you were not aware she was phoning the police. You telling the truth?"

"I was in the bathroom. Didn't want no argument."

"I say you grabbed the phone because the call went dead. She phoned the police back. You caused that."

"Not see her with no phone."

"Because you knew the police were on the way."

"No. Would've stayed there if I knew she'd phoned police."

"Not true, is it?"

"Is true."

"I put to you that you smelt of alcohol. You did not spill any over your jacket. You were absolutely drunk."

"Not true."

THE CROWN'S case was that Kenwyne Jameson intentionally beat up Alisha Turner and threatened her with a knife. The making of a threat to kill is an offence wherein the defendant intends the victim to fear it will be carried out. It is immaterial whether it is premeditated or said in anger.

The truth in the trial was there somewhere, but neither claimant nor defendant was entirely convincing which would hardly have helped the jury in its deliberations.

13

KENWYNE JAMESON: Common assault; threats to kill

THIS WAS a strange one. Among other things, Kenwyne Jameson was accused of weeing in a bedroom waste paper bin, one of the more unusual allegations in a Crown Court trial.

The so-called common assault left the claimant with a "slight reddening" to her left arm but not to her face where, she said, she had been struck three times. Alisha Turner never mentioned to the police that Jameson had allegedly held a knife to her throat as she subsequently told the jury or that he threatened to kill her.

It was no surprise when the jury returned a verdict of not guilty to both charges. If a claimant fails to mention to the police something as serious as a knife to the throat the Crown's case is severely weakened.

14

AZIZ ABDUL: Affray

AALEM POYA: Affray; possession of an offensive weapon; theft

TALL MAN, SHORT MAN
AND PLANK MAN

KABIR PAWAN and his girlfriend Manja Filipović went to a local kebab shop, parking the car a couple of minutes' walk away.

As they strolled to the shop Pawan bumped into — literally — Aalem Poya who was with his friend Aziz Abdul. According to Pawan, an off-duty police officer, he was initially the victim of pick-pocketing by Poya who stole his wallet.

Pawan grabbed it back and went with Manja to the kebab shop where he realised, the Crown said as it opened the trial, £100 was missing. A short while later Pawan was attacked by a number of males and knocked unconscious by one who struck him with a plank of wood.

Police found Abdul hiding behind a bush while Poya was arrested a few days later after handing himself in at a police station.

The prosecution told the jury the fact that Pawan was an off-duty police officer was irrelevant and he should be looked upon like any other claimant.

The jury was shown a 20-minute CCTV compilation tape which did not feature the attack, just the defendants, claimant and witness during the period leading up to the incident.

Affray, the Crown explained, is a public order offence whereby a reasonable member of the public would fear for his or her safety.

MANJA FILIPOVIĆ was asked by the prosecution about the evening in question.

"We were at home. It was about 10 and we decided to get some ice cream from Tesco. We did that and headed to a kebab shop. We parked up and walked towards the shop."

"As you did this did you meet anyone?"

"Yes. Two men walking towards us."

"What happened as they passed you?"

"One male pushed my partner on the shoulder."

"Did you notice anything about him?"

"He was tall and wore a grey hoodie."

"Anything said?"

"The tall male said: 'What's happening'?"

"What did you do?"

"I was trying to get my partner to move on. I didn't want any trouble. Then my partner realised he'd had his wallet stolen."

"Where was it?"

"In the taller man's hand. My partner tried to snatch it back which he did. I just wanted to get away."

"Once he got it back what happened?"

"The taller male got his belt out. It had a buckle at the end. He hit my boyfriend on the head with the belt. We then made our way to the kebab shop where he realised £100 was missing from the wallet."

"What did he do?"

"He wanted to find the people responsible and call the police. I called the police."

"So you left the shop to search for the males."

"Yes. We found them and my partner asked for his money back. They swore at him. The taller male swung the belt with the buckle at my partner. The shorter one went to a dustbin, got a bottle and broke it against a wall. He said: 'I'll kill you.' I didn't say anything."

"What happened then?"

"The taller male shouted and some people appeared. I didn't see where they came from. They were all male. One had a metre long plank of wood. He hit my boyfriend across the back with it."

"What did you do?"

"I tried to stop it. I was afraid. I tried to scare them off by saying the police were coming. They all ran away down a back alley. My partner ran after them because he wanted to keep them in sight until the police arrived. The man with the wood hit my partner on the head with the plank."

THE DEFENCE barrister for Aziz Abdul suggested to Manja Filipović that Kabir Pawan was the instigator of the trouble.

"Your boyfriend bumped into the taller male."

"No, the other way round."

"Whoever orchestrated the collision… there was friction."

"More them."

"It became quite heated. Your partner was angry and got into a fight with the taller male."

"No."

"You had to pull him away."

"No."

"He wanted to fight."

"No."

"Yes, he did. No wallet was taken."

"Yes, it was."

"The second male tried to stop your boyfriend getting into a fight outside the kebab shop."

"No."

"He wanted to fight. He was angry."

"No. He just wanted a closer look at them."

"There was no point at which your boyfriend checked his wallet."

"Yes, he did."

"When he had his back to the CCTV camera, was that when he checked?"

"No."

"He could have observed them from a distance and called the police."

"I'd already phoned them."

"That's a lie. All calls are recorded, you know. He found the men and they attacked him. You didn't phone the police [when you said you did]."

"I did."

"No, you didn't. You phoned the police after the fight. You're lying,

121

aren't you?"

"No."

"What happened was, your boyfriend got into a fight with the taller male who called out for men in nearby flats to help him which they did. You say plank man attacked your boyfriend and someone took a bottle out of a bin and smashed it on a wall."

"Yes."

"You said this was the shorter male. Was every guy in the group Asian?"

"Yes."

"Could you have been wrong with the identity?"

"No."

"Nobody broke a bottle and waved it at you."

"They did."

"You say all this happened while you were on the phone to the police."

"Yes."

"They were shouting 'fuck you' and 'I'm going to kill you'. You thought you were going to die, yet you followed potential murderers down an alleyway."

"My boyfriend did."

"He didn't need to get that close for a description. He's a trained police officer. Why follow him?"

"I was with my partner."

"You say you dialled 999 as you left the kebab shop."

"A few minutes."

"Why not earlier? Your boyfriend had been belted and robbed."

"I was so shocked."

"He picked the fight."

"No."

"Only when other men came down did you phone the police."

"No, before."

The defence read out some of the transcript of Manja's phone call to the police.

"We was just attacked. Please come here. Oh my God he's bleeding. So many boys attacked us. They hit him in the head. He is bleeding so

bad. They've robbed his money. They are running away with the money. He's a police officer."

"No one had a metre of wood, did they?"

"They did. It was my way of describing it. It was how I saw it."

"It seems fairly descriptive. You were on the phone [to the police] for six minutes. Nowhere are there any threats [heard]. It didn't happen, did it?"

"It did."

"You phoned the police when you realised your boyfriend had done more than he could handle."

"No."

"The shorter man did not threaten either of you."

"He did."

THE DEFENCE for Aalem Poya — the taller male — put it to Manja Filipović that she was trying to protect her partner.

"No."

"No one stole his wallet."

"They did."

"So he grabbed the wallet back and noticed £100 was missing."

"In the kebab shop."

"I suggest the tall male used a belt to defend himself because your boyfriend came at him."

"I disagree."

"He wanted to fight him."

"Not true."

"Did your boyfriend use force at any time?"

"Only to defend himself."

KABIR PAWAN, who confirmed he had his warrant card with him at the time of the incident, was cross-examined by the prosecution.

"What happened when you first saw the two males?"

"The tall male bumped into me. I didn't think much of it, but he was very close to my face and he said: 'What's up?' I'd never seen him before in my life. He went for his belt which had a large buckle. I went to walk off, but maybe two or three seconds later I noticed he had my wallet."

"Where was it on you?"

"Front pocket of a zipped-up jumper."

"What did you do?"

"I turned back and said: 'My wallet.' I snatched it from his hand. He took his belt off and hit me three or four times with the buckle. His mate tried to pull him away. We ran to the kebab shop to get away. There I realised £100 was missing. I said to my girlfriend: 'He's stolen the money, call the police'."

"What happened next?"

"We left the kebab shop and saw two males walking down the road about 30 metres away. I shouted: 'Give me my money back or I'm calling the police.' The tall man turned round, came at me and started hitting me with his belt which was wrapped around his fist."

"What did the shorter male do?"

"He went to some rubbish bin and picked up a bottle which he smashed on the ground. He waved it in our faces. We were in a block of flats and the tall male shouted: 'Ali, come down, kill that bastard'."

"What happened next?"

"My glasses were snatched. My vision is blurred without them. I was on the ground protecting my head as I was being hit. Someone walked down with a large piece of wood and hit me on my back, the back of the head... everywhere. Eight or 10 times."

"Of the original two?"

"The tall male was hitting me with his belt. I could taste my own blood. I fell down and lost consciousness."

THE DEFENCE barrister for Aziz Abdul put it to Kabir Pawan: "In your statement to the police you said you smelt alcohol on the tall male's breath. You did not mention that in court. Are you changing your view?"

"If it says that on my statement, that's what I said."

"Did you smell alcohol on his breath?"

"He was very aggressive."

"Can you answer the question?"

"I can't remember."

"It was a pretty significant incident."

"Yes. One that will stay with me for the rest of my life."

"Let's talk about when you bumped in to each other. How did you not see your wallet being taken?"

"Because my wallet was not there."

"So he had his belt in one hand and took your wallet."

"Yes."

"It does not make sense to take someone's wallet and hold it in front of them."

"I don't know."

"When did he take the money?"

"I don't know."

"You are, as a police officer, used to situations where you have to be alert to threat."

"Correct."

"Someone threatened you with a belt. What did you do?"

"I ran away."

"That's a lie."

"It's the truth."

"You were involved in a fight with the taller male outside the shop."

"No."

"You wanted to fight him."

"Not correct."

"Why did you not call the police?"

"I wanted to follow them to see where they went. To get a description."

"You wanted to confront him."

"No. To follow them and know exactly where they were."

"When the police arrived, you were taken to a van to see a male. It was the shorter male. You said you thought he was involved, but did not hit you. You made it clear the second male did not hit you. You also made it clear he threatened you with a bottle. Why did you not mention that?"

"I had just been hit. I was shaking... bleeding."

THE barrister for Aalem Poya said to Kabir Pawan: "You're a well-built male."

"I train, yes."

"A police officer."

"A very proud police officer."

"I suggest you bumped into the taller male. You barged him."

"I disagree."

"You're a proud man. Guy swearing at you in front of your

girlfriend. You took offence. You were embarrassed."

"I've had it before with work."

"He took his belt off because he felt he was going to be attacked. You wanted to fight him."

"Not true."

"You wanted to sort it out yourself."

"Not true."

"You said you'd been pickpocketed. He snatched your wallet. A professional pickpocket knows what to do which is not standing in front of you with your wallet in his hand."

"I saw it."

"You've invented all this."

"I disagree."

AZIZ ABDUL had admitted in a police interview he had initially lied when he said he had not been with Aalem Poya when the wallet was taken. "I was scared," he said. The defence barrister asked him to enlarge on this.

"It was something I had never been through before. I was frightened."

"So what did happen?"

"I was at a friend's house with Ali [Poya]. I smoked some cannabis. Me and Ali left for the off licence about nine. We got some Remy Martin and planned to go back to his flat. I saw two people coming towards us and something happened, some confrontation between Ali and the guy. They were trying to push each other."

"Did you see a belt used?"

"No."

"A wallet taken?"

"No."

"Do you know if a belt was used at all?"

"Only on the second confrontation."

"Then?"

"We started to walk back to his flat. He didn't say what had gone on. Then the guy came to Ali and pushed him in the face. Ali used his belt to defend himself. Three others came down from the flats."

"Did you see anyone with a plank of wood?"

"No."

"Did you pick up a bottle and smash it?"

"No."

"Then?"

"I ran towards an alleyway. I was really scared. I did not want to be associated with it. I hid behind a shed."

"Did you threaten anyone?"

"No."

"Use any violence?"

"No."

THE CROWN put it to Aziz Abdul: "When Poya went for him with his belt you joined in."

"No."

"Threw a few punches."

"No."

"You got involved when it all kicked off."

"No."

"You've tried to fit your account in evidence to get off."

"I was silly to lie. I was scared. I ran away."

WITH THE jury out of the courtroom the defence barristers argued that wearing a belt is not an offence per se. There has to be a pre-existence of some intent. Wearing a belt does not mean you are going to use it. This was, they argued, a spontaneous event and no one was carrying a weapon with intent.

The judge told the jury that count two — being in possession of an offensive weapon — had been withdrawn from the indictment. He also told the jurors there was no evidence how the money was taken from the wallet "so do not speculate."

IN ITS summing up the prosecution said: "Poya had the opportunity to tell you what happened. He chose not to. There are some questions you might like to have had answered. How Mr Pawan picked up his injuries? How was it when the police arrived, they all ran away? You are entitled to ask yourselves whether the answers could have been self-incriminatory.

"You heard the call to the police by his partner. She was hysterical. Was she making this up to justify something?

"There is no reason to doubt how foolish Mr Pawan was to come out of the kebab shop because he ended up being attacked by a group with weapons."

AZIZ ABDUL'S barrister, who said that Kabir Pawan had looked "cocky and self-satisfied" in court, told the jury to carefully consider the evidence by the claimant and his girlfriend. "The issue is not why they might be lying, but might they be lying? Is there consistency in their evidence? You might feel certain parts of it do not hold true. Was the bottle broken on the ground or against a wall? No broken bottle was found by the police. You might think that's odd.

"A skilled pickpocket does not fight because it gains attention. But why would he take £100 out of the wallet? The claimant did not notice the money being taken. This does not hold up to even the most basic premise."

THE barrister for Aalem Poya said: "He exercised his right to remain silent. Remember, he was not arrested at the scene. He handed himself in a few days later.

"Kabir Pawan was smiling at me while being cross-examined as if he found it amusing. He was out of uniform, but police officers have to behave in a certain way. He wanted to sort it out himself.

"How can you open a wallet and pull money out without it being noticed? He said he only followed them for a description. He'd been face-to-face with them. Come on…"

THE JURY had to decide whether one, both or neither of the defendants was guilty of the charges. For affray, it is not enough for the prosecution to prove that unlawful violence has been used. There has to be violence of such a kind that a bystander would fear for their safety.

It must be proved that a person has used or threatened unlawful violence towards another. The seriousness of the offence lies in the effect that the behaviour of the accused has on members of the public who may have been put in fear. There must be some conduct, beyond the use of words, which is threatening and directed towards a person or persons. Mere words are not enough.

While any trial must be judged on the evidence heard in court, when a police officer is the claimant, whatever the jury might have thought of his performance in the witness box, it would understandably present it with an unusual dilemma in its deliberations.

14

AZIZ ABDUL: Affray;

AALEM POYA: Affray; possession of an offensive weapon; theft

KABIR PAWAN may well be a very proud policeman, but his performance in the witness box showed an arrogance rarely seen from a claimant, let alone a police officer. He smiled throughout cross-examination, giving the impression of superiority and being untouchable.

Even Dynamo Magician Impossible would struggle to take someone's wallet and remove £100 from it with one hand presumably out of action because it had a belt wrapped round it — and without the owner seeing the money stolen.

There are no hard and fast rules about police officers carrying their warrant card while off duty. Pawan had his ID with him and police officers are expected to put themselves on duty whenever required. For reasons not asked or explained PC Pawan did not immediately arrest Aalem Poya when he stole his wallet.

The growing impression during the trial was that Pawan had bitten off more than he could chew with the initial confrontation and ended up the loser as the defendants had a little help from their friends in what may be perceived as street justice but, of course, is against the law of the land.

The evidence of the claimant was, in my opinion, so obviously flawed and as I could not be sure Poya had stolen Pawan's wallet and money there were questions about his subsequent claims, despite the injuries the claimant sustained.

Which shows how wrong you can be when you second-guess a jury. I was surprised when the jury found Poya guilty of affray and particularly theft. Ditto that Aziz Abdul, who admitted he had lied to the

police about his evidence, was found not guilty.

It is difficult to understand how the jury could have not had any doubts about the manner in which Pawan claimed the wallet was stolen... how Poya still had it in his hand so Pawan could snatch it back... and how £100 had been removed without the claimant seeing this.

Yet the jury found Poya guilty of theft. Poya chose not to be cross-examined, as is his legal right, and the jury can draw whatever inferences it puts on this. But any negatives for Poya's silence were countered by Pawan's non-explanation of the wallet and money episode which was, after all, the start of whatever else may have happened.

For this observer, with so much doubt and zero credibility regarding the wallet/money incident then the rest of Pawan's evidence — not least the way he delivered it — would have been treated with care. Perhaps it was because he was a police officer the jury thought he must — somehow — be telling the truth, even though it appeared to barely stand up to any credible measure of reliability, especially the wallet incident.

Unknown to the jury, Poya, 23, had appeared in court on nine occasions for 18 offences, mainly motoring and cannabis possession. The judge said that "however cocky" Pawan was and that "it would have been far more sensible had he stayed in the kebab shop" Poya was "the driving force" behind the violence that saw the claimant attacked, even though the defendant did not cause the more serious injuries.

"You started the whole thing by acting aggressively and a serious fracas occurred," the judge told Poya who was sentenced to two years' imprisonment. As he had spent 220 days on curfew that amounted to 110 days credit plus the three weeks in custody, making a total of 131 days. Poya would serve half his sentence in prison before being released on licence so he was in jail for around eight months.

15

JAMES NICHOLLS: Rape; sexual assault

DID HE RAPE THE MOTHER OF HIS SON?

JAMES NICHOLLS claimed that virtually every time he saw Miss T during their 11-year friendship they had sex.

Both parties agreed the last time he went round her house it ended with the pair having sex. Nicholls maintained the intercourse was consensual. After Miss T told her best friend Sue Welch that "he made me have sex with him" Welch telephoned the police to report the allegation.

The 30-year-old Nicholls was charged with rape and sexual assault.

THE CROWN'S case was that Miss T was in a long-standing, controlling and violent relationship, though, when she was asked by the defence whether James Nicholls controlled her, she said: "No."

The claimant had called the police on three occasions to report violence on her by Nicholls, but the Crown Prosecution Service decided each time there was insufficient evidence to proceed with the case and no further action was taken.

Nicholls and Miss T had a son who was six at the time — the defendant also had five other children by three different mothers; two were in court each day during the four-day trial.

The friendship between Miss T and Nicholls was weird though on the surface far from wonderful. For whatever reason both had gone along with it.

Miss T tried to explain their relationship in her police interview. "There's been so much stuff over the years. I just fell for everything. It's been on and off over the years. He had a baby with someone else. We've not been together for four years."

THE PROSECUTION asked Miss T about the three incidents where she had called the police.

"For the first [six years ago] you were in a car park. What happened?"

"I can't remember."

"Was there an argument?"

"Yes, I think so."

"The police were called."

"Yes."

"By who?"

"Me."

"Why?"

"We'd had an argument. It was so long ago."

"Was anyone hurt?"

"We had, like, an argument, a fight. I don't remember it."

"OK. Five years ago, the police were called to James's house. Do you remember who called them?"

"I don't remember. It was something to do with messages on a phone."

"You confronted him."

"They were about him and another woman."

"What's wrong with that?"

"He was always saying we were together. He was lying to me."

"What happened?"

"I don't remember. I went to get some of my things from his house and he smashed my TV."

"Did he do anything to you?"

"Yes, but I don't remember."

"Roughly speaking."

"There was an altercation."

"You phoned the police."

"Yes."

"But you don't remember the details. OK. The third time — does that ring any bells?"

"No."

On the day of the third incident Nicholls had driven to the claimant's home. Miss T, who had just started a new relationship, was reluctant to let him in, but agreed to meet him in the car park. "He said he wanted to go to the loo," she told the jury. "I thought 'I'm not stupid, he just wants to get in the house.' He said to give him the house keys and he'd let himself out. I thought 'no way, he could do anything.' He did not seem aggressive so I agreed he could use the loo and leave straight after."

THE DEFENCE tried to discover more about the relationship between James Nicholls and Miss T.

"He messed you around."

"Yes."

"You were never in a conventional girlfriend/boyfriend relationship."

"Not really."

"You had a child by him."

"Yes."

"You told the police he sold you dreams."

"Yes. Not all the time over the 11 years, but there comes a time when you realise, they won't happen. He was promising me the world."

"You really wanted a relationship."

"At some time, yes."

"He didn't want it. He pushed you away."

"He didn't push me away."

"He'd turn up and you'd have sex."

"In the past, yes."

"You found out he had at least two other children with other women. Was that upsetting?"

"Initially."

"You had a choice, whether to stay involved with him."

"Yes."

"He helped you with money for your son."

"Not consistently."

"You told the police he controlled you."

"He did, but not in the past few years. He's not able to control me like he used to. If you love someone you try. I wanted things to work out. I felt I deserved more. I'm not saying he didn't provide that to someone, but not to me."

"When did you last have sex [together]?"

"Last year."

"In March when the incident took place, he allowed you to use his car. That was amicable."

"Yes, he did help. Things were not perfect, but I wanted more from him."

"He would quite often come round for a chat."

"Yes."

"You watched TV together."

"Yes."

"So it wasn't unusual for him to come round."

"No."

"Did you leave a key for him?"

"Not regularly."

"But it did happen."

"Yes."

WHEN he was arrested, the police asked James Nicholls about his relationship with Miss T.

"We have a son together. We get on well and speak every day on the phone. I pick my son up every Friday and drop him back to her house or his nan's on Sunday. We'd also spend time together, relaxing, watching TV, have a drink together during the week."

"In the last three weeks, how many times have you been there?"

"Two or three."

"Was she a friend, a lover, the mother of your child or what?"

"It's a weird relationship. Not really say it's a relationship, but we still slept together. She became like a best friend."

"You had other women, they had your children. How did she perceive this?"

"She wanted to be in a relationship. She was insecure."

"How often did you have sex?"

"Every time we saw each other."

"Even when you were with other women?"

"Yes."

"Was there ever a time she refused?"

"No, never, not once."

"Were there any problems when the police were called?"

"Arguments, that's it."

"Any end in violence?"

"No."

"She described her relationship as a very different picture. She said there was time when there was no sexual activity."

"Last year we did not speak for three months. That was the only time we were not sleeping [together]."

"When was your previous sexual contact?"

"Two weeks ago, at her house."

"She said not since last year. Can you prove consensual sex took place — texts, maybe?"

"No, not texts."

"Tell me about the day of the incident."

"I called her at nine, she did not pick up. I called her again, not pick up. I was near her house on the way to work so I went there. She opened the door with a phone in her hand."

"Was there a chain?"

"No, she was standing in the doorway. She said she'd come outside to talk to me. We sat in the car and chatted, I said I needed the toilet. She said I just wanted to check inside. I said I didn't care if there was anyone inside, I just wanted the toilet."

"So you went in her home."

"Yes, I went to the toilet. We were chatting, I checked the door to the garden as she was always forgetting to close it. I pulled her forward, gave her a kiss on the cheek and told her I did it [check the garden door] as I cared about her and our son. After that we carried on talking."

"What happened then?"

"My hand went to her bum and she said she felt like she was coming on [period]. She took off her trousers and said she would check. Then she was sitting in the bedroom wearing a pink towel and a grey top. We chatted about our son. I had my shoes on her bed and she said I should take them off. She said I should also take my work track-suit bottoms off. I put my arm round her, cuddling, we then kissed and carried on kissing and we had sex."

"What went where?"

"What do you mean?"

"There are a lot of different ways to have sex."

"My dick went in her vagina. She said she didn't like it [this way] so we changed to doggy style."

"Did you ejaculate?"

"Yes."

"Inside her?"

"Yes."

"Did you use a condom?"

"No."

"Did she have an orgasm?"

"She was enjoying it."

"How do you know?"

"She closed her eyes."

"You could see that doggy style?"

"No, when I was on top."

"Was she on her period?"

"No. When she went to the bathroom, she said it was just spots."

"So you did not have sex when she was on her period."

"Not in full flow, no."

"Was there any indication she wasn't enjoying it?"

"No, she would have told me."

"And then?"

"We both went to the bathroom and washed off. She said: 'Look, I've come on.' We joked about it being a near miss. We went into the lounge and she started to talk about her new guy, Shaun."

"Had your son said anything about him?"

"No, not at all."

"So you did not rape her."

"I would not rape anyone, not the mother of my child. How could I ever see him then? We've had our arguments, but rape is a bit… intense. I'm devastated. It's shocking."

The interview returned to when Nicholls entered the property.

"Why did you check the garden door? Why would that be your business?"

"My son is there. She forgets to close the door."

"She said you went from room to room."

"I did not do that."

"She said you touched her breast. She said she did not want sex. She told you: 'If you want sex have it with your girlfriend.' She repeated it over and over again that she didn't want sex. You pulled her trousers and knickers down, pushed her on the bed. She felt degraded by the [period] blood. You said: 'One more time, like a last supper'."

"I did not say one last time."

"She said you put her hand on your penis."

"No."

"She said she just let you do it, put your penis in her vagina. Your hands were holding her tightly. She said it ended when you asked her if she wanted you to stop and she said 'yes.' She did not want it to start. You said: 'I hope your conscience is clear now you've cheated with me'."

"Not true, not true at all. She's a big girl, I'm a smaller guy. It would have been easy for her to stop me."

THE DEFENCE asked James Nicholls why he went to see Miss T on the day in question.

"To give her the car, my car, so she could take our son to school."

"How would you get around?"

"A work colleague was going to pick me up and drop me back so I could pick up the car."

"What did she say to you when you chatted in the car?"

"She asked me if I'd come here to do security. We were laughing and joking."

"When you were in her home, in the kitchen, what did you do?"

"I had an apple juice with a shot of vodka."

"You were going to work, why vodka?"

"It was only a cap-full."

"You had sex, who instigated it?"

"Both of us. We kissed and it went from there."

"How was she?"

"Relaxed."

"Did she say 'no'?"

"No."

"At any point?"

"No, she didn't."

"Did you say anything about her conscience being clear?"

"No. I said I was happy she'd found a relationship."

"How long did you stay afterwards?"

"About 15 minutes. My colleague phoned and I had to leave."

"Did you speak to her later?"

"I had a missed call."

"The next day you went to the police station."

"I went to work and my brother called to say the police had been round. I wondered why they'd come."

"When you heard rape…"

"I was shocked."

"Did you rape Miss T?"

"No."

JAMES NICHOLLS was asked by the prosecution if he agreed that he micro-managed Miss T's life.

"No."

"Interfere at all?"

"No."

"Telephone her at nine to see if your son went to school?"

"Every day I did that."

"Do you phone the mothers of your other children?"

"Yes, daily."

"You like freedom to come and go."

"Not if I meet the right person."

"What time did you say you got to her property?"

"At 9.45."

"You were supposed to be dropping the car off. Why not just give her the keys?"

"I did not have the opportunity. She was on the phone when she answered the door."

"Why not say 'I can see you're busy, here's the keys'?"

"Didn't have the chance."

"You had vodka and apple juice."

"Yes."

"Did you ask?"

"No."

"You don't like apple juice so you put some vodka in to hide the taste."

"Yes."

"This was you making yourself comfortable and you could do what you like in her house."

"I always have a drink when I'm round."

"Why not just go?"

"I wanted to relax and wait for my colleague."

"You went to the bedroom."

"Yes."

"You had sex."

"Yes."

"You forced her to have sex."

"No."

"Any time she complained about anything apart from your shoes?"

"No."

"How long were you in bed?"

"No idea."

"I suggest you know that you got there at 11.45."

"No."

The prosecution produced Nicholls' mobile records that showed he made calls to the claimant at 12.36, 12.44 and 15.05.

THE CROWN'S closing speech highlighted alleged inconsistencies in James Nicholls' evidence.

"The case is fundamentally a bedrock of controlling behaviour towards the claimant. He would not commit, but at the same time would not leave her alone. He was always just there. They had a child together, but no relationship.

"There were allegations of pushing her, grabbing her hair, threatening her and damaging her property. There was never a conviction, but as a fair-minded jury you will be able to decide if this was a pattern of behaviour. The defendant claimed he arrived at 09.00, then 09.45 and then 10.45, He was completely inconsistent on this evidence, a strong sign he was fabricating. He had to fit the facts around what really happened.

"She said she never mentioned it [rape] to the police. She would not have done it unless her best friend hadn't made her. Did she lie to her friend? Why would she make it up against the father of her son?"

THE DEFENCE did not try to paint the prettiest of pictures of its client. "He would not be a candidate for boyfriend of the year. He treated the claimant badly. He strung her along, sold her dreams, but did not come up.

"Their relationship and arguments are not on trial, though. They are only a background to the indictments. You should not judge him on those allegations because not one was proved. The prosecution suggested they showed a pattern of behaviour by the defendant. Or do they show a pattern of behaviour by the claimant?

"She reported three alleged assaults to the police. She doesn't get back at this man and decided to complain about rape. The most telling of all was when she was asked about any controlling behaviour and she said 'no.' That shows what her mindset really is.

"We all tell fibs that can take on a life of their own. She tells her friend something on the spur of the moment and immediately it gained momentum. She was almost forced to go to the police. If she went back on what she had said she would be branded a liar.

"She made it up because she had let herself down. She called 101, the non-emergency number, twice but did not mention any sexual offence. You may think that is telling."

THE JUDGE told the jury while the unusual relationship between claimant and defendant may help to put in context events of the day [of the alleged offences] the defendant must not be judged by this. He said: "The only common ground is that the defendant penetrated the vagina of the claimant with his penis. Did she consent? If not, did the defendant reasonably believe she consented?

"Did he intentionally touch her breast? If you are sure he did, then decide whether the touching was sexual and did he reasonably believe she consented?

"There is no suggestion that in any of the three incidents the defendant used violence against the claimant to have sex with her. If you are not sure they happened they will not assist you. If you are sure [they did happen] do they establish a propensity of violence against the claimant and whether they are relevant to the alleged rape?"

140

15

JAMES NICHOLLS: Rape; sexual assault

THIS trial was one of the most difficult to predict. James Nicholls was unfaithful — and some — though that is not a crime (in law anyway). Some of his evidence was unconvincing, but the claimant's refusal to report the rape and saying "no" when asked if Nicholls was controlling was perhaps significant.

The jury's deliberations went into a third day, a sure sign of uncertainty. Would Nicholls really rape the mother of his son? He was, presumably, having regular sex with his partner and probably a few other girls, too, given his record, so he could hardly have been desperate for some old-fashioned relief.

Sometimes, a single line can make me sure a witness, either the claimant or the defendant, is telling the truth. In this trial it was when the claimant said the defendant told her after they had intercourse: "I hope your conscience is clear now you've cheated on me."

That was an obvious reference to the claimant's new boyfriend and it did not strike me as a line that could be made up or one that would have been said after consensual sex.

I have no idea what swayed the jury to its guilty verdict but, like me, it presumably felt Nicholls' evidence had too many holes.

Nicholls was sentenced to nine years in prison.

16

JUAN CARLOS DÍAZ: Sexual assault

DÍAZ'S DANGLY AT
THE BUS STOP

MISS B was waiting for a bus in a busy area on a warm summer evening. She'd had a long day at work and after a drink or two with friends she wanted to get home. What she didn't want was, she claimed, a male brushing his penis against her on two occasions while she was by the bus stop.

Juan Carlos Díaz was charged with sexual assault; the particulars were intentionally touching Miss B and the touching was sexual. She did not consent and he did not reasonably believe she did. The Ecuadorian, who spoke through a Spanish interpreter, denied the single charge.

The jury was shown CCTV footage from a camera on a nearby lamp-post and from inside the bus. Díaz was interviewed twice by the police and on each occasion, he replied "no comment" to virtually every question under advice from his solicitor, he said.

THE CROWN called Miss B to the witness box.

"You were waiting at the bus stop."

"Yes."

"Where had you been?"

"At work and then I had a couple of drinks with friends, two gin and tonics."

"The bus stop was crowded."

"It's always crowded at that time of the evening and was no different."

"What happened?"

"It was a sunny day. There was a crowd of people. I was a little way back from the road, almost on my own. I felt something on the back of my left leg, quite high up. It brushed against me, quite subtle it was. I wasn't quite sure what it was. I turned around and noticed a man pretty close to me, just behind my left shoulder. I started to move away. At that point I knew it was his penis because of his relative height."

"What did you feel?"

"Initially a regular brushing movement. I moved away quickly."

"Did he need to be that close to begin with?"

"No. There were a lot of people. No one else was in the immediate vicinity. I'd stepped apart from the crowd."

"What sort of distance was there between you and anyone else?"

"A metre, a metre and a half. There was no need for him to be standing next to me."

"What did you do?"

"I think I made a disparaging noise. He lost his footing a little and fell forward. He stumbled forward a bit."

"Did he say anything?"

"He said 'sorry' twice and seemed to back away a little. I thought he could be drunk or it was a mistake. I wasn't sure."

"Why drunk?"

"Because he was standing so close to me and stumbled."

"How did you feel?"

"Puzzled. I just wanted to get away from him. The bus pulled up and everyone surged forward. I just joined the queue for the bus."

"How far had you moved from the initial standing spot?"

"Couple of metres, maybe more."

"What happened then?"

"I felt exactly the same thing on my leg. I knew it was him again. It was the same part [of my leg] and the same feeling."

"What did you do?"

"I pushed him. I think I put two hands on his shoulders. Not very hard, just to get him away from me."

"Did he say anything?"

"I told him to stop touching me and said he was creepy, or words to that effect. He took a step back and said 'sorry' again two or three times. He was very calm. He put his hands up, like it was an honest mistake."

143

"When you said 'stop' did he say anything else?"

"I asked if he wanted to get on the bus and he stood in front of me. He didn't say anything. I just pushed my way onto the bus to get away from him. I went to the top deck and sat down."

"Did you see him again?"

"No."

"Did you call the police?"

"I told my sister and she said I should call the non-emergency number. I was still in shock. I think if it had just happened once, it could have been an accident. But when it happened a second time, I knew it wasn't an accident. I had moved away and told him I did not welcome that close contact."

Ten weeks later Miss B attended a police station and identified the man who allegedly touched her.

THE DEFENCE began cross-examining the claimant.

"Why did it take 19 days for the police to get hold of you? They had left messages on your voicemail."

"I would have returned any calls."

"The police tried several times to arrange a statement."

"I don't remember there being any difficulty to organise this."

"If the police left a voicemail, you'd get straight back?"

"Yes."

"When did you leave work?"

"About seven."

"Did you eat while you were out?"

"If I did it would have been a snack."

"You told the jury you had two gin and tonics. In your police statement you said 'no more than two gins and tonics'."

"It was 19 days after it happened, I guess. I wanted to tell the truth."

"You said the bus stop was very busy."

"Yes."

"You felt something brushing against your leg. You told the police it was 'semi-soft and dangling.' You've no idea what really happened."

"No, not the case."

"You said someone was 'ridiculously' close to you."

"Yes."

"So you thought it must be his penis."

"I knew what it was."

"You said it went on for a while."

"Seconds."

"A bit different from a few seconds."

"The second time did not go on very long. First time was a few seconds."

"You said no one else was around and you immediately moved away."

"My memory is no one [else] was standing close by me."

The CCTV was shown to the jury.

"The only point of contact was to the top of your left leg."

"Yes."

"When you said the second incident took place everyone had surged forward."

"Yes."

"Quite a crowd of people."

"I was at the back."

"Did you tell the bus driver what happened?"

"No."

"Did you say to anyone 'stay with me, there's a man touching me'?"

"No. I just wanted to get away from him. I just wanted to get home."

"The defendant does not speak English."

"He said 'sorry' twice."

"Why did you go upstairs and not stay on the ground floor nearer the driver?"

"I just wanted to sit down. I was in shock. I felt safer."

"Not safer closer to the driver?"

"No."

"What were you wearing? "

"A T-shirt and jeans that were quite thick."

"Where did you feel the brushing?"

"The top of my left leg."

THE POLICE officer in charge of the case told the jury the defendant had been traced because he paid for his journey via a debit card. While Juan Carlos Díaz answered 'no comment' to most questions at the police interview he did say that he was "quite drunk." The officer also confirmed it had taken three attempts to contact the claimant, despite leaving voicemails. The jury was told Díaz was a man of good character with no previous convictions.

JUAN CARLOS DÍAZ took to the witness box with an interpreter. The defence asked him where he was from.

"Ecuador."

"How old are you?"

"39."

"When did you come to the UK?"

"April 2010."

"Are you entitled to be here?"

"Yes. I have permanent residency. I was married in 2014."

Díaz said he worked in the construction industry and on the day of the incident began at eight o'clock, finishing at four, returning home at five.

"What did you do then?"

"I went with Diego, my wife's uncle, for a drink at about six."

"Did you eat before you left?"

"Chicken and potatoes."

"You went to a pub?"

"Yes."

"How much did you drink?"

"Four beers, four pints of lager."

"How drunk were you?"

"On a scale of 10? Three."

"When did you leave the pub?"

"About eight, to go home."

"How did you feel?"

"Fine."

"We know you went to the bus stop."

"Yes."

CCTV was played to the jury again.

"As far as you were aware did you touch anyone as you moved forward?"

"No."

"The first part of the allegation is that you intentionally pushed your penis towards the left upper leg of a lady at the bus stop. Did you do that?"

"No."

"The claimant said you said 'sorry' twice."

"I did not say 'sorry' at any point."

"Did you say anything?"

"Nothing."

"On the CCTV it looks like words were exchanged."

"No."

"She said when everyone was moving forward to get on the bus, for a second time you pushed your penis against her. Did you do that?"

"No."

"Because you do not remember or it did not happen?"

"It did not happen."

"Did you intentionally touch anyone at the bus stop?"

"I did not touch anyone intentionally or sexually."

"You've answered my next question. When you were interviewed by the police why did you say 'no comment' to most answers?"

"My solicitor told me to."

"The same solicitor as you have now?"

"No. It's why I changed them. Because they said say 'no comment' and maybe I could have said something at the time."

THE PROSECUTION continued the cross-examination of Juan Carlos Díaz.

"You've been here for eight and a half years, seven years at the time of the incident."

"Yes."

"Been in construction all that time?"

"No. Only for just over a year, six months at the time [of the incident]."

"Before that?"

"Kitchen porter."

"Working alongside English people?"

"I worked alongside one man. I didn't know where he was from."

"So who else?"

147

"Poland and Colombia."

"So you could speak in Spanish to one, but you understand little English."

"I went to college for six months, but that's all."

"On the evening in question you had four beers."

"Yes."

"Four beers a normal amount?

"Probably, some days more."

"Did it affect your memory?"

"No."

"Affect your functions?"

"No."

"Is it fair to say the video shows you had more than four [beers]?"

"That day I was very tired."

"Did you have more than four?"

"No."

"The video seems to show you staggering."

"Yes. Maybe the four beers affected me."

"I'd say they affected you quite a lot."

"Yes."

"I suggest you deliberately touched the claimant with your penis."

"No."

"Accidentally with any part of your body?"

"I don't know. There were a lot of people getting on the bus."

"You recall apologising?"

"No."

"So she's wrong."

"Yes."

"It possibly happened or you don't remember?"

"I remember well and it didn't happen."

"Anyone claim you touched them or upset them?"

"No."

"Nobody pushed you."

"No."

"You remember what happened."

"Yes."

"No one accused you of touching them."

"No. We were all getting on the bus together."

"Not accidentally touch anyone with your genitals."

"No."

"The CCTV looks like you said something to the claimant."

"I didn't say anything to her."

"So not exchange words with anyone."

"No."

"When you were interviewed by the police six weeks later, you remember what you were talking about?"

"I said 'no comment'."

"That is not what I asked. I asked if you knew everything you were talking about?"

"Yes."

"You did nothing wrong."

"No."

"Not touch anyone."

"No."

"Something you'd never do."

"No."

"I accept you were given advice, but I suggest you are hiding behind what your solicitor told you."

"No."

"You wanted to tailor your evidence to what came out."

"No. My solicitor told me not to comment."

"We say you deliberately touched the claimant with your penis for your own gratification."

"I did not touch her."

THE PROSECUTION summed up its the case to the jury: "CCTV has its limitations and you cannot see a sexual assault taking place, but it may be helpful to decide if the defendant was pushed or they spoke.

"Sometimes the best evidence is from an eye-witness. Do you believe the evidence of the claimant? There was no reason for her to lie. There was no prior axe to grind, no reason to tell lies about a complete stranger.

"Maybe you could give him the benefit of the doubt about once, an accident, but he followed her and rubbed himself against her again. If you had accidentally touched a woman's leg with your genitals, would you not go out of your way to make sure it didn't happen again?

"Either the defendant was so drunk he didn't know what he was doing or he's lying."

THE DEFENCE told the jury: "It's just as well there was CCTV. Thank heavens they got that. If the claimant was accurate, consider she said there was a metre around her. You can't see that on the CCTV. She said something brushed her leg and it went on 'for a while.' She put two and two together and it must have been his penis.

"I don't wish to be too graphic, but she said it was 'semi-soft and dangly' yet she felt it through her thick jeans. If it was his penis, would she not feel the rest of his body against her too?

"No one is saying she is lying. Perhaps mistaken. The police officer said he left several messages for her before she got back. She said she would have got back when she received a message.

"And if mistaken, she thought she had better exaggerate."

THERE WAS little reason to suppose Miss B was not a reliable witness. She presented her evidence eloquently and emotionally. Using an interpreter Juan Carlos Díaz was unable to communicate with the jury in such a way.

The CCTV was inconclusive so the jury had to base its deliberations on the evidence from the claimant and the defendant. Why would Miss B lie to convict someone from South America she had never met? Whether four pints of beer had affected Diaz's manhood is one thing, but could the claimant have felt "something dangly"?

The jury had to agree one or both touches were intentional and sexual.

16

JUAN CARLOS DÍAZ: Sexual assault

THE claimant remained in court throughout the trial, which is unusual and was an indication of how seriously she took the charge.

It is hard, no pun intended, to think of a reason why the claimant would fabricate a story about a man from South America whom she had never met. On the other hand, the Ecuadorian was helped by the weakness of the prosecution's evidence, not least that Miss B felt "something dangly" brush against her. Had the defendant's penis been erect, her claim would have had more credibility and surely his body would somehow have also made contact?

Those considerations no doubt played a major role in the jury finding Juan Carlos Díaz not guilty.

17

GARY BROADBENT: Two counts of grievous bodily harm with intent

DID MAKE-UP HELP TO MAKE UP ALIBI?

IT WAS 6 a.m. on a Saturday. The morning after the night before. Gary Broadbent and his cousin were sitting in a bus shelter outside a Kentucky Fried Chicken shop. On the other side of the road were Joe Wilkins and Harry Brown, making their belated way home from a party.

Those facts were not in dispute. The jury had to decide what it believed happened next.

According to Wilkins and Brown, Broadbent called them "cunts" — when they went to confront him, he pulled a knife from his rucksack and stabbed them both in the thigh before running off.

Broadbent claimed he never said a word. Instead, he alleged, Wilkins and Brown crossed the road and Wilkins became abusive before pulling a knife from his waist-band. Broadbent said he used his knife in self-defence to ward them off.

When arrested, Broadbent said in a prepared statement: "I accept stabbing the victims with a knife. I don't know why I had a knife, but it was an act of self-defence to counter their attacks."

Broadbent was charged with two counts of unlawful wounding with intent to cause grievous bodily harm. It was explained to the jury that unlawful means not in self-defence while maliciously wounding [GBH] meant the breakage of skin requiring stitches.

JOE WILKINS was first in the witness box to be cross-examined by the prosecution who asked him where he had been on the night in question.

"We had been in a pub before going to a party at midnight," he said.

"We left the party together about 5.30."

"What state of drunkenness or sobriety were you in?"

"Not too drunk… the same with Harry."

"What happened on the road?"

"One person called me a 'cunt' several times. I ignored it at first, but we crossed the road to ask him why he was calling me a 'cunt'."

"Then what happened?"

"He was waffling. I couldn't really understand him. He was swaying about. We had a little argument and the next thing I know he [Broadbent] pulled a knife out and stabbed me."

"There was no physical exchange."

"No."

"What sort of knife was it?"

"The blade was about two inches long. He stabbed me in the leg. He then tried for my chest, but I jumped back into the road. It all happened so quickly."

"Did either of you do anything to provoke this?"

"No. We just crossed the road to ask why he called me a 'cunt'."

"Was there anything unusual about his appearance?"

"He had eye-liner on."

THE DEFENCE put it to Joe Wilkins: "He had eye-liner on. Was that why you approached him?"

"No. Because he called me a 'cunt'."

"You had some sort of weapon."

"No."

"You got drunk, you were looking for trouble and Mr Broadbent tried to defend himself."

"Not right."

"You went to the hospital and all they did was to wash the wound."

"No. I had an operation."

"So neither of you had a weapon."

"I don't carry weapons around."

The police recovered a knife which Gary Broadbent admitted was his.

The jury was shown photographs which Wilkins claimed were his injuries, though the defence put the point to him that they were of someone else.

"How am I going to get a picture of a stabbed leg?"

GARY BROADBENT told the jury his version of events under cross-examination by the prosecution.

He said: "I admit I did it, but it was self-defence. They crossed the road and started to be aggressive to me. It was a threatening situation. He [Wilkins] went for me first. He pulled a knife out and swung it at me. I was protecting my cousin. My actions were to ward off the attack."

Broadbent was asked what he had in his rucksack.

"Shower gel, shampoo, change of underwear, T-shirt, pen and pencils and a utility knife, a short knife for kitchen use. I use it for opening cans of food."

"As a general rule you cannot carry a knife around."

"Yes."

"It would be different if you had a fork."

"I didn't have a tin opener."

"Why did you carry the rucksack?"

"I was sofa-surfing, occasionally sleeping rough."

"Where was the knife exactly?"

"In a separate part of the rucksack from my other things."

"When you pulled it out were you not worried about cutting yourself?"

"The blade was not sharp enough to cut myself."

"So one of the boys pulled something from his waist-band — a knife-style object?"

"Yes, to my recollection."

"You then armed yourself with a knife from the rucksack."

"Yes, I knew where it was."

"You had to unzip the compartment to find it in the dark."

"Yes."

"You weren't injured?"

"No."

"And they both ended up with knife wounds."

"Yes."

"How did you avoid being injured?"

"By fleeing from them."

"You were close enough to be stabbed, yet you received no injury."

"No."

"There were two of them and one of you."

"Correct."

"You decided to teach them a lesson."

"That is not how it happened."

"You intended to hurt them."

"No, it was only self-defence."

WAS THE defendant's eye-liner a valid reason for Joe Wilkins to be aggressive? The jury may have thought the presence of a knife in Gary Broadbent's ruck-sack and the time it took him to retrieve it was unusual.

Broadbent admitted using the knife, but claimed it was in self-defence.

The jury's job was to decide who was telling the truth and who was lying.

17

GARY BROADBENT: Two counts of grievous bodily harm with intent

NO WEAPON allegedly used by the two boys was ever found. The defendant admitted wounding them with a knife, but claimed it was in self-defence.

The jury found Gary Broadbent not guilty on both counts of grievous bodily harm with intent.

And I have no clue how it came to its verdict.

Sometimes you leave the court shaking your head at the decision of the 12 good men and true. This was certainly one of those occasions. Broadbent's excuse that "I accept stabbing the victims with a knife. I don't know why I had a knife" lacked credibility. How can you not know why you have a knife? One of many unanswered questions after the trial.

18

COLIN PHELPS: 18 indictments including anal rape

NO FUN AT THE FAIR
40 YEARS AGO

IT WAS the publicity surrounding accusations concerning Jimmy Savile that prompted the claimant, who cannot be named for legal reasons so will be referred to as Male Y, to belatedly tell the authorities what allegedly happened to him over 40 years earlier in a care home.

Colin Phelps was charged with 18 indictments involving Male Y, including anal rape.

Opening the case, the prosecution told the jury: "This is one person's word against another's. How can you be sure of something that happened 40-odd years ago and which happened in private? Why the delay? But why would the claimant make up such allegations? It is up to you to decide who is a truthful and reliable witness."

MALE Y, now 54, said he could not remember the incident, but was told by siblings that their mother barricaded the children in the front room while she threw out the father.

Aged seven, Male Y was sent to Gilbert House along with two brothers. It was here he met Colin Phelps, one of the people in charge of the home. "At the time I was vulnerable and in need of affection," said Male Y. "I was easily led."

When the children bathed, they had been supervised by a couple who previously ran the home, but only to ensure they "washed behind their ears." Soon after Phelps arrived, Male Y claimed he took a more hands-on approach — literally.

"He would stroke me all over, caressing and rubbing me," Male Y told the jury. "He would then rub my genitals, washing under my foreskin which gave me an erection. He just said 'enjoy it' which, because I didn't really know what was happening, I did.

"On other occasions he would play with my genitals, working the lather around towards my buttocks and then slipping his finger inside. When he bathed me, he touched me every time, maybe two or three times a month. This happened until we were nine, around two years on, when we were considered able to bath ourselves.

"In my mind as a child it went on forever... the finger penetration... probably not as long as I imagined, but it felt forever. This must have happened eight or nine times, using the tip of his finger."

Male Y claimed Phelps also started to visit the bedroom he shared with his two brothers. He said: "I was in bed and woken in the night by someone feeling me. I opened my eyes and there was a hand over my mouth. I would see from the hall light who it was. He put his finger to his lips and said: 'Go back to sleep,' and left.

"He put his hand in the hole in my pyjama bottoms, but stopped when I woke up. My brothers, who are heavy sleepers, didn't wake up. This happened quite frequently and overlapped with the bathroom activity. I wanted to tell somebody, but didn't know how or who."

Male Y claimed there were similar instances in a van owned by the home "numerous times."

As Male Y, then aged 11, had been ill when the other boys went on a day out, Phelps took him to Battersea Fun Fair to make up for this. "Afterwards we went to a restaurant," he said. "I had steak. I'd never had steak before. I was also poured a glass of red wine which I drank. It made me feel a bit woozy.

"I had to be assisted back to the car. He was rubbing my leg and feeling my crotch. He undid my shorts and pants and slid them down. He straddled me over his lap. He liked to be kissed on the lips. I could feel his hand fumbling down on me. He had one hand on my shoulder. I then felt something inside me. I thought it was his finger, but it wasn't as his other hand was also on me. I felt a sharp pain in my backside.

"That is the last I can remember. I guess he carried me to bed."

Male Y recalled another incident and told the jury: "I remember a time when no one else was in my room. I woke up and could hardly breathe. All I could see was his face. I would smell the tobacco and wine on his breath. He was rubbing his genitals against mine. It seemed to go on forever until he eventually stopped, threw back the bed clothes and left."

According to Male Y, Phelps would spank boys who had misbehaved. "He would ask me what I had done wrong, what did I think about it? He'd want you to say 'spank me.'

"He'd say 'assume the position,' and he'd take off my trousers and pants, put me over his knee and while holding my genitals in one hand would spank me with the other. This happened as often as he could make it. No matter how much I denied what I was supposed to have done, he would just call me a liar."

MALE Y was 16 when he left the home. The first person he told about what had happened was a foster aunt. She and her husband owned a pub and one day Male Y saw a male spanking his child. "I flew at him," said Male Y. "That's when I told her, but we never spoke about it again."

He also subsequently told his ex-wife, without too many details.

Male Y was asked how it had affected his life. "Any love I had... it had to have conditions, usually preceded by pain. I lost my job through my own stupidity. Likewise, I threw away the only person who loved me [his ex-wife]. I've spent most of my life chastising myself for waking up in the morning. I've tried to take my life half a dozen times."

In 2013, the Jimmy Savile allegations and other similar historical cases hit the headlines and "it had a real effect on me," said Male Y. "I just wanted closure on my early life. As far as I was concerned, Phelps was a 35-year-old and I was seven. Nothing would come of it."

But something did when Male Y contacted Social Services "because I didn't want it to happen to anybody else." After hearing his story, he was told the police had to be informed and Phelps was arrested.

THE PROSECUTION revealed Colin Phelps had previously pleaded guilty to three counts of sexual activity involving young boys in May 1980. However, though Phelps had pleaded guilty, he maintained his innocence.

"A police sergeant told me if I didn't plead guilty, they would hold me in custody for several months while they carried out investigations," said Phelps. "If I pleaded guilty, he said I'd do no jail time. This was put to me a few days before the trial."

He was fined £120 for each of the three offences.

Phelps was asked why Male Y would have singled him out.

"This is the question that has tormented me and my family for two and a half years," he said.

Under cross-examination by the Crown, Phelps denied every allegation Male Y had made. He said he only helped to wash boys' hair and backs, insisted that the door to the bathroom was always open, that no boy had ever been in his car or the school van with him alone and that he had never touched Male Y's penis or buttocks.

"Were there any rules about touching a penis or a bottom?"

"There were no rules as such, but it wasn't done."

"Were there any circumstances where the [bathroom] door would be closed?"

"No."

"Was there any occasion when you took a boy out in your car alone?"

"No."

"Can you ever recall being alone with Male Y?"

"I cannot recall that, no."

"What was your relationship with him at the home?"

"The same as with all the boys."

"Did you ever take him to a fun fair?"

"No. I don't recall this. You just wouldn't go anywhere with one child."

"A restaurant?"

"Not recall that."

"Did you give him alcohol and assault him?"

"No. I would not give a child that."

"Did he ever see your penis?"

"No."

"Did you bugger him on the back seat?"

"Absolutely not."

"Why would he make all of this up?"

"No idea."

"You maintain nothing happened?"

"Absolutely."

Was it a fantasy of someone who had been affected by more recent publicity surrounding child abuse? Or was Male Y still a reliable witness even after all these years?

18

COLIN PHELPS: 18 indictments including anal rape

BEING SURE of what may have taken place almost half a century ago is a challenging job for a jury. The three main questions for it to deliberate with this trial were: why would the alleged victim have lied? How credible was his evidence of so long ago? And did Colin Phelps make a reliable defendant?

One line of Male Y's evidence rang particularly true. When he spoke of being taken to a restaurant after the trip to Battersea Fun Fair aged 11, he said: "I'd never had steak before," which smacked far more of reality than fiction.

Maybe this helped the jury to find Phelps, 70, guilty of five of the 18 indictments. He was sentenced to five years, reduced to four on appeal.

Phelps was cleared by the jury of one count of attempted buggery, where the victim had accused him of trying to have sex with him after a visit to Battersea Fun Fair and nine other counts of indecent assault. The jury failed to return a verdict on three other charges of indecent assault, which were left to lie on file.

This was a new trial, the previous jury having been discharged late in the initial trial which the present jurors were unaware of. Two of the original jurors began to fight so the jury was dismissed.

RECENT high-profile trials for sex offences committed between the 1960s and 1980s have raised many questions about how those convicted of historic offences are dealt with by the courts and how the consequences of such a passage of time between offence and sentence should be considered.

The Sentencing Council's policy is that when a defendant is sentenced it should be according to the law at the time the offence was committed, not the law at the time when they are sentenced.

It is a general legal principle that the law should not be applied retrospectively. Sentencing levels have been increasing over the past few decades and changes to the law relating to sex offences are a good example of this trend. It reveals much about how attitudes towards these offences have altered over time.

For example, sentencing levels for indecent assault on an underage girl have undergone several changes over the years. Between 1957 and 1960 the maximum was two years' imprisonment. It was changed in 1961 to a maximum of five years if the victim was under 13 and in 1985 it was increased again to 10 years.

The Sexual Offences Act of 2003 redefined sex offences and indecent assault was replaced by new offences such as sexual assault and assault by penetration. While the maximum sentence for sexual assault remained at 10 years, it was increased to 14 years in cases where the victim was under 13 while assault by penetration was given a maximum sentence of life.

Some sentencing levels have decreased. If someone had been sentenced for murder in the early 1960s, they could have faced the death penalty and some may think that if people have to be sentenced as the law was at the time of the offence, they therefore should get the death penalty. However, the entire sanction has been abolished. In short, it is no longer legal for anyone to be executed in any circumstances, so even if it applied at the time of the offence, the type of sentence cannot be resurrected and used today.

In sentencing offenders for historic offences, judges will use current sentencing guidelines for the purposes of assessing the harm to the victim and the culpability of the defendant. However, the law only allows them to pass sentences within the maximum that would have been available at the time.

In some cases, particularly if there has been a long period between the offence taking place and a conviction and sentence, the offender may be quite elderly. Judges are not obliged to take that into account when sentencing, but may do so depending on the circumstances, such as if the defendant is very ill or frail.

There is no inflexible rule governing whether sentences should be structured as concurrent or consecutive components. The overriding principle is that the overall sentence must be just and proportionate. If the aggregate length does not meet this yardstick, then the court should consider how to reach such a sentence. With historical sex cases a judge may feel that if the sentence at the time was five years and the defendant was found guilty of two or three offences then 10- or 15-years' imprisonment, with the sentences running consecutively, may be more appropriate.

19

LORNA BARCLAY: Aggravated burglary

WAS A GUEST, PARTY TO VIOLENCE?

PARTIES are supposed to be fun. A time when friends meet, people chat and laugh. Perhaps new friendships can be made. A party at the house where Ben Robinson lived proved to be anything but fun. It was the catalyst for five people returning and breaking the claimant's right leg in a sickening attack.

In the dock was Lorna Barclay who was charged with aggravated burglary; effectively being responsible for arranging and participating in the beating Robinson sustained. In a case of aggravated burglary, it can mean breaking into to someone's property as a trespasser with a view to causing grievous bodily harm.

Robinson had a flat in the house where another tenant, his cousin Emmanuel, hosted the party. Barclay had been told about it by a "friend of a friend." At some time during the party, she claimed her phone had been stolen, though Barclay and Robinson had significantly different recollections of what eventually happened that night — or more significantly, the following morning.

There was no dispute that Robinson sustained a broken femur [thigh bone] in a sustained attack by a number of unidentified males. There was no argument that Barclay had far too much to drink. Apart from that there was little common ground between the defendant and the claimant as the trial progressed.

Barclay alleged Robinson and another boy assaulted her, throwing her out of the party. Robinson maintained she was merely escorted from the property.

The defendant and two friends, Sham and Shaquila, had arrived at the party around 11 p.m. An hour or so later Barclay became aware her phone was missing.

She said Robinson, after being told what had allegedly happened, was angry that someone at the party could be a called a thief. He turned the music down and asked if anybody had seen Barclay's phone. No one answered and the party continued.

The defendant who, by her own admission, was "not a good drinker," became drunk… so drunk she was sick in the toilet. She was in there for around 15 minutes before being helped out and put into Robinson's bed.

The party ended around 7 a.m. Robinson and his cousin, Emmanuel, went to their respective bedrooms for some belated sleep. At lunch-time this was disturbed in a violent manner.

THE PROSECUTION cross-examined Ben Robinson and asked him what he was doing when the gang broke in his house.

He said: "I was in bed. Suddenly I was hit in the face. Then a baseball bat hit my femur. Then the bar from a dumb-bell hit me round the head."

"So you were in bed."

"Yes. Two black guys came in, then two more."

"What happened?"

"They targeted my right leg. It was broken."

"Was anyone else there?"

"The girl I had escorted out [of the party]. She was there, a few feet from me."

"What was she doing?"

"Shouting that I deserved it."

The jury was told a white male also joined in the attack.

"How long did the attack last in all?"

"Three to four minutes."

"How long was the girl in your sight for?"

"Twenty or 30 seconds."

"You'd seen her before."

"Yes. The whole night at the party."

"Had you seen the black guys before?"

"No."

"The white male?"

"No."

"Can you describe him?"

"No."

"How old?"

"Forty-ish, well-built."

"Anything distinctive about his voice?"

"No."

"You sustained a very serious fracture [to your right leg]."

"Yes."

"You had surgery and a plate and a rod were inserted into the leg."

"Yes. They are permanent."

"Any other injuries?"

"A cut head, this was cleaned, no stitches needed. My jaw, where I was punched, now makes a cracking noise."

"How long were you in hospital?"

"Four days. The physio is still ongoing [eight months later]."

THE POLICE subsequently showed Ben Robinson nine images of different females and was asked if he could identify the girl who was present during the attack. He pointed to the photo of Lorna Barclay.

"How sure were you?"

"One hundred per cent."

Robinson was also shown images of nine white males, but was unable to identify any as the one who was part of the beating.

THE DEFENCE took over the cross-examination of Ben Robinson.

"You gave a description of a girl who was drunk and put out of the house."

"Yes."

"Did you describe her to the police [after the attack]?"

"Yes."

"How much had you been drinking on the day of the party?"

"Two cups of brandy."

"Cannabis?"

"No."

"When you gave your description, you said she might have had a scar on her cheek."

"Yes."

"You recall that?"

"Yes."

"About five feet five inches, early twenties, met her a few times before… think I've seen her a few times before… that's what you told the police. In court you said once before — which is it?"

"Once before that night and the night."

"Whoever assaulted you must have been very upset with you."

"Yes."

"You say she came back to your house sometime around 12.40 with a group of males to assault you."

"Yes."

"Anyone wearing a mask or a bandana?"

"No."

"You say the attack lasted three to four minutes and the defendant was there for the last 30 seconds. During the assault you mention a white male. He was in your view for a significant period yet you were unable to identify him."

"My focus was on protecting myself, my safety, not looking at faces. I was focused on his hands. People who break in usually have knives or guns."

"Your statement said that 'a white male wearing a black coat pinned me down and hit me' and he said: 'You've beaten up my daughter'."

"Yes."

"I appreciate your priority was to survive, but you had a face-to-face encounter with a person. You should be able to identify him."

"He was beating me up. I was only concerned with defending myself and surviving."

"But you identified the defendant."

"I'd seen her before."

"She does not have a scar on her cheek."

"OK."

"Did you make your own inquiries into who the person might be who arranged the assault? On social media, perhaps?"

"No."

"You sure?"

"One hundred and ten per cent sure."

"I'm suggesting you know the defendant had no part in it and she was not there."

"She was there."

"I suggest you are looking for a reason why you were assaulted and you have made this up. The defendant was not there."

"I did not invent it."

THE DEFENCE asked Ben Robinson: "Do you have many enemies?"

"None."

"At least one, clearly. You say the defendant brought a group of men to your house."

"Yes."

"A merciless attack, you said."

"Yes."

"You know the defendant said she was assaulted by you."

"I didn't [assault her]."

"You manhandled her, grabbed her hair, pulled her down the stairs. You say it didn't happen."

"It didn't."

"You didn't allow her to put her shoes on."

"I don't remember."

"Then someone else dragged her down the stairs, insulted her. You were there."

"No."

"You said there came a point when the defendant was drunk."

"Yes."

"Was this before or after she said her phone was lost?"

"After."

LORNA BARCLAY took her place in the witness box to be cross-examined by the defence. She was asked: "Would you say you were still drunk when you were outside?"

"No."

"What did you do after the police left?"

"I went to the bus stop, took a bus and then a tram to Sham's house."

"When did she leave [the party]?"

"Before me. She had work."

"What happened when you got to Sham's?"

"I was crying. She tried to calm me down. I told her what had happened. She said I should call the police again."

"A call is recorded at 09.52 when you said you were assaulted, but the police did not take it seriously. Is that correct?"

"I said it did not matter about the phone, I'm calling mainly about the assault."

"At this point had you told anyone else?"

"Not at that point."

"How long did you stay at Sham's?"

"Quite a while."

"You said you got home about 11."

"Yes."

"Why did you go home?"

"I didn't want to fall asleep in her bed. I felt really sick."

"Did you see your mum and stepdad?"

"Yes."

"Did you say what happened?"

"They could see by my face and hair, so I told them. I said I was assaulted and the police did nothing. I felt humiliated."

"Are they protective of you?"

"Yes, they are a lot. My stepdad said: 'Why didn't you call me when it happened?' They were angry, like all parents would react."

"Was the possibility of going round there talked about?"

"Yes, that's what happened. The possibility was raised. I told them to just leave it. The only way they'd have known where to go was if I'd told them. I said not to go there or order anyone to go there. I'm not a violent person."

THE PROSECUTION continued Lorna Barclay's cross-examination. "What was the party like when you arrived?"

"Chilled… respectable people… everyone dressed casually."

"Did you know anyone?"

"Not apart from those I was with."

"How did the night progress?"

"I went into the kitchen, talking and drinking. I put my phone down on the side, went back into the kitchen and when I got back it was gone."

"How long had you been away?"

"Three, maybe four minutes."

"What did you do?"

"It was not taking calls [when a friend dialled my number]."

"What did you think?"

"Someone had turned it off. I know it was fully charged."

"Who did you speak to?"

"He [Ben Robinson] said 'no one would take your phone.' He turned the music down and said 'anyone seen her phone?' 'No' was the answer."

"What did you do?"

"I had insurance on it so I stayed at the party and carried on drinking."

"What did you drink?"

"Shots of vodka."

"There came a point when you were drunk."

"I was unable to move. I was physically vomiting in the toilet when a friend stood me up. I got more sick."

"How long were you in there [the toilet]?"

"Fifteen to 20 minutes. I had to get out because other people wanted to use the toilet. Sham helped me to another room. I don't know whose room it was."

"Were you sick any more?"

"No."

"How long were you in the room?"

"Till around five or six."

"What led you to leave?"

"Shaquila woke me up. She was quite drunk and said: 'Come and dance with us.' That's when the defendant started screaming and shouting at me."

"What was his demeanour?"

"Very aggressive. I wasn't going to say 'no'."

"You said you'd drunk a lot. You sure of this?"

"I'd slept for four, five hours, so pretty sure, yes."

"Did you dance?"

"No. He told me to get out. I tried to put my shoes on. I only got one on. He started to say: 'Get out of my house.' He grabbed me by my hoodie, pulled me out of the room and downstairs. I was, like, on the stairs trying to put my shoes on and trying to do my hair. A different guy grabbed me and called me a tramp… a whore… a drunk… my belongings were thrown on the pavement."

When she was outside the house Barclay said she waved down a passing police car. She told the jury: "I said: 'Can you help me? Someone's assaulted me in the flat.' They knocked on the door and people came down. They spoke to them and came back to me and said there was nothing they could do as there was not enough evidence."

According to PC David Timms: "At 06.39 there was a very drunk female in the street shouting she'd lost her phone. She was incredibly drunk, loud and slurring her speech. She said she'd been kicked out of the party. She was so drunk she was not making perfect sense."

The police officer spoke to Robinson and others still present. "His account was the same as all the others, so I judged it did not happen. She was shouting at everyone instead of talking. She wanted him arrested for dragging her out of the party. We spoke to her friend [Shaquila] and even she agreed she'd been escorted out."

Barclay's response to this was: "Not correct. I did not shout about the phone. I never said anything about the phone."

DC MICHAEL ARTHUR, the officer in the case, was next in the witness box.

The prosecution asked: "A number of people were involved in the attack on Ben Robinson. Any leads?"

"Only forensics, no concrete evidence."

"No arrests?"

"Correct."

Robinson had failed to pick out Lorna Barclay's stepfather in a video identity parade, selecting the wrong person.

The defence asked DC Arthur whether the defendant was a person of good character.

"The first time she had been arrested."

LORNA BARCLAY had drunk half a bottle of wine and shots [of vodka] with an energy drink. She said she was not so drunk she could not remember what happened. She could remember clearly what happened, she claimed. Throughout the course of the day, she insisted she was not drunk to the point where she was unable to function.

DC Michael Arthur was asked by the defence: "During her police interview she was answering every question?"

"Yes."

"No hiding… no 'no comment'."

"Yes."

"Only when you made reference to a white male and she spoke to her solicitor that she returned with 'no comment'."

"OK."

"Did the mention of the white male trigger the 'no comment' in your opinion?"

The judge ruled the police officer was not able to comment on what triggered a 'no comment' in someone else's mind.

The defence continued: "She gave an alibi for the time [of the assault]. She was somewhere else."

"She said she was at home."

"During the course of the interview she was giving full details until the reference to the white male being her [step] father?"

"Yes."

"The defendant made it clear what her movements were. Did you not corroborate with her Oyster card and bus CCTV or did you not deem this necessary?"

"No."

"The defendant's stepfather was arrested."

"Yes."

"He made a 'no comment' interview."

"Yes."

"He was charged."

"Yes."

With no one to corroborate the evidence of the defendant or the claimant the jury was left to decide which it believed the most. And whether that belief was strong enough to be sure, beyond reasonable doubt, to find Barclay guilty of aggravated burglary.

Was she present at the attack? Did she play a part in it? Or was she at home? "Probably" is not enough to deliver a guilty verdict. The jury had to be sure.

Why would Robinson lie about the behaviour of the defendant during the party or as she left? At the same time, why would the defendant, a person of previous good character, make up a story that had such a devastating ending for Robinson?

The jury retired and its deliberation lasted one day.

Page 177 de\leted in error

19

LORNA BARCLAY: Aggravated burglary

THERE WAS little doubt, despite the lack of concrete evidence, the group that attacked Ben Robinson did so in a revenge beating. While homeowners can, thankfully rarely, find themselves the victims of an attack by strangers (almost inevitably part of a burglary) the chances of four or five people forcing their way into someone's property and breaking their right leg in a random act of brutality are so slim as to be discounted.

The easier part for the jury was linking the attack on Robinson with the incident a few hours earlier involving Lorna Barclay. But would it decide the 20-year-old with no previous convictions, not an arrest, a reprimand or a caution, was part of the beating that saw Robinson hospitalised for four days? Robinson could only identify her, no one else. Was he doing so because she was the only familiar face?

The jury decided that Barclay was guilty of aggravated burglary. It believed she was with the men as they punched, kicked and hit Robinson with weapons while she joined in the frenzied attack with a belt.

Barclay was sentenced to nine years' imprisonment, losing half of her Twenties because of a revenge attack. It would have been interesting being a fly on the wall to hear the conversation between Barclay and her stepfather when he visited her in jail.

AS A RULE of thumb, a person is released at the halfway point of their sentence if it is between 12 months and four years. If the sentence is over four years they can apply for parole when they have served half their sentence. If they are granted parole, someone from the probation service will regularly check on them after they are released.

Being on licence means that you are still serving a prison sentence, but you can live in the community instead of being in jail. While on licence, there are rules that must be followed. If you break the rules, you have to go back to prison [be recalled] which are standard rules if you are on licence.

They include: you must be well behaved and not commit any further offences or do anything that could put members of the public or your friends or family in danger; you must keep in touch with your probation officer and do what they ask you to do; you must not be late for appointments or turn up under the influence of drink or drugs; if your probation officer needs to visit you at home or somewhere else, you have to agree to this; you have to to live at an address that your probation officer has approved; you must tell your probation officer in advance if you plan to leave that address or stay at another address, even if it's for just one night; you have to tell your probation officer if you change your phone number; you can take up work only if your probation officer approves it; you must not travel outside the UK without the permission of your probation officer (permission isn't usually given); if you are on home detention curfew, you have to keep to a curfew which usually runs for from 19.00 to 07.00.

Failure to abide by these conditions can result in breach of proceedings, resulting in a recall to prison to serve the remainder of the sentence. If the accused does commit further offences, then they will be sentenced for these as well as having to serve up to all of the time of the previous sentence.

20

STEVE PILKINGTON: Exposure

SIZE MATTERED FOR
FLASH STEVE

MISS I was on maternity leave. To boost her income, she took a cleaning job with a family who lived nearby — two hours at £10 an hour. She went to see the Pilkingtons, she was shown around the house and agreed to start the following week.

When she arrived, only husband Steve was there; his wife and son were out. Within a minute, Miss I told the jury under cross-examination by the prosecution that Pilkington had started to behave "very inappropriately" which ended with him exposing himself and masturbating.

Miss I said: "I had only just walked in when he made a remark about my false tan. He touched my back and then asked me if my breasts were tanned. He also asked if I shaved my genitalia.

"I brushed it off. I have worked in the construction business so I am used to men being, well... men. I just told him I wanted to start cleaning which I did, but I felt a little uneasy.

"I was upstairs when he came down from the loft extension where he worked, asking me if I had called him. I hadn't. He began telling me that he only had sex with his wife once a month and it was boring so he preferred masturbating. He said that he designed an escort web site which his wife did not know about."

"How did you feel at this point?" the Crown asked.

"Uncomfortable."

"What did he say next?"

"He asked me if I had ever thought about becoming an escort. He then said I should go up to the loft extension as I may have to clean it next time. We had to climb a ladder to reach it.

"Up there, he told me I was curvy and could do well as an escort. At that time, I thought 'enough is enough' and wanted to leave. I had almost finished, but wanted to go. He said that his wife was anal about cleaning."

At this point the judge intervened: "Anal?"

"She means fussy," explained the prosecution.

Miss I continued: "There were three cups in the sink which I washed up. As I turned round Mr Pilkington was there with his exposed erect penis and was masturbating. I said to him: 'What would your wife think of that?'

"He said that she would never find out. I felt disgusted. He had a wife and child. How would his son feel if he knew what his dad was doing? I asked him to put it away. He replied that it was too big to be put back in."

Miss I was asked for confirmation about the size of Pilkington's penis. Her answer would no doubt have improved the defendant's ego, if not his chances of an acquittal, as he sat in the dock.

"He had an extremely large penis."

"What happened then?" asked the prosecution.

"I took the £20 which was on the kitchen surface and left. As I was leaving, he asked me if I'd give him my number."

"What did you do then?"

"I tried to call his wife. I couldn't get an answer so I left a message. Before she got back to me, I phoned the police. When she did get back to me, she didn't believe me."

THE DEFENCE asked Miss I why her first call was not to the police.

"I was in shock. I was disgusted by what he did. I thought she [his wife] had a right to know. If my husband had done it I'd want a heads-up. I phoned her first so it would not be such a shock when the police contacted her."

"I suggest at no stage did you go to the loft."

"I can tell you what the loft extension looks like."

"When he came to the kitchen, he asked you if you wanted a drink."

"No. He had a Coke."

"When he asked about work, you said you were good at

manipulating people and getting money out of them."

"I never said that."

"He never exposed himself."

"He did."

"What happened was you embellished what was jovial banter."

"I didn't."

The defendant decided not to give evidence.

Banter or a boner was the deliberation for the jury.

20

STEVE PILKINGTON: Exposure

MISS I was the most credible witness I heard. Her evidence, given from behind screens, was so obviously honest and reliable it was staggering that Steve Pilkington had pleaded not guilty. It took rolling the dice to a new level.

Pilkington may be well-endowed, but exposing his manhood cost him a large withdrawal from his bank account after the jury found him guilty. He was fined £1,000, the judge also ordering him to pay £4,000 prosecution costs after what amounted to a spurious not guilty plea .

Pilkington had allegedly exposed himself to three different girls before, though the cases were never proceeded with. As proud as he may be of his penis, he will hopefully realise some things are best kept under wraps.

21

ZAK WARDLE: Actual bodily harm; aggravated burglary; grievous bodily harm; criminal damage

LIES, DAMN LIES AND EVEN MORE LIES

THE CASE involving Zak Wardle was memorable for many things, none of them good. For starters, the defendant was arrogant and barely on first name terms with the English language while Christina French was a foul-mouthed lying claimant who withdrew all of her original statements against Wardle.

When the police entered French's flat, she must have set a world record for the number of times "fuck" was said in 15 minutes. She seemed incapable of completing a sentence without using an expletive. French claimed to have a personality disorder. In fact, she made Jekyll and Hyde seem well balanced.

In the wake of one accusation against the defendant by French, armed police stopped a bus to arrest Wardle who had in his possession a... screwdriver.

The trial gave an insight to a relationship that appeared to be love at first fight.

Oh, and French wanted sex in a court cell.

ZAK WARDLE was charged with five counts on three different dates involving Christina French:

1 — Actual bodily harm to Christina French

2 — Aggravated burglary and grievous bodily harm on Christina French

3 — Possession of an offensive weapon in public

4 — Damaging property

5 — Going equipped for burglary

THE PAIR had an eight-month relationship which Christina French ended though, the Crown said, Zak Wardle was unhappy with this. What followed was an incredible tale of lies, deceit and wasting police time with the jury having to decide who, if either of the lying lovebirds, was telling anything resembling the truth.

French was a reluctant and hostile witness who was in court only because she had been told if she did not appear she would be issued with a witness summons. A mother of four whose children were all in care, her personality disorder extended to announcing in the court lobby during a lunch break: "I'd love to be in the cells having a bunk-up."

As you do.

THE PROSECUTION told the jury details of the case. On February 27 Christina French discovered the lock on her door in the block of flats where she lived was broken, apparently by a lodger.

As she felt vulnerable, she phoned Zak Wardle. It was two months after their relationship had ended, though they remained in contact, to see if he could come over to fix it. He agreed and, French said in her police statement, he slept on the sofa. In the morning, the prosecution said, Wardle became angry because he felt the relationship was being rekindled and when he was mistaken… he assaulted French, injuring her.

Two weeks later French woke up one morning to find Wardle had gained entry to her flat and was standing by her bed holding a screwdriver. He allegedly told her: "Good job you woke up, if you'd been asleep, I was going to stab you." The prosecution said: "Maybe he wouldn't have done this, but it was still a nasty thing to hear."

Three days later French heard a knock on her door. When she attempted to look through the spyhole, she found it was broken. Outside was Wardle, kicking and screaming, it was claimed. She called the police, but Wardle had left by the time they arrived. He was arrested on a bus by armed police (more of which later).

ZAK WARDLE and Christina French gave dishonesty a bad name. The judge warned Wardle not to smirk or shake his head — as he had — while evidence was read out in court. For her part, French was clearly unhappy at having spent the previous day at court only for the start of the trial to be delayed because of another case over-running.

Cross-examining a hostile witness is always challenging and the prosecution soon discovered the claimant was in no mood to be helpful. French told the jury her statements to the police were "all lies... made up." She had withdrawn them because, the prosecution said "she still had feelings for the defendant."

The Crown Prosecution Service can still proceed with a case because it has a duty where multiple accusations of various crimes have been made, even if later withdrawn.

The prosecution began cross-examining French: "Your door was broken by a man."

"No."

"Do you remember the date?"

"Vaguely."

"There were problems with the door."

"Someone tried to gain access, but not Mr Wardle."

"You couldn't shut the door properly."

"No."

"You rang him for protection."

"Yes."

"Were you still an item at the time?"

"On and off."

"Were there any problems the next morning?"

"Not that I can remember."

"Did you argue?"

"Probably. We didn't get along too well. That's why we're not together. I don't deal with emotions too well, especially in the morning. I can be quite aggressive."

"Was there any physical contact?"

"Probably. By me, yes."

"Do you remember calling the police?"

"I wanted an ambulance as I was having a panic attack, but the police turned up. Nine of them. I counted them. They took me to a mental health unit."

"Do you remember having pictures taken later that day?"

"Yes, vaguely."

French was given the relevant photos.

"Are they a true likeness of your arms and legs?"

"They are obviously my arms and legs."

"How were the wounds sustained?"

"I was taken away in the back of a police van. I was verbally abused and I was being thrown around the back of the van quite a bit. I was manhandled while the driver would suddenly stop. I was annoyed at being taken away."

"Do you remember the statement you made [about this]?"

"I can't remember that far back."

French was handed her statement.

"I have explained I lied in the statement. I don't need to read it again. What I said then I made up, to get him into trouble… to get him out of my life."

French refused to read her statement so the prosecution took the initiative.

"You said: 'Zak lost it. He smashed my TV and I smashed a lamp over his head'."

French said: "I said he was responsible for my injuries. If I had just said he smashed my TV he'd have got a NFA [no further action]. I thought I'd let him have a taste of his own medicine."

"Later in the day the police turned up."

"They forced entry. They harassed me, made me feel intimidated."

Because French was so unhelpful it was decided there would be little point in showing the jury the expletive-filled video filmed by a body-worn camera when police officers arrived at her property.

"Do you remember another occasion when you made a complaint?"

"What was it about?"

"Someone in your bedroom."

"Oh yes, I remember. I said Mr Wardle had broken into my house, which was wrong. I allowed him in. I lied. I made it up. I told the police he had a screwdriver and threatened to kill me. There was no struggle though he did tip out the contents of my bag. I can't remember if I told him to p-off or he left."

"Were you distressed?"

"I said I was, but I made it up. I lied. I wasn't [distressed]."

"Did he threaten to kill you?"

"No."

"Let us move on to the third incident. Was there a knock on the door?"

"Yes."

"Was there a problem with the spyhole?"

"Yes."

"Who broke it?"

"The police when they forced their way in. I said Mr Wardle broke it, but he didn't."

"Did you call the police?"

"Yes."

"Did you tell the police he had an object?"

"I said he had a gun."

"A real gun?"

"Yes."

THE DEFENCE cross-examined Christina French.

"You have been diagnosed with a mental disorder."

"Yes."

"What are the symptoms?"

"I become compulsive and aggressive at times. In my head I do things I think are funny, but they aren't really. I have depression and panic attacks. I know this is not acceptable which is why I am having treatment now."

"This had not been diagnosed at the time [of the incidents]."

"No. At the time I did not really understand when I was doing wrong. It was in the heat of the moment. I just flipped."

"Looking back, was one thing you did in the heat of the moment to call the police?"

"Yes."

"They gained entry into your home with an enforcer."

"Yes. I was on the other side of the door laughing, but I can see now it wasn't funny. I had a lot of issues. I knew something was wrong, but didn't know what."

"What happened when they went in?"

"I was clapping my hands. I told them to fuck off or else I'd jump off the balcony."

"You accused one officer of purposely injuring you."

"Yes."

"You even said your arm had been broken."

"Yes."

"You also made a statement, a subsequently withdrawn statement, to say your previous allegations were not true."

"Yes."

"You explained that you had issues that caused you mental health problems."

"And my kids were removed from my care which didn't help. I wanted my kids back so I put the blame on him rather than me. I didn't want it to go against me."

THE LAST accusation, where Christina French alleged Zak Wardle had a gun, was declared a firearm incident by the police. At 00.28 a bus was stopped in Catford, south London. Wardle was the only passenger as armed police boarded the vehicle.

"Armed police — hands up," yelled the first officer on board. Wardle was hand-cuffed and taken to a police station. The bus was searched. No firearm was found, only a small green screwdriver squeezed between two seats.

It is logical to wonder why French was not charged with wasting police time or even perjury. Her withdrawn statement had no bearing on the decision to prosecute Wardle. The CPS decided to push ahead with the case based on her original statements. It believed Wardle had a case to answer in what was becoming a fascinating, bizarre and confusing trial.

THE JURY was read a transcript of Zak Wardle's first police interview regarding actual bodily harm and burglary at Christina French's flat. The jurors were also shown four photographs of injuries sustained by French which comprised bruises and cuts to her right wrist; a bruise to right forearm below elbow; lower left leg bruise; lower right leg by ankle showing bruises.

The police officer, who had surely never experienced an interview like he was about to, began by asking Wardle if he caused the injuries sustained by French on February 9.

"I may have caused some, not in the way she said. You see, she had let a room to another geezer, which pissed me off. You know, some bloke sauntering in. The geezer came round to get some things, but couldn't get in and he broke the lock. I called the Old Bill. He was going off on one. The door was fucked."

"Miss French asked you round that night for protection, shall we say."

"Yup. I didn't sleep on the sofa though. I was in her bed, you know, cuddling all night. I was there all night. She's saying I slept on the sofa. I ain't a fucking prick, mate, know what I mean? She's a head-fuck. I was butt naked, man. She's 30 and damaged in the head, mate."

"Why do you say that?"

"She comes at me all the time, but I still love this girl. I woke up, you know, eyes all scratchy, not even had a fag and she's in my face, putting scissors in my face. I restrained her a bit, not slap her or punch her. The bruises could have been caused by restraining her or when she fell off the bed, mate."

"She said you grabbed her by the throat and punched her."

"No."

"Did you have any injuries?"

"Few cuts, like. I love the girl. It's not what you'd call agg [aggravation] or nothing. I just pushed her away. She's caused so much crap since I've been with her, mate."

The police officer moved on to the incidents on February 27.

"Oh my God man, that's a lot of bullshit, mate," said Wardle.

"Where were you that day?"

"I was at my auntie's chilling like. She [French] texts me like saying she wants to see me. 'Come over about half nine, babe.' I went over there, the door was fucked. She opened it. If that's breaking and entering, I don't know what fucking is mate."

"Did you have a screwdriver?"

"No."

"Did you stand over her?"

"I don't know where she gets it from. She smokes too much puff. She came at me with a lamp saying: 'I'm going to kill you.' She attacked me, I defended myself. I thought 'fuck this for a laugh' and left."

"What happened then?"

"She texted me saying she loved me to bits."

"Why do you argue so much?"

"I don't get her, mate. She's been puffing for 15 years and that fucks with your head."

The police officer finished his questioning with events on March 30.

"What happened that night?"

"I knocked on the door, went in, she made me a cup of tea. We chilled. I didn't do any damage to the door."

"Did you have a screwdriver?"

"Yes."

"Why?"

"I forgot it was on me. I'm a handyman."

"Did you threaten to kill her?"

"Man, we chilled. Had a bit of a joint and I left cos we started to argue."

"Did you have a gun?"

"No."

The prosecution decided to withdraw count 3 "because there was no evidence to establish the weapon was used in a public place, only a private flat" and count 5 "because the evidence is not the strongest." Counts 1, 2 and 4 remained.

ZAK WARDLE walked to the witness box with an arrogant swagger, looking bored and surly.

The defence asked Wardle what Christina French was like.

"She can he hard work, but I really love her. One minute she can be OK, but once she's got a bee in her bonnet she can scream, shout, attack, call the police."

"Tell us about the first incident."

"The door was damaged. The geezer was under the influence of alcohol so I called the police. When they arrived, they escorted him away."

"In the morning, what happened?"

"She was OK at first, but she can change quickly. We argued about something. She came at me. I tried to calm her down. At first, she had a bottle of perfume, then scissors. I pushed her on the bed so I could leave."

"Where did you grab her?"

"The wrists."

"Then?"

"I walked out, went to my auntie's."

"When were you aware of police involvement?"

"When she was sectioned. She sent me a text saying: 'Oh look I've been sectioned.' We got back together two or three days later. If you love someone you get through it."

"Before you met Miss French, were you in trouble [with the police]?"

"Couple of cautions. One for throwing a brick. Can't remember the other."

"Criminal damage."

"Oh yeah. Was it a motor car?"

"It was damage to your family home."

"Oh right."

"On March 27, what did you do? Argue?"

"Probably. She goes off onto one. It was usually about whether I was looking at another girl or seeing someone else. I walked out."

"And March 30?"

"Probably round Christina's."

"Do you remember an argument?"

"She had it in her head I was doing something. I took her skunk puff [cannabis] and left. Taking that made her go, mate."

"What did you do?"

"Got on a bus. She was calling saying 'come home.' I thought 'sod her, let her have a taste of her own medicine.' Then a rapid response unit, firearms, stopped the bus."

"Did they find anything?"

"A screwdriver. I had it on me. The rest of my tools were round Christina's."

"You are aware of allegations you had a gun."

"Ridiculous. I thought 'what has she said now?' Cos they don't just come out."

THE PROSECUTION began cross-examining Zak Wardle.

"If all circumstances were favourable, would you be back together again?"

"I hope we could work it out, yes."

"On February 9, did you grab her wrists? Just enough to stop her doing anything?"

The defendant was shown the photos of French's injuries.

"Could have been from me when I was holding her. She had scissors. I placed her on the bed. She was erratic, she rolled off. She could have done it then."

"Do you think you might have kicked her?"

"No."

"Struck her? Or over-reacted?"

"No. I've never laid a finger on her."

"Do you think the injuries were caused by any factor other than you?"

"As Christina said, in the back of the police van."

"You have a turbulent relationship and one condition of your bail was not to contact her, which you did."

"I appreciate that. My love for her over-ruled that, really. Her mindset is that if she thinks I've done something then she has to get back at me at the time. We just forgive each other. Something happens and five minutes later she regrets it. Like 'sorry I called the police,' know what I mean? If you love someone, know what I mean, it sounds crap, but you put these things aside to make it work."

A JURY normally has to decide who is telling the truth. Here, it was more a case of which of the claimant and defendant was the lesser liar.

The judge told the jury that Christina French's original allegations are accepted in the indictments. "She is a witness who has changed sides. Someone can make an allegation that is true and then, because of divided loyalties or love can be changed."

French was a hostile witness and it was the jury's task to decide the credibility and reliability of her evidence, notably her police statements and the statement when she withdrew her original statements. It was difficult to give either the defendant or the claimant the sympathy vote or the benefit of the doubt.

Whatever its verdicts, it would be a trial the jury would not forget as it deliberated the decisions on the three remaining counts against Zak Wardle. Would the jury find him guilty of all or any of:

189

1 — Actual bodily harm to Christina French

2 — Aggravated burglary and grievous bodily harm on Miss French

4 — Damaging property.

Could the jury be sure the original allegations by French were true and had been withdrawn because of ongoing feelings for Wardle? The jury had to decide each of the remaining counts individually.

The 12 who had to decide this unusual case would not have expected jury service to be quite like this.

21

ZAK WARDLE: Actual bodily harm; aggravated burglary and GBH; criminal damage

LISTENING to the evidence of Zak Wardle and Christina French was like witnessing a display of lying.

There were three counts to consider against Wardle and I was left wondering whether there could be a hung jury with the 12 unable to reach any majority decision because of the lack of credibility of the two people concerned.

A tale of the unexpected fittingly had a surprise ending. Wardle was found not guilty of all counts, which may not be too much of a shock, though he was taken back to prison as he remained in custody for breach of bail conditions.

There was more and this was not made public at the time, but the pair were involved in a second scenario with Wardle once again being accused of various offences by French who, for the second time, later withdrew her original evidence.

You will be spared more of the same.

22

MICHAEL KWAME: Rape

SEXY DANCER'S LOSS
OF MEMORY

THE SILVER PALM was a popular club for Ghanaians. It enhanced the culture of the country and Miss L, who had worked there, went back to see some old friends and customers.

One, Michael Kwame, had some drinks with Miss L and took her back to a friend's house where he was staying. While there was some consensual sex, Kwame was accused of rape (penetrating the vagina of the claimant with his penis).

Miss L was "extremely drunk" the jury was told when she went home with Kwame. They had sex. He said she was a willing partner; she was horrified when she found out what had happened. Miss L claimed she was so drunk she had no memory of what may have happened on the night — or to be precise, the morning — of the incident.

The judge gave the jury some legal guidance before the trial began. The prosecution had to prove Miss L was so drunk she lost the capacity to choose whether to have sex and the defendant knew or ought to have known she was not able to consent.

As the evidence unfolded it seemed far from a straightforward case for the jury to decide.

MICHAEL KWAME is from Ghana, the claimant — Miss L — is an African American. Miss L had previously worked at the Silver Palm club, but on the night in question she was there as a client and knew Kwame as a customer among the predominantly Ghanaian clientele.

Miss L did not ask for screens as she gave evidence, unusual in a rape trial, as the jury was told of the incident from 21 months previously.

Inevitably, it was one person's word against another's; the jury's task was not helped by contradictory evidence from witnesses while Kwame's pregnant wife listened to explicit details of her husband's infidelity from the public gallery.

CCTV FOOTAGE showed Miss L arriving at the club at 01.17. She was sober, she said, and wearing white shorts, a sheer black top with no bra and black high-heel shoes.

The defence asked Miss L whether the Silver Palm was different from other clubs.

"From a culture aspect, yes."

"Would you say your clothes that night clashed with the culture?"

"Debatable."

"Different bars and clubs have different dress codes."

"Yes."

It was never made exactly clear how much Miss L had to drink at the club, but she admitted having two Courvoisier and double Baileys mixed, two glasses of rosé wine and a couple of tequila shots.

"You told the police the dancing you did was described as grinding."

"Yes."

"What does this involve?"

"The male is behind with the female gyrating in front of him, going up and down."

"Where precisely?"

"The penis area."

"In essence the female is moving against the male penis."

"That's right."

CCTV showed Michael Kwame and Miss L, who had been chatting to each other, going outside at 02.45.

"You went on your own free will."

"Yes."

"It was friendly."

"Yes."

"You kissed of your own free will."

"Yes."

Miss L said she was aware there were customers she knew from her time working at the club in the car park while she complained Kwame had bad breath.

"When he was asked to stop [kissing] he did."

"Yes."

"He did not try to carry on."

"No."

The pair returned inside. Miss L had told the police in a statement she was drunk and fell over as she went to the bathroom.

However, the defence put it to Miss L: "Rather than fall by being intoxicated, I suggest you were trying to run in high heels and stumbled. Would that be fair?"

"Yes."

Miss L had told the police that following the "falling over" incident her memory was "almost non-existent" apart from one more dance "which she remembered the next day." The next thing she could recall was waking up at about 11.00 later that morning in the house of Kwame's friend, Malc, next to the defendant on a duvet on the floor.

The jury was shown CCTV footage at the club from 03.12 where Miss L is dancing with a male, not the defendant.

"You were dancing up and down in the style you spoke of earlier."

"Yes."

"At 03.15 [after the dancing had finished] you were able to walk by yourself to the bar where Kwame was standing."

"Yes."

"You made physical contact with the defendant of your own free will."

"Yes."

"You were dancing with your rear in Kwame's penis area."

"Yes."

"You kissed of your own free will."

"Not going to say free will. I won't agree to that, no."

"I suggest you left the club with the defendant."

"I cannot remember."

"I suggest you walked to the cab by yourself."

"I cannot remember."

The club manager told the jury: "She was sober when she arrived. Later she was dancing very inappropriately and did not appear as sober as when she came in. At around 3 a.m. she was at the bar with Kwame. She had her arms round him. They were kissing… what I'd call an attractive kiss. I assumed they were boyfriend and girlfriend. I saw them walk out around 3.15. I'd say she was in control of herself, yes."

The doorman confirmed the manager's evidence. He said: "I remember her arriving, she did not appear drunk. The way she was dressed, I could see her breasts. By 3 a.m. she looked like she needed help. On a scale of ten with zero sober and ten drunk I'd say she was a seven. The defendant never let her go as they went to the cab."

The taxi driver had a slightly different recollection of events. He said: "One of the bouncers helped her to the taxi. The defendant was behind him. The bouncer was holding her hands all the way to the car otherwise she might have fallen over.

"The man in the back [the defendant] asked her if she was up for a party. She said: 'Maybe, not now, but maybe.' Within a couple of minutes, they started kissing. I just focused on driving. He seemed a decent chap, well-mannered."

The defence asked the taxi driver about the bouncer, suggesting his assistance to Miss L did not happen.

"I'm telling you what I saw."

The defence pointed out that in the taxi driver's statement to the police he had said Miss L had said of a party: "Maybe, not now, but maybe *later*."

"Yes."

"And she understood the question?"

"Yes."

"In long parts of the journey, the claimant and defendant were talking."

"Yes."

"Was he taking advantage of the situation?"

"It did not feel like it."

"Did anything not seem right?"

"No."

"How was she when you arrived at the destination?"

"In a slightly better condition than when she got in."

"In your statement you said she was very, very drunk when she left your car — eight out of ten."

"Listen, it made no difference to me. I was just concerned about getting my money."

BACK TO Miss L and the defence cross-examined her about what happened at Malc's house.

"You started kissing the defendant."

"I can't agree because I can't remember."

"You performed oral sex on him."

"Sorry, I don't recall that."

"You told him you wanted him inside you. He put on a condom and you had sexual intercourse."

"I don't remember."

"During sex you asked him to say he loved you."

"No."

"He eventually pulled his penis out, you remember that?"

"No."

"You then put your clothes back on."

"No."

Miss L agreed that when they woke up in the morning Michael Kwame performed consensual oral sex on her.

"I played along. I did not want to be, you know, confrontational."

MICHAEL KWAME was cross-examined by the defence.

"Did you have sex with Miss L without her consent?"

"No."

"You believed she consented."

"Yes, she did."

"When did your wife find out?"

"A few days later. I realised I'd let her down. I was not happy. We've done counselling to fix our marriage."

"Had you ever made advances to Miss L before?"

"No. I was a customer and she was a bartender."

"How did you feel about kissing another woman?"

"At the time… it was the moment. I let myself and my wife down."

"Did any security guard help Miss L to the cab?"

"No."

"What was her state?"

"Tipsy, but not drunk."

"In the cab?"

"She started kissing me, touching my chest. She put her hand on my penis, but I pulled it away because I did not want anything like that in a cab,"

"And inside the house?"

"She made sure Malc had gone to bed. I turned around and she came to me. I thought: 'OK, she's up for it.' And I followed on. We started kissing, then more passionately. She pulled my zipper down, reached for my penis and started sucking me off. She was at ease. When she stopped, she said: 'I want you inside me.' I said I needed to get a condom. She said I didn't need one, but I put one on. She had pulled her shorts and knickers down. I went to penetrate her. She was making noises like 'keep going.' We moved from the sofa to a duvet on the carpet. She was happy, I could tell. She wanted me to tell her I loved her. She asked three or four times, but I wouldn't. She started to hold me tighter, it became too physical. I took my penis out and lay next to her. She put her clothes back on and so did I. It had been a long day and we fell asleep. When I woke up in the morning, I still had the condom on."

"What happened then?"

"I got up, took the condom off, washed my face. We had oral sex, me going down on her."

"With her consent?"

"Yes."

"Did she ask you what you'd done that night?"

"Not at all."

"She called you later."

"Yes, and asked if we had sex. I said: 'Yes, of course we did. What are you driving at?' She said she felt used. As far as I'm concerned, we had consensual sex. I was getting confused. She called me back later. She said: 'I'm not happy, I feel cheated.' I told her I thought we had resolved this. She said: 'You have to pay me.' I told her I didn't see her as the type of person who would do this. We had consensual sex, no way was I going to pay her money. I'd done nothing wrong."

DID MICHAEL KWAME take advantage of a girl who was too drunk to consent to sexual intercourse? The jury retired to deliberate whether Kwame had raped Miss L or whether the sexual intercourse was consensual.

22

MICHAEL KWAME: Rape

A POPULAR reason given by girls who claim they have been raped is that their drink was spiked. In fact, the biggest common danger to a female's safety is excessive alcohol, not anything secretly added to it.

Rohypnol, one of the most commonly claimed date rape drugs, is available on prescription in England, used by those suffering from acute insomnia. To help to ensure its product could not be used illegally, the manufacturer put a vivid purple colourant in rohypnol which discolours any drink in which it is dissolved.

"Everyone thinks that rohypnol is a problem," said Michael Scott-Ham of the UK's Forensic Science Service. "But alcohol is by far the biggest problem."

Miss L said she had drunk three Courvoisier and double Baileys, two glasses of rosé wine and two tequila shots — a potent mix of different alcohols. No illegal drugs were found in Miss L's blood sample taken the following day.

After a day and a half of deliberating the jury sent a note to the judge saying it was unable to reach a unanimous verdict and did not think it would be able to do so. The judge told the jury he would accept a majority verdict of 10-2 or 11-1.

A day later the jury returned with a majority verdict of not guilty. It had to be sure Miss L suffered a mental blackout even though she was dancing just before she left the club. Maybe the consensual kissing in the car park and being the willing recipient of oral sex in the morning made the jury unsure that the sexual intercourse was non-consensual.

As much as anything, Michael Kwame was lucky his wife stood by him, also supporting him in court where she heard intimate details of her husband's infidelity.

23

BARRY MORTON: Grievous bodily harm with intent; GBH

DID HE USE GLASS OR FIST
TO HIT CLAIMANT?

BARRY MORTON had known Fred Molyneux for about 20 years. As a teenager, his parents used to take him to a pub where Molyneux was the manager. The pair had kept in touch, though when Morton started to go out with a former girlfriend of Molyneux's it appeared their friendship became strained.

On FA Cup final day in 2019 Morton, his girlfriend and some friends went to a local pub where Molyneux was drinking. The day ended with Molyneux suffering injuries to his head and face following an altercation.

At 22.54 police and an ambulance were called to the pub where Molyneux was initially assessed by paramedics before being taken to hospital where superficial cuts to his head and face were treated. Police went to Morton's house just before 02.00 and one officer described him as "appearing drunk… his speech was slurred, his eyes were glazed and he was unsteady on his feet."

Morton was arrested for grievous bodily harm. At the police station, he was kept in a cell overnight and interviewed at 10.30, but answered "no comment" to every question, as is his right.

THE DEFENCE asked Barry Morton what happened on the day of the incident.

He said: "I went to the pub with some friends to watch the FA Cup final. We got there about two. I did not drink [alcohol] all day. I drank Coke most of the day. When Fred [Molyneux] came in the pub he had a funny grin on his face. He was staring at me and grinning. He wanted me to say something. It went on for an hour and a half. I felt intimidated as he had friends with him."

"Why did you not just leave?"

"I didn't want any trouble. I just ignored him."

"How much alcohol had you drunk?"

"Four or five pints of Carling."

"How did it affect you?"

"I was jolly… fun, not drunk."

"On a scale of one to ten, with one being stone cold sober, what were you?"

"About four."

The jury watched CCTV which showed Morton going outside for, he said, a cigarette. He approached Molyneux who was smoking.

"What did you say to him?"

"I said: 'Can I have a word?' I wanted to know what his problem was. I wanted it out in the open. I thought it was the best thing to do at the time. He was quite aggressive to me and said: 'What?' I said to him: 'What's the matter, mate?' He was aggressive and said: 'What's it got to do with you? You fucking mug. I'm going to do you.' I thought he was going to hit me with his glass."

"Why did you not walk away?"

"I wish I had. It was a heat of the moment thing."

"There were no hands raised."

"No, but he was very aggressive in his manner. I thought he was going to hit me so I threw beer over him."

The CCTV was unclear whether Morton had a glass in his hand as he appeared to strike Molyneux. He denied this, claiming that as he threw beer over Molyneux he dropped his glass which shattered. Molyneux fell backwards to the ground.

"What was your intention at the time?"

"I felt threatened and acted in self-defence. I honestly felt he was going to glass me."

As Molyneux fell backwards, Morton claimed he struck his head against a wall "which accounted for the cut on his head," said the defence. Morton was seen hitting Molyneux as he lay on the ground, but said: "He was still threatening me and calling for his friends. I thought if he got up, he'd do something. He kept saying 'you're dead'."

It took two bystanders to pull Morton away from Molyneux. The defendant left the pub and went home.

THE PROSECUTION asked Barry Morton why he drank both alcohol and Coke.

"Because I didn't want to wake up with a hangover."

"The police said you appeared very drunk when they came to your house."

"Wrong. No."

"Your eyes were glazed."

"When you have a drink, your eyes get glazed."

"They said your speech was slurred."

"I had a couple of Budweisers when I got home. My speech, even when I've not had a drink, some people can't understand me."

"You say [Fred] Molyneux gave you a funny look."

"Yes. I felt intimidated and he had friends with him."

"Did you want to start on him?"

"No, just clear the air."

"If you felt intimidated, why did you go to him?"

"To find out what his problem was. To get it sorted by talking to him."

"He was simply having a cigarette and minding his own business."

"He was aggressive and had a glass in his hand."

"You flew off the handle."

"You're wrong."

"How was drenching him going to stop him attacking you?"

"I threw drink over him to put him off balance."

The prosecution estimated that Morton punched Molyneux six times and kneed him four times while he was on the ground.

"You were drunk."

"No."

"This was an unprovoked attack."

"No, it wasn't."

BARRY MORTON claimed self-defence. There is nothing in law that states a person has to be struck before defending themselves. However, even if the defendant can show that they honestly believed the force used was necessary in the circumstances, it is up to a jury to determine whether the degree of force used was reasonable in the circumstances.

A person is entitled to use reasonable force to protect themselves, members of their family or even a complete stranger if they genuinely believe that they are in danger or are the victim of an unlawful act, such as an assault. An individual may even take what is known as a pre-emptive strike if they honestly believe that the circumstances demand it.

This is what Morton said he did.

Would the jury agree? If it did not, would he be found guilty of grievous bodily harm with intent or the less serious GBH?

23

BARRY MORTON: Grievous bodily harm with intent; GBH

HAD I been on the jury I would have asked myself how Fred Molyneux could have fallen backwards to the ground if only beer had been thrown over him. I would then have asked myself if striking Molyneux 10 times while he was on the ground was self-defence and reasonable in the circumstances.

I would have concluded that while CCTV was unclear, Barry Morton must have struck Molyneux either with his fist or with a glass in his hand for him to fall as he did. And I would not have considered punching and kicking Molyneux, who never hit Morton, as reasonable in any way.

My view would have been that this was an unlawful, unprovoked attack on another person, fuelled by alcohol and no doubt related to the girl they had both befriended.

Maybe those thoughts were discussed by the jury as it reached its unsurprising guilty verdict, not of grievous bodily harm, but of the more serious wounding with intent to cause GBH. It came to the conclusion that Morton had hit Molyneux with a glass, effectively a weapon.

Morton had three previous convictions connected to alcohol, though not violence — in 2002 and 2011 he was found guilty of being drunk and disorderly; in 2004 he was banned for a year after driving with excess alcohol.

The judge did not count these as bad character, showing a pattern of offending for the same offence, and sentenced Morton to 40 weeks' imprisonment. Morton would serve 20 weeks before being released on licence.

Section 18 (GBH with intent) carries a maximum sentence of life imprisonment. Among factors indicating higher culpability are a significant degree of premeditation, use of weapon and deliberately causing more harm than is necessary for commission of offence. Morton certainly appeared to tick those boxes, so to spend just five months in jail for such a nasty offence seems little more than being sent to the naughty step.

24

MAURICE RICHARDS: Sexual assault; rape by penetration; indecent assault; actual bodily harm

13 CHARGES AGAINST
A 'LOVING FATHER'

ACCORDING TO Maurice Richards, he was a loving father who never raised a hand to his stepdaughters.

However, according to his stepdaughters Child J and Child C he was a violent sex pervert. Richards' response to their accusations was that the girls were after compensation in the wake of his divorce from their mother.

To add more intrigue to the trial, when the divorce was finalised Richards remarried his first wife.

MAURICE RICHARDS married Christine in 1980; he became the stepfather of Child J and Child C, later adopting them. From a very early stage, they claimed they were shouted at and physically chastised... he would talk to them inappropriately and indecently assault them.

The charges against Richards were:

Count 1... Between 1981 and 1982, he put a finger inside the bra of Child J [aged 13] and rubbed her nipple

Count 2... Between 1981 and 1982 he put his finger in the vagina of Child J

Count 3... Between 1981 and 1982 he put his finger in the vagina of Child J

Count 4... Between 1981 and 1982 he put Child J's hand on his erect penis

Count 5... When she was aged between 14 and 17 he put his finger inside the vagina of Child J

Count 6... On at least five occasions, he groped Child J, feeling her breasts

Count 7... He hit Child J so hard it caused injury to her lip — occasioning actual bodily harm

Count 8... Between 1982 and 1985 he punched Child C in the face, causing two black eyes — ABH

Count 9... When Child C was 15 or 16, he punched her in the face — ABH

Count 10... There was no lock on the bathroom door, he would come in and stare at Child C when naked, also beating her — indecent assault

Count 11... On at least seven occasions the defendant would pay Child C £1 to massage his foot which he placed in the area of her vagina, wriggling his toes — indecent assault

Count 12... Between 1984 and 1987, when Child C moved, on at least five occasions he committed the same offence as in Count 10

Count 13... In the late Nineties when Child J had moved to Cornwall, the defendant touched the breasts of her 11-year-old daughter, Child H.

IN 2002, Child J told her mother she had been sexually abused. "Why did you have to bring it up now?" was her mother's response. The allegation was put on the divorce papers which were signed by both parties.

In 2018, Child J phoned ChildLine who contacted the police. Maurice Richards, 82, denied all the offences. He gave no evidence in court, but made a statement to the police when he was arrested in August 2018.

Christine (name changed for legal reasons), the girls' mother, had started divorce procedures in 2002 when Child J told her she had been sexually abused by her stepfather.

IN COURT, Christine said that when she heard the news [about the allegations], she told Child J: "He's been a good father and husband," and Child J replied: 'Yeah... right.'

"Child J then said there was a programme on TV she could relate to, but didn't say which one. She put the phone down on me. I called her back and asked her if she meant rape. 'No, fingers,' she said.

"I told Maurice he had one of two choices — to leave or I call the police. 'Why bring it up now?' he asked me. His face looked like a deer caught in the headlights. I didn't want a divorce. I did love my husband. I was not aware at the time of him beating up the girls. If it happened, I wasn't there.

"After we married, he became more dominant. You know, no sweets or TV. But I never witnessed any incident causing injury. I remember once he asked Child J for a hug and she refused. I said: 'That's not very nice.'

"The children had to do chores to earn pocket money, which is not unusual. In front of me he was a good father and husband."

INTERVIEWED by the police, Maurice Richards was asked about his "admission" of sexually abusing Christine's daughters in the divorce papers. Richards said: "I did it to help the divorce through. I have been a loving father and have never raised a hand to the girls."

"But if you had not sexually assaulted anyone, why did you admit it by signing the papers?"

"She wanted a divorce. If she wanted to do it then let her do it. I just wanted it out of the way. I just let her have her own way. I know it doesn't make any sense, but I just wanted to get rid of it."

When Richards allegedly placed his finger inside her vagina for the first time, Child J said she was "shocked and confused." She claimed Richards said: "You must have known it was going to happen." Richards told the police: "Ridiculous. It never happened. I don't know where she's getting this from."

The next time it happened, Child J claimed he told her: "You must have enjoyed that — your panties are damp." He told the police: "Hand on heart it never happened. You don't do that to your daughter. I don't know where she's getting these ideas from. I'm an affectionate man. I didn't want a divorce. These allegations are invented to help Christine get a divorce and go to the USA [where she eventually re-married]. They are jumping on the Jimmy Savile compensation bandwagon. Violent? Never in my life. I don't believe in it. I did not hit them, not once."

SUMMING UP, the judge read out character references from Maurice Richards' family. From his first wife, who he remarried: "He has three sons — I was the disciplinarian. I never saw him violent. He is a generous person who thinks the best of everyone."

His eldest son said: "He isn't aggressive. He's very soft. I have two daughters and he's never done anything inappropriate to them." One of the daughters said: "He's never smacked me. He's a good granddad. He's very kind."

Another son said: "He never smacked me. Mum did. He didn't have a lot of bottle… rather wimpy."

The judge told the jury that it should take into account the good character of the defendant, who had no convictions or reprimands. "Someone of good character can mean he is less likely to commit the offences," he said. "It is his right to give no evidence in court and it is up to the jury what relevance it thinks this may have.

"Just because he made no comment, you cannot convict wholly on this. Perhaps he did not wish to speak because of his age and the stress it may cause. Maybe he did not want the quality of his defence tested in cross-examination.

"All 12 of you must agree or disagree, one way or the other."

24

MAURICE RICHARDS: Sexual assault; rape by penetration; indecent assault; ABH

MAURICE RICHARDS was a lucky man. The jury found the 82-year-old guilty of all 13 charges. Why lucky? Had the judge been able to use 2018 sentencing guidelines then Richards would have faced a possible life sentence.

However, the defendant had to be sentenced under the guidelines from the Eighties, so he escaped with a four-year prison term.

"This is a sorry case," said the judge. "You are guilty of a gross breach of trust on your stepdaughters. It is painfully obvious that what you did to them has had a massive effect on them. Digital penetration could now result in life imprisonment."

However, at the age of 82, two years in jail before being released on licence may still have been life for Richards.

25

GARON GREENE: Violent disorder, unlawful wounding; possession of an offensive weapon; grievous bodily harm with intent

MICHAEL MacINTYRE: Violent disorder; unlawful wounding; possession of an offensive weapon

CUZZIES... BRUVS... LITTLE
BOY A... AND THE RIGHT BUM

THIS TRIAL was like an Agatha Christie novel. It started with the jury needing to decide the guilt or innocence of two defendants and six charges, but ended with them deliberating just a single count against one of the accused.

Garon Greene did not like JT — street name Da Big Man — and the feeling was mutual. The pair had "previous" in the shady world of local gangs. Greene claimed he had been beaten up by "people who knew JT." So when he went out of his manor he carried a knife "for protection."

One day, around lunch-time, Greene saw JT on a bus. He and his three "cuzzies" [cousins] boarded it. JT, who was upstairs, noticed the four getting on and while Da Big Man was over six feet, he was outnumbered.

What to do?

Perhaps aware he might find himself up against more than just fists and feet, JT waited for the bus to come to a halt so he could hopefully have a fast getaway. Needing to defend himself somehow, he took off his belt and swung it around as he ran down the stairs.

Four against one was always going to be demanding odds to overcome, especially as Greene had his "protective" knife. Greene proved to be a challenging opponent and a challenging defendant —

difficult to hear and difficult to understand with the jury treated to an unexpected lesson in street English.

THE PROSECUTION kicked-off proceedings by asking Garon Greene if carrying a knife made him feel safe.

"Uh huh [yes]."

"You knew JT."

"Uh huh."

"He is known as Da Big Man. Do you have a street name?"

"No."

"Did you like him?"

"Scared of him."

"If you are scared of someone, you can't like them."

"Uh huh."

"You took a knife if you went out of your area."

"Uh huh."

"So that day you took a blade."

"Uh huh."

"How long was the blade?"

"Four, six inches."

"It was tucked in the side of your trousers."

"Uh huh."

"Was this comfortable or uncomfortable?"

"Uncomfortable."

"It was just for defence."

"Uh huh. I only walked with a knife cos [it] made me feel safer."

"When was the last time you had seen JT before the incident?"

"Bout a year ago."

"Forty-five minutes before getting on the bus you'd had some cannabis."

"Uh huh."

"Is it fair to say you had a buzz?"

"Unlikely."

"You targeted JT."

"No."

"You were with your cousins?"

"Me cuzzies, yeah."

"And you were all scared?"

"Uh huh."

"If all four of you were scared, why did you not let the bus go by?"

"I did not think he'd attack us."

"So why were you paranoid?"

"Cos of previous incident."

"So you thought he might do something."

"It's why we stayed downstairs."

"Why risk it?"

"Not think he'd attack us. There was a lot of people on the bus. It was daylight and there was four of us."

"You deliberately positioned yourselves by the doors."

"No."

"Why did you separate?"

"I didn't know what he was thinking, so easier to see what he was doing."

"Boy A [who cannot be named for legal reasons] was the first to kick JT."

"He's little. He can't fight, but can defend himself."

"Why did you not put little Boy A behind you?"

"Not think he'd attack anyone, just get off the bus and go about his business."

BEFORE the cross-examination of Garon Greene continued the following morning, he pleaded guilty to violent disorder, unlawful wounding and possession of an offensive weapon.

Co-defendant Michael MacIntyre also pleaded guilty to violent disorder and unlawful wounding — he was dismissed from the dock. It left the jury with one charge against Greene to deliberate — wounding with intent to cause grievous bodily harm.

THE PROSECUTION put it to Garon Greene that JT came down the stairs lashing with his belt defensively to "ward you and your friends off him."

"He should've come down the stairs like a normal person."

"The bus had come to a stop. If there was nobody in his way he could have got off."

"No one was in his way. He ran at Boy A and hit him with his belt."

"You were up and ready for him."

"No, that was not our intention."

"CCTV footage seen by the jury showed Boy A kicking out at JT. You say little Boy A's not a fighter."

"No, but he can defend himself. A normal person would walk down the stairs and leave. He decided to run down the stairs and assault little Boy A."

"When Boy A attacked JT he had no right to do that."

"You're right, but JT's over six feet and I saw me little cuz under threat and in danger."

"Why didn't you stay in the baggage area and just let JT off?"

"I knew what he was getting ready to do. He was saying: 'Four v one, come on.' He wanted four v one, I swear on my mum's life he said that. He was saying: 'C'mon bruvs'."

"You produced a knife and waved it around."

"Yeah. I wanted to defend a family relative. If I wanted to stab him, I could have gone upstairs and done it. I only did it when he assaulted Boy A. If I had wanted to hurt him badly, I would not stab him in the right bum. I did it to slow him down."

ONE WITNESS said the cut to JT's buttocks was "really big, the size of a small fist." She "packed" the wound until the paramedics arrived. The cut to the arm went so deep it reached the bone and tendons, for which Garon Greene apologised.

When police officers and the London Ambulance Service arrived, they found the 21-year-old victim suffering from stab wounds to his arm and buttock. He was taken to hospital for medical treatment and later discharged.

After the victim was stabbed, all four suspects ran off. Detectives from the Trident and Area Crime Command launched an investigation. Michael MacIntyre was quickly identified from the CCTV footage by officers and arrested the following day.

Officers also arrested Boy B on the same day. Just over two weeks later, acting on intelligence, officers — assisted by the Territorial Support Group — attended an address. They forced entry and found Greene and a 17-year-old boy [Boy A] inside. The teenager attempted to resist arrest. He was detained and both were taken to a local police station.

They both refused to answer any questions despite being shown images taken from the bus's CCTV and were charged.

THE ISSUE for the jury was to decide whether they were sure Garon Greene had the intention to cause really serious injury or whether the knife was just for self-defence.

25

GARON GREENE: Grievous bodily harm with intent

THE FOREMAN of the jury replied "guilty" — as opposed to "uh huh" — when asked by the clerk of the court if it had found Garon Greene, 19, guilty or not guilty of wounding with intent to cause grievous bodily harm. He had previously pleaded guilty to violent disorder, unlawful wounding and possession of an offensive weapon. Greene, of no fixed abode, was jailed for six years.

Michael MacIntyre, 19, unemployed, had pleaded guilty to violent disorder, unlawful wounding and possession of an offensive weapon. He was jailed for two years.

Two 17-year-old boys, who cannot be named for legal reasons, pleaded guilty to violent disorder. Boy A was sentenced to an eight-month Detention and Training Order; Boy B was sentenced to a 12-month Detention and Training Order.

The judge said: "When you stab someone with a knife it can hardly be 'a warning'. It must be with the intent to cause GBH. Knives can kill, maim and cause serious harm.

"This was a violent assault on board a bus on a Friday lunchtime. The defendants attacked the victim as a pack with complete disregard for the safety of other passengers. It is fortunate that the victim did not sustain more serious injuries which could have ended his life.

"The fact that two of the group were in possession of large knives with the blades being at least 12 inches long shows that they had every intention of causing serious harm."

There was more to come, though.

SIX MONTHS later Garon Greene was back in court where he pleaded guilty to two counts of unlawful wounding and possession of a bladed object in a public place. The incident had taken place two days before the attack on the bus and the jury in question was unaware of this.

Hassan Kukak was on his way to have a cup of coffee, but his path was blocked by 10 black males. "Can you move over, man?" Kukak said waving his hands to illustrate what he was asking.

"Don't use your hands to me," said Greene.

"Why?"

"I'll shank [cut] you."

After a brief exchange Greene went to a bag which was in some bushes and took out an eight-inch knife as the other nine boys took off their belts. "I was very scared," said Kukak in a statement. "I knew I was in trouble."

Greene swiped the knife towards Kukak's right leg; when he looked down, he was bleeding profusely. The cut was one and a half inches wide and the claimant was kept in hospital for four days. A year later he was still unable to run or play any physical sport while the emotional scars had also yet to heal.

The gang ran off. Two female French students recognised Greene who attended the same college as them, though they did not know his name. Initially they were too scared to assist inquiries, but were shown photographs by the college of various students and identified Greene plus Michael MacIntyre and the two 17-year-olds who were to be implicated in the bus incident. However, the other three were not charged.

Kukak also identified Greene as the person who stabbed him. Greene had previously been found guilty of robbery after the victim was hit with a bottle before his phone was stolen and being in possession of a bladed object in a separate incident.

Within a three-day period, Greene had stabbed two people and of the Kukak knifing the judge said: "This was a truly deplorable incident by you again. This was wicked behaviour and you should be ashamed of yourself. For a young man of 19 you have a serious record of violent behaviour."

Greene was sentenced to six months for possession of a bladed object and 18 months for unlawful wounding, the sentences to run concurrently. However, the 18 months would be served consecutively to the six years for the bus stabbing, meaning Greene was given a total of seven and a half years for his two knife attacks.

26

JAMES LAWRENCE: Actual bodily harm; indecent assault; assault on a child; sexual assault

THE SPANKING PASTOR

GOD, so the saying goes, can work in mysterious ways and James Lawrence, a pastor in the Christian Fellowship, certainly had unusual religious methods to help three female members of his congregation. He spanked them.

Lawrence, 73, claimed the sessions were "deliverance counselling" and had to be done "flesh to flesh" on the bare bottom to cast out evil spirits or, in one case, to attempt to rid the woman of her depression. The pastor maintained the smacking of the three women was consensual. With one of the women, he spanked her between her legs to "cure her frigid spirit" and performed a sex act on her with his finger.

The jury was asked to put its religious feelings aside as the trial began. Lawrence denied seven counts of sexual assault; one count of assault by digital penetration and two counts of indecent assault, against three women between 1991 and 2013. He also denied four counts of child cruelty against three different youngsters and a charge of causing actual bodily harm to one of the women, all between January 1969 and February 2008.

THE PROSECUTION claimed James Lawrence ran the church "more like a cult" ...that he "brainwashed his followers" and "manipulated vulnerable women" into submitting to spanking sessions for his sexual pleasure. Lawrence's defence was that the deliverance was "not sexual."

The defendant told the jury that one of the women had asked him to spank her as she thought it might help with her depression and he agreed.

Lawrence said: "She wondered if it could help with her depression. I thought it could. It depends if you see depression as an illness or an evil spirit. If you smack somebody it could free an evil spirit."

Lawrence cited the example of Smith Wigglesworth, a Pentecostal faith healer who claimed to be able to cure cancer by punching sufferers.

The prosecution told the jury that Lawrence had helped one of the women to find a job, as well as paying her bills. "Those things would be great if they didn't come with the flip side," the Crown said.

"Once he had drawn her in with apparent kindness and significant generosity... once he'd done that, made her trust him and rely on him, things took a turn for the worse."

THE DEFENCE said James Lawrence was not a "charlatan" or a "megalomaniac," just a busy pastor trying to do his job. "He helped men and women in need, both practically and spiritually.

"The purpose of deliverance isn't sexual and is a part of a charismatic Pentecostal church. It may be hard to get your head around. Deliverance, for example, is actually a widely held belief and there's nothing wrong with it.

"Context is so important. What about the use of extreme force on a very young child? Is that permissible on a very young child? Actually yes, because what about circumcision of an eight-day-old baby which is a tenet of Judaism?

"If you want to engage in Christian Domestic Discipline, you have the right to do that."

The defence told the jury there was "no evidence" that Lawrence had used subliminal control patterns to "brainwash" his congregation and said the women who had made complaints against him "bore grudges."

THE JURY had to be sure James Lawrence had committed the offences and that the claimants did not willingly participate.

26

JAMES LAWRENCE: Actual bodily harm; indecent assault; assault on a child; sexual assault

THE so-called spanking pastor was found guilty of six counts of sexual assault with no penetration; also, of neglecting a child and assaulting a child while he was a Christian Fellowship minister.

James Lawrence was cleared of one count of actual bodily harm, two counts of indecent assault, two counts of assault on a child, one count of sexual assault with no penetration and one count of sexual assault by penetration.

He was jailed for six years and ordered to sign the sex offenders' register for life.

The judge said: "These are serious offences involving a gross abuse of the trust that was invested in you, and in your position in the church. Indeed, custody is inevitable."

Lawrence had spanked one woman on between 10 to 20 occasions "hard enough, on one occasion, to bruise her" and during one of the sessions he even photographed her afterwards while she was naked on the floor of his office, before showing her the pictures and deleting them.

The judge added: "You had persuaded her to believe that what she was agreeing to was some form of therapy."

27

TERRY QUINN: Deliberately harbouring

'HE WAS ON THE RUN?
I HAD NO IDEA'

TERRY QUINN cut a sad figure in the dock and the registered alcoholic said: "I've lost everything."

Would he subsequently lose his freedom after pleading not guilty to deliberately harbouring Harry Samuels who had escaped from custody while at hospital receiving treatment?

The jury was not told what Samuels had been charged with. A few weeks later the police received information Samuels was at the flat where lifelong friend Quinn lived.

After legal arguments between the prosecution and defence "harbouring" remained a subjective term which could be interpreted in various ways.

Harbouring is assisting an offender, giving him shelter, to maintain him secretly.

But does providing somewhere for a fugitive to have a beer, a shower and a change of clothes constitute a safe haven? Was Quinn aware that Samuels was wanted by the police when he offered him a helping hand and he stayed the night at his flat? And how long does someone have to be in a property before they "stay" there?

Legal arguments. Bloody hell.

HARRY SAMUELS had known Terry Quinn since the former, half the defendant's age, was five. Both were familiar with the inside of a courtroom, Quinn since the age of 12, though over the previous 10 years most of his offences were drink-related.

Acting on a tip-off, five police officers arrived at Quinn's flat, three guarding the rear entrance. The officers were familiar with Quinn, whose door was ajar when they arrived. "Terry, it's the police," one shouted. "Don't come in," said Quinn who quickly appeared wearing only a towel.

"It seemed we had disturbed him and his good lady," an officer told the jury. "He seemed a bit flustered." The officer said he told Quinn: "We're here to look for Harry Samuels. We believe he's here." Quinn said he wasn't and the police were "welcome to have a look" which they did.

The officer told Quinn that he would be committing an offence if he allowed Samuels to stay there. "Harry's wanted, you know. He has absconded from lawful custody."

He said Quinn replied: "Our kid? Look, don't be so stupid." Quinn was told if he wanted to speak to the police anonymously, he could phone 101.

Six days later the police returned to Quinn's flat and one officer shouted: "If you do not open the door, we will force entry."

"You ain't fucking breaking the door down. I'm behind it," was Quinn's reply.

He opened the door and greeted the police, this time wearing just his underpants. As one officer thought Quinn was going to hit him — "he drew his right fist back" — he was hand-cuffed.

"Terry, you have an escaped person at your address."

The police said Quinn responded: "I don't know."

Samuels was in the lounge and he, too, was hand-cuffed. Quinn was arrested for aiding and abetting a person at large.

Quinn denied he knew Samuels was on the run. He claimed he had not seen Samuels for seven or eight years until one day he turned up on a nearby estate, the Shanklin — "I call it the Wanklin," said Quinn. Samuels was staying with a family friend and went to visit Quinn.

"I'm not sure why he came round," said Quinn. "He stayed for an hour or two, I can't remember exactly."

THE PROSECUTION asked Terry Quinn about his conversation with Harry Samuels: "What did you speak about?"

"Mainly about moving flat. Angie [Quinn's latest partner] let him in. He was soaked right through. I gave him some track-suit bottoms. I was drinking heavily."

"What was a typical day?"

"It could vary. Maybe 12 cans of Stella, on another day two bottles of whisky."

"What can you remember the police telling you [on their first visit]?"

"I went to bed because I'd had a lot of whisky. I heard a noise and saw some police in the house. They said they were looking for someone, but there was nobody there."

"Did they say who they were looking for?"

"To be honest, I don't know. I'd been drinking heavily. They were looking for someone. I don't know who. I carried on drinking."

"On August 24 you were arrested. Harry Samuels was found in your flat. Had he stayed there up until then?"

"Only the one night, the previous night. Me and Angie were having a drink, whisky I think, the security phone downstairs went. Harry wanted to pop in with his girlfriend, Lauren, who I'd never met."

"Do you know why he wanted to come round?"

"Just to pop round, I suppose."

"What happened?"

"We sat in the front room. The girls looked at some photos."

"By then did you know the police wanted to find him?"

"Only when the girls were speaking, I heard something. I said: 'If you [Harry and Lauren] want to be together you must sort this out.' I thought he'd failed to appear at a police station or something. I didn't want him to have the life I've had. You know, in and out of courts, messed up relationships, not seeing my kids."

"Was it your intention to prevent arrest?"

"Never in a million years. One thing I do know is you can't get away from the law. It may take three years, but they'll get you. It's too late for me now. I've lost everything."

"You are saying you were not aware he had escaped from prison?"

"I swear on my babies' ashes. For me, he had just not appeared at a police station."

"You say you told him to surrender, to what offence?"

"Whatever it was."

"You let him stay to avoid arrest."

"Never. I tried to make him surrender. I'm not his legal guardian.

He's a young lad. I let him come round, have a bath. I mean, if you're dirty you need to wash. I fed him, changed his clothes, had a beer, know what I mean? I can't make him give himself up. I didn't know what he'd done. The police came round. I was stark bollock naked. They said they had info or something. I never knew what he'd done until the police told me. I just thought he hadn't turned up at a police station."

"The police know you. Some days you can communicate better than others."

"I don't know. I've never interviewed myself."

THE POLICE officers who saw Terry Quinn on their two visits denied he appeared in a state of inebriation on either day, though the jury may have been aware of his apparent discomfort caused by not having a drink for several hours as he gave evidence.

Quinn became a registered alcoholic after the break-up of his marriage in 2004, his ex-wife taking their children with her. In 2011 Quinn remarried, but a year later his second wife died.

How much of a sympathy vote this would draw from the jury as it reached its verdict remained to be seen.

27

TERRY QUINN: Deliberately harbouring

STILL battling the demons of alcohol addiction, Terry Quinn had claimed he had no money and had to walk the seven miles home one night and then back to court the following morning. While he had convictions dating back 40 years to when he was 12, it was difficult not to have a degree of compassion for a man whose life had been wrecked by his addiction.

The jury seemed to agree, though most of all it appeared it felt Quinn's ability to take in facts and his memory were affected by his condition. Quinn was found not guilty of knowingly harbouring Harry Samuels.

28

ALEX McDONALD: Three counts of sexual assault

PORN FREE — HOW DID IT AFFECT TEENAGER?

WHEN a defendant is accused of three sexual offences against a girl who was nine at the time, it is natural even for the most impartial and non-judgmental of jurors, not to sympathise with the alleged victim.

Child Z was 13 when she gave evidence against Alex McDonald, initially at a police station (her mother, Laura, was there) with a Child Protection Team officer and then in a Crown Court where the teenager had a responsible adult by her side.

The alleged events took place at the house of Ioni, a childhood friend of Laura who baby-sat for her daughters Child Z and Child Y while Ioni worked. The defendant was a friend of Ioni and a frequent visitor to the house.

CHILD Z claimed during her police interview that Alex McDonald had "touched me inappropriately... between my legs, my labia... he rubbed inside with his fingers" as she went to the bathroom to clean her teeth.

"He wanted to touch my reproductive organs. I said 'ouch' when he was poking me, fiddling with my labia. He wanted to do it to me again. I didn't know what to say. I didn't tell my mum because I thought I might get into trouble."

Child Z was asked what McDonald's exact words were.

She replied: "'Can I look at your private parts?' 'Do you want me to?' 'Can I have a feel?' She said she told him 'no'."

Child Z was then asked when she started having periods.

"When I was 10."

"What about when you started to wear a bra?"

"Before secondary school."

THE LAST two questions became easier to understand as the trial proceeded. The defence had to tread a delicate path between needing certain questions to be answered on behalf of its client while respecting Child Z's age.

Child Z was asked about Robin Wright, a former boyfriend of her mother who had not told her he was on the Sex Offenders Register for life after an earlier conviction.

"Did you know Robin Wright?"

"Yes. He was a friend of mum's."

"Did he look after you when mummy was working?"

"No."

"What was he like?"

"Kind."

"Did he ever do anything you didn't really like?"

"Not really."

"Did he ever touch your private parts?"

"No."

"Did he ask you to touch his private parts?"

"No."

The defence moved on to ask Child Z about Alex McDonald.

"You said you met Alex eight to ten times at Ioni's house."

"No, a couple."

"You mean two?"

"More than two."

"More than five?"

"Six."

"OK. I now want to ask you about films. What films do you like?"

"Celebrities."

"Have you seen adult films involving real people?"

"Yes."

"Did they touch each other's private parts?"

"Yes."

"Do you know what pornography is?"

"Yes."

"Have you seen pornographic films?"

"Yes."

"When did you start to look at them?"

"When I was two or three."

"When did you last see them?"

"Thirteen [her present age]."

"Because you have seen pornographic films did you pretend Alex touched your private parts?"

"No."

"What did he do to you?"

"I was in the bathroom and he put his hands on my shoulders. I went into the bedroom and I was on my back with my knees bent."

"Are you jealous of your sister's friendship with Alex?"

"No."

NEXT IN the witness box was Rachael Harman, the mother of Child Z and Child Y.

The prosecution asked her: "How old was Child Z when you started the relationship with Robin Wright?"

"Six."

"How long were you with him?"

"Six months."

"Did he ever stay the night?"

"Yes."

"When you started the relationship, what did he tell you of his past?"

"That he'd had an affair with a 17-year-old."

"The police made you aware of Robin Wright's past. That he had sexually assaulted girls aged 13 and 14, touching their breasts."

"Yes. I ended the relationship then."

"Is it right Child Z was diagnosed Autistic Spectrum Disorder?"

"Yes."

"She also has learning disorders and sleeping problems."

"Yes."

"Have you seen her draw pictures of people's sexual organs?"

"Yes."

"When did this start?"

"When she was eight or nine."

227

"Did you ask her why she did this?"

"She loves art."

The mother said that her daughter had told her McDonald had touched her. She confronted McDonald who denied the claims.

THE DEFENCE cross-examined Child Z's mother.

"When your brother, Errol, came to stay, he had some pornographic magazines which you caught your daughter looking at."

"Yes. She took them out of a bag, I told her not to look at such things."

"And she had watched material on an adult channel."

"I think she was flicking through and it came up."

IT WAS then Child Q's turn to give evidence, the 14-year-old wearing his school uniform.

"You are the son of Ioni?"

"Yes."

"What was the house like?"

"Busy... mad... six kids in one room... three girls, three boys."

"Where did you get changed?"

"In my mum's room. Child Z would sometimes come in wearing her bra and knickers which was annoying."

"What did she watch on her laptop?"

"Female wrestling, but there would be sex pop-ups and I'd say: 'That's disgusting, you shouldn't do that.' It was Russian girls with their tops off touching each other."

"What about Alex?"

"He'd come over maybe once a week. We'd play FIFA, but he wasn't any good. He was a cheerful, happy guy."

"Were he and Child Z ever alone?"

"No, never."

"Is Child Z the sort of girl to tell a lie to deliberately hurt someone?"

"Not sure."

"Have you ever heard her do something to get a person into trouble or isn't she like that?"

"Not sure."

SARAH DANCE, who lived at Ioni's house, was cross-examined by the defence.

"What was Child Z like?"

"Kinda weird. She'd stare at you or start laughing for no reason."

"Was there a time when Child Z and Alex McDonald were alone?"

"Not that I know of. It was a busy house."

"Did he ever act improperly towards anyone?"

"No."

"Was there anything unusual about Child Z?"

"She developed at a very young age. She had a lot of pubic hair which can be confusing for a child."

LOUISE THOMSON lived at the house for three years. She was cross-examined by the defence who asked her about Child Z.

"She was always in her own little world. When she was getting dressed in the morning, I'd hear people say: 'Put your clothes on, don't stand in front of the mirror [in the corridor] naked'."

"What was Alex McDonald like?"

"Kind, humorous, down to earth."

"Did he ever act improperly?"

"No, not at all."

JO TOMKINS, Louise's mother, was asked by the defence about Alex McDonald.

"He's very nice. To me, he would play a vital role in the community. He's a people person. I've never heard any complaints about him."

McDonald could only deny Child Z's accusations when in the witness box, while some glittering character references were read out about the defendant.

THE JURY had to decide if Child Z had made up such serious accusations about the defendant. And if so, why? The teenager obviously had some problems with learning difficulties, but would they contribute to fabricating sexual allegations against Alex McDonald?

28

ALEX McDONALD: Three counts of sexual assault

THE DEFENDANT must have been wondering about the judicial system as he reflected on being cleared of all three sexual assault charges against a troubled and unreliable Child Z.

Alex McDonald was also no doubt thinking that the people who instigated such a system have no grasp of the dangers to the real victims of effectively believing someone who made a spurious sexual accusation and then decides there was a case to answer.

The claimant's evidence was so lacking in credibility that this observer almost had sympathy for the prosecutor who was forced to clutch at the thinnest of straws. All the witnesses said that the house was so small and so crowded that it was impossible for Child Z and McDonald to have been alone together in the bathroom with no one aware of anything untoward happening.

"But it is possible it could have happened?" the prosecutor repeatedly asked witnesses, which was almost like saying: "But it is possible for David Beckham to knock on the front door?" Well, yes, possible, but let's move into the real world.

McDonald will have to live with the unfounded allegations for the rest of his life. How it affects him will be like throwing a pebble in a pond with the ripples going on forever. An obviously innocent man was needlessly put through a sexual trial that will be a tattoo for life.

Why Child Z chose to make the accusations will probably never be known. She is a child who, in some respects, became an adult far too early and it must be hoped the relevant authorities can help a teenager who had developed an unhealthy interest bordering on obsession with pornography.

29

CRAIG MURDOCH: Possession of indecent material

HE THOUGHT THOSE INVOLVED
WERE OVER 18

DOWNLOADING pornographic still images or videos of men and women who are aged over 18 having sex is not unlawful. Watching porn is something couples can do before the real thing, to get them in the mood. Maybe it is better than what is on television on a rainy Thursday.

However, when the recorded participants are under 18 it is a different matter. Very different.

The term "indecent" isn't defined in law beyond that which any "ordinary right-thinking member of the public" would consider so. Basically, if it's naked, a topless girl, contains genitals or sex acts including masturbation, then it will be perceived indecent. It is illegal to take, possess, make (i.e., download) or share "indecent images" of anyone under 18 even if you are the person in the picture. A "child" is anyone under 18 (it used to be 16, but was changed in 2003 to 18).

Craig Murdoch admitted he liked looking at videos of 18-plus males involved in sexual activity. He claimed that he was not aware the images and videos police found on his laptop contained pre- and post-pubescent males. In his mind, the models were all aged 18-plus.

THE PROSECUTION told the jury it would not have to view the images. "The issue is not whether the images are indecent or the age of those involved. It is how those images got on to the defendant's laptop and USB stick. The defendant said he has never knowingly downloaded anything involving anyone under 18. We say he intentionally downloaded them.

"There are three categories — A is penetrative sex; B is nonpenetrative sex, masturbation and sexual touching; C is indecent images that do not fall into categories A or B."

The Crown said that officers raided Craig Murdoch's home. Forensic examination found 14 still images of naked boys aged 12–14 in the shower; a male aged about 15 with an erect penis; a naked boy aged 12–14 with an erect penis; naked males aged 14–15 with their genitals showing; a moving video of prepubescent males and females demonstrating masturbation.

INTERVIEWED by the police, Craig Murdoch said he did not download anything for gratification purposes.

He was asked: "Why did you keep them?"

"I had a Channel 4 sex education show and I was looking to do a documentary showing the different attitude towards sex then and now."

"Boys drinking naked on a bed?"

"I do not recall that, no."

"Which then turned sexual."

"All I can say is, I mean, I can't specifically recall that one. I would have believed they were all of legal age, but if they were children…"

"You spoke of your sexual preferences."

"I'm talking 18-plus. It is not an easy subject to talk about. I use blogs which say those taking part are 18-plus. I know you cannot necessarily rely on that, but I did not seek out."

"You know it is illegal to possess under-18 pornography."

"Yes."

"You used [name of site given]."

"It said 18-plus. To my belief, and I could be wrong, any pornography I have, the participants were 18-plus. I can absolutely appreciate why. I do not know if anyone believes me, it's a judgment call. One blog article said it [what was downloaded] was on Belgian TV. It even had proper closing credits which was another factor in me believing it was not under-18 pornography."

"Pictures of boys masturbating?"

"I believed they were all over-18. I had no intention to actively seek out illegal material."

"Have you ever knowingly downloaded anything under-18?"

"Definitely not."

"Did you view everything you download?"

"Not always. There could be three or four subsequent links."

"So you download links not knowing what you have downloaded."

"Yes. I know that sounds reckless. I like ginger guys. I can download them and look at them later. I can't promise you I'll watch everything on the computer."

"You ever produced anything?"

"Programmes, yes. Previously I made ads. I wanted to do something on the changing attitudes towards sex education."

THE JURY had to sit through an afternoon of evidence from two digital forensic investigators, one for the defence and one for the prosecution. The problem was, you needed to be a digital forensic investigator to understand much of what they said.

It was blinding the jury with science. The most significant factor was that neither expert could say who had downloaded the "indecent" files.

CRAIG MURDOCH, who lived with his [male] civil partner, was cross-examined by the defence.

"How did the police come to have a search warrant for your address?"

"A Canadian company passed on my details to the Toronto police who informed the UK police. I had bought a naturist video from them."

"Naturism is something that interests you."

"Yes. My stepfather had an interest so I was familiar with the naturist lifestyle when I was 10 to 15. The reason I came across it [the site] was I was seeking naturist videos and the site purported to sell them."

"Naturism is not a sexual case."

"No, not at all."

"Why did you want to view the naturist videos?"

"In pursuit of the lifestyle, seeing families going for a walk, playing golf, exploring the countryside."

"Did you find it sexual?"

"Not at all."

"What did you buy?"

"Two videos. I viewed them, but there was nothing of naturist pursuits, nothing outdoors. There were children aged 14 to 16 in swimming trunks."

"What did you do?"

"I contacted them and asked them to take me off their mailing list and destroyed the videos."

On the day of Murdoch's arrest police took away 15 items, including computers, laptops, videos, an Xbox, an iPad mini and a tablet.

When the defendant was interviewed at the police station, he declined the offer of a solicitor.

"Why?"

"I believed I was innocent, if I told the truth, I'd be OK. I tried to be as open and thorough as possible."

"There was some perfectly legal pornography on the computer."

"This is not something I am proud of. My civil partner of six years is disabled and we are not able to have a sexual relationship."

"What sort of videos do you prefer?"

"My interest is in men under-30, but over-18, smooth-chested and slim."

"How did you find the videos?"

"Go to homosexual pornography sites, enter 'twink' [a slang term for young males in their late teens and early 20's]. Then follow the link to the blog."

"How do the images get to your computer?"

"Right click, save as."

Murdoch admitted he was "hopeless" at keeping various files separate, with pornography often alongside bank statements.

"Tell me about the Belgian video."

"It was an historic TV transmission and I wanted to look at it for changes in sex education."

"What did it show?"

"I did not think it was anything pornographic, just an old-fashioned sex education video."

"It showed young boys masturbating."

"Yes. It was a mistake I made because I did not consider it to be pornographic. It had a sound track and closing credits plus copyright. In Belgium, 1991, it was not pornographic."

"There were drunken boys having penetrative sex."

"I was not knowingly seeking videos with children."

"How did the still images get there?"

"One thing that may be possible is that when I downloaded material, multi-images were also downloaded. When the police showed me the images… I'd never seen them or on a web site or downloaded them."

THE PROSECUTION cross-examined Craig Murdoch.

"You had an idea when the police arrived what they were there for."

"Yes."

"The company you bought videos from had been in the news."

"Yes."

"Your credit card details were on their data base."

"Yes."

"Recognised as a past customer."

"Yes."

"The reason for you buying the DVD's from the company was an interest in naturism."

"Yes."

"Nothing illegal about that, but what you received was children in swimming trunks wrestling."

"Correct."

"They billed themselves as a naturist site, naturism being liberated of clothes in areas of natural beauty. That was the attraction for you."

"Yes. I have fond memories of it as a boy."

"So the reason you bought the videos from the site was for naturism in Crimea. Was there not a way of doing this for free?"

"I didn't believe so from my research. The videos were billed as videos of Crimea, not children in trunks."

"You seemed so uncomfortable you considered going to the police."

"More accurately I considered confessing I had the videos."

"To hand yourself in."

"Essentially, yes. But I decided against it as I did not consider the material illegal. I disposed of them [the videos] as they were of no interest to me."

"Did it put you on alert about material over the internet?"

"Yes, but overage. When looking for material I did my utmost to ensure that what I downloaded was not children. I never tapped in terms that would bring inappropriate videos."

235

"What did you key in?"

"Twink mostly. Some sites say 'teens' but that can be 18 or 19. If I had any doubts or if the site didn't state the age I didn't go beyond the front page."

"The three pictures of a 15-year-old with an erect penis, how did they get there without your knowledge?"

"The only explanation I can give is I right-clicked to save a text link. When I was shown the image by the police, I didn't recognise it."

"But you caused it to come on your computer."

"Yes. But it was not what I had downloaded, just from a link."

"How do you explain the duplication of images?"

"Computer generated."

"So it must have been viewed."

"I've been racking my brain, I realise the conclusion is I downloaded it. If I did, it was not intentional. I did not seek them out."

"If you are looking for young, gay, hairless, athletic boys isn't it likely some would be under-18?"

"I believe I'm as careful as I can be."

"I believe you are careful to cover your tracks and delete internet history. Why is there no internet browsing record of the Belgian video?"

"No idea."

"You used Eraser software to clear internet browsing history."

"I was unaware it had that capability."

"What did you use Eraser for?"

"In my job, my boss sent me some sensitive documents that had to be deleted for security reasons."

"The Belgian sex education video was 41 minutes long and includes images of prepubescent children masturbating. "

"I bought it as a sex education video. I was thinking about making a programme of changes in sex education. I have made them about sport. It never came to anything as I didn't have time."

THE INDICTMENT was changed from 14 category C images to two because it was accepted it was impossible to prove the defendant had personally downloaded the other 12. He also faced three counts relating to category B and two of category A

In its summing-up the prosecution urged the jury not to believe Craig

236

Murdoch's "cock and bull excuses" and for the defendant "not to pull the wool over your eyes."

The Crown continued: "The defendant's gay, but that is neither here nor there. Many people enjoy naturism which is nothing sinister. It's not for everyone, but it's not unlawful. He ordered films about naturism in Crimea — his interest was nude boys, not health and efficiency.

"It is also nonsense what he said about the Belgian video. It depicts young children masturbating — he is a clever, but devious man who lied to cover his tracks."

THE DEFENCE pointed out that around 2,500 pornographic but legal images were found on the defendant's computer and USB. "Only 17 images were those of children. If someone was deliberately downloading child porn or indecent images, would there not have been more? Seventeen is not a large number. Of course, one is too many, but the amount has to be put in focus.

"A forensic expert said there was no evidence of indecent web sites or Eraser had been used to delete files. There was also no evidence of searching for children."

CRAIG MURDOCH had, as the defence told the jury, around 2,500 images of adult (over-18) pornography on his laptop. That is not illegal. It may not be to everyone's taste, but the jury was told to put any prejudices or preconceptions aside when deliberating. The judge said that these images must play no part in the jury's decision-making process. It must decide its verdict only on the evidence it has heard regarding the indictments.

It was not just a question of what had been downloaded by Murdoch. The prosecution had to prove to the jury that the possession or making of the images was deliberate and knowing.

The word "making" in this area of law can be somewhat confusing. The court regards the act of voluntarily downloading an indecent image from a web page on to a computer screen as "making" an image. Also, if an image was copied from a web page, but in both instances the act has to be intentional.

The jury had to be sure that when Murdoch made the images either he knew what he was making was an indecent image of a child or it was likely to have been an indecent image of a child.

It was accepted the images were indecent so the jury did not have to see any. It did not have to decide the age of the children. The prosecution had to make the jury sure the defendant was deliberately seeking out child pornography.

29

CRAIG MURDOCH: Possession of indecent material

IT TOOK the jury a couple of hours to conclude Craig Murdoch was, as the prosecution had suggested, a clever but devious man who had lied to cover his tracks. Murdoch was found guilty of all charges.

He was sentenced to carry out 150 hours of unpaid work over a 12-month period and ordered to pay prosecution costs of £1,000. Murdoch was placed on the sex offenders' register for five years.

30

VIHAAN JINDAL: Grievous bodily harm

WHO DELIVERED KNOCKOUT BLOW TO POSTMAN?

BIPLOP RAJAH was doing his usual job for Royal Mail, delivering packages with his partner Anthony to an area he knew well. However, not for the first time, apparently, one package had been delivered to a wrong address. It was not even Rajah's error, but it saw him savagely assaulted, sustaining two fractured ribs, a punctured lung, a cut forehead, swollen eyes and two teeth missing.

The attack was, the prosecution said, a joint-enterprise between Vihaan Jindal and his father, Abdul. The jury was told Abdul had pleaded guilty to grievous bodily harm so only Vihaan, who was also charged with inflicting GBH on Rajah, was on trial. The son was deemed to be the main assailant in the beating that saw the claimant off work for six months.

"The initial attack was by the father," said the Crown in its opening speech. "The son finished it off, delivering the blow that resulted in more serious harm."

A near neighbour, Sue Rollance, was driving along the road where the incident occurred and saw two men shouting at each other. She claimed it was the son who delivered the final blow, not the father. This was backed up by a second witness, Renato Cardosa, though another, Hilda Brookes, who refused to come to court to give evidence, said in a statement that it was the father, not the son, who caused the severe injuries sustained by Rajah.

However, as she did not appear in court her evidence could not be tested by cross-examination which the jury would have to take into

240

consideration.

Abdul was arrested later that day, Vihaan 10 days later. Vihaan told police he was at home when the parcel had been delivered to the wrong address — "we've complained before." He heard his father shouting, went outside and claimed he saw the postman with a fist raised saying: "Go fuck your mother."

Vihaan said he pushed the postman away. Having done that he never looked back as father and son walked home. He acted as he did because "I thought a violent man was going to attack my dad." He said he saw his father use no blows to the claimant.

The jury had to decide whose evidence it believed. There was no dispute that Rajah sustained serious injuries, but were they caused by an initial violent attack or the result of a peace-maker simply pushing away the man he saw as the aggressor?

CROSS-EXAMINED by the prosecution, Biplop Rajah was asked: "Was your partner, Anthony, with you?"

"No, he was in another road."

"You were on your way back to the van."

"Yes."

"What happened?"

"A male aged 50 to 55 was waiting for me by the bus stop. He said I'd delivered a package to the wrong house, but I hadn't delivered it."

"Did you know him?"

"No, but I know his house."

"What was his tone?"

"Angry. He was speaking half English, half Hindi."

"What did you say?"

"He came quickly to me. I said I did not deliver it, it must have been my partner, but he did not want to listen."

"How close did he get to you?"

"Right in front. Ten metres."

"What happened?"

"He said I'd delivered the parcel to the wrong address. I told him I hadn't delivered anything at all to him. It must have been my partner."

"Did you know the male?"

"I have worked the road for two years so in that respect I knew him."

241

"When he came to you how did he seem?"

"Very angry."

"What happened next?"

"When he got to me, he punched me in the face. It made me feel dizzy. I told him not to punch me or I'll call the police."

"What did he hit you with?"

"His right hand, clenched fist."

"What did you do after he hit you?"

"I put my hands up to defend myself."

"Did you stay standing up?"

"Yes, but I was dizzy."

"What happened next?"

"I cannot remember clearly what happened, but I heard him call to his son in Hindi. I can understand a little. I was aware of a second male coming [towards me] from his house, 30 or 35 metres away."

"Had you seen him before?

"Sometimes."

"What happened next?"

"He missed me with his first punch. Then he punched me in the face with a metal bar or something metal. I saw it glinting in the sun."

"What effect did the blow have?"

"I was unconscious. I came round in hospital. I was in that hospital for four days and another [hospital] for three days."

"In all of this incident did you use any force?"

"No."

"Threaten anyone?"

"No."

THE DEFENCE resumed the cross-examination and said to Biplop Rajah: "Quite a punch then?"

"Yes."

"You said the older man shouted to his son. I suggest he said 'Rob'."

"No."

"When the younger man appeared, you were wagging a finger."

"No."

"Did you tell him to fuck his mother?"

"No."

242

"You 100 per cent sure?"

"Yes."

"I suggest the younger male merely intervened."

"No, he punched me straight away."

"There is no doubt you sustained horrible injuries. You say you were punched by the older man, but told the police it was difficult to be sure what happened next."

"Yes."

SUE ROLLANCE was next in the witness box. The Crown asked her: "Where were you at the time of the incident?"

"Driving along Broom Road."

"What took you attention?"

"An argument between two gentlemen, one a postman, I could see his uniform."

"Could you hear what was being said?"

"No."

"What did you do?"

"I slowed down to about 10 miles per hour. In my wing-mirror I saw a male following the postman who was walking away."

"What did you think he [the postman] was trying to do?"

"Just get away."

"How did it develop?"

"I saw the male swing at the postman and the punch caught him in the eye. I stopped and put the hand-brake on."

"Tell us about the hit."

"The male, with his right hand, hit the postman before he really knew what was going on."

"How would you describe the punch?"

"Malicious."

"What effect did it have?"

"I got out [of the car] and shouted: 'Oi, I can see what you're doing.' The postman was on the floor. He knocked his head when he fell and was unconscious."

The witness was asked exactly what she saw when the punch was thrown.

"It, like, knocked him [the postman] off his feet. He sort of went up a little like and was knocked to the ground."

"What happened next?"

"There were a few people watching, three males. The guy who hit the postman went back to his house."

"How did you know it was his house?"

"Assumption, I guess."

"What was the male wearing?"

"Black T-shirt."

THE DEFENCE asked Sue Rollance how she knew the two males were related.

"They came from the same house."

"You did not see the older male outside the house?"

"No."

"You accept you only saw snippets of the incident as you were initially driving?"

"Yes. But I saw the male swing and catch him [the postman]."

"I suggest maybe you got things mixed up."

"Absolutely no."

RENATO CARDOSA came to the witness box. The defence asked him: "Where were you when this happened?"

"Vehicularly opposite to where it happened, in a car with three friends."

"When did you become aware of anything?"

"When I heard the arguing between the postman and an older man. Swearing and that, it caught our attention. We stopped as it looked like there'd be a fight."

"What sort of argument?"

"At first, thought it was a family argument."

"How far away were you?"

"Kerb to kerb, two car lengths."

"How did it develop?"

"They were shouting and swearing at each other. The postman shouted 'fuck your mother' or something like that."

"Next?"

"The older man slapped the postman across the cheek."

"How hard?"

"I heard it from across the road. My friends went 'ooh.' It dazed the postman who was not steady on his feet."

"Then?"

"The man kinda held on to the postman, grabbed hold of his shirt. He turned around and started calling someone from the house."

"Do you remember what was said?"

"No, different language."

"What did you see then?"

"A younger man exited the house and ran straight towards the postman. Initially I thought he was gonna stop it as I thought it was a family issue. But he punched the postman straight away."

"Did the punch connect?"

"No, it missed."

"What did the postman do when the punch was swung?"

"He turned around to run away."

"Then?"

"He threw a second punch, the younger man. It directly hit the postman who was basically knocked out before he hit the floor."

"What sort of punch was it?"

"Pretty hard, yeah, on the side of the face. He fell to the ground, his face, the side of it, hitting the ground first."

"What did you do?"

"I crossed the road to help him, put him in the recovery position. He wasn't moving at all. His face was bleeding, blood pouring out."

"What did the younger man do?"

"Rushed inside the house. The son was saying something, didn't hear it. It was 'fuck' or something."

"I'm going to suggest the younger male pushed the postman. Could you have been misunderstood?"

"Definitely not."

"I am going to suggest there was no physical contact apart from pushing."

"Disagree."

VIHAAN JINDAL maintained he was a peace-maker, not a person who inflicted grievous bodily harm on Biplop Rajah.

When asked for his version of events by the defence Jindal said: "We received a letter from the postman given to the wrong address. I'd complained about 10 months earlier, but no one seemed to take any notice, I just felt like we weren't getting the service.

"Dad said he would go to talk to him [the postman]. I'd just woken up [about 13.30]. I was in the living room. I heard some shouting and my name was called out by dad who sounded in distress. He was calling 'Rob' which is like a nickname. He said it twice.

"I ran out, went to investigate and ran towards them. The postman was swearing and dad was like moving backwards. I saw the postman about to hit dad. I separated them and pushed him [the postman] out of the way. I just, like, pushed him away with my hands. A big shove, yes. I said 'let's go home' to dad and we walked back home.

"I did not look back. I didn't see he [the postman] was on the floor. I didn't see what it could have done to him. At home I saw him on the floor so I thought I must have pushed him on the floor."

Vihaan did not call an ambulance "because I heard someone else doing it."

The police arrived and arrested Abdul. "They cautioned him, he didn't know what a caution was because his English isn't so good," said his son.

THE CROWN, in its closing speech, told the jury: "The mere fact the defendant's father pleaded guilty to the same offence does not help to determine the guilt or innocence of the son.

"What sort of state was the claimant in when Vihaan arrived? Why did he need to defend his dad? We say there was no need to. He got involved and acted out of a sense of anger, arrogance and frustration about a parcel… misguided loyalty to his dad. He punched the claimant viciously and this is based on the evidence of witnesses who came to court to be cross-examined.

"There is no doubt the injuries were severe, but consistent with a push?

"Hilda Brookes is a neighbour, though the defendant doesn't know her. She said she did not see the son do anything. Even the son admitted he shoved the claimant pretty heavily. Is there something a little strange there?

"After Vihaan shoved the postman, he said he did not look round.

He said he was protecting his dad against this crazy postman who was about to hit his dad, yet suddenly he was no threat at all."

THE DEFENCE summed up: "There were contradictions and inconsistencies in the evidence of the other witnesses, yet the evidence of Mrs Brookes is dismissed by the Crown as valueless. Why is the evidence of the other witnesses not valueless?

"My submission is that the evidence falls well short of the high standard needed for a guilty verdict. One witness said the defendant hit the postman with his left hand, another with his right.

"I am not saying anyone was lying, but people get things wrong, they get the wrong end of the stick. All gave different versions of what happened. If they get something so wrong about the colour of the T-shirt, can you rely on the rest of the evidence?"

WHILE the charge of maliciously and unlawfully inflicting grievous bodily harm on another person may appear straightforward, the judge ran through the points of law the jury had to consider.

GBH means the skin of the victim is broken and the injuries sustained are serious. The central issue was whether the injuries Biplop Rajah sustained were inflicted unlawfully by the defendant.

The jury had to consider three issues:

1 — That the defendant punched the claimant with a view to inflicting injury

2 — This resulted in the claimant suffering really serious bodily harm

3 — That the defendant's actions were unlawful, that is not in defence of his father.

The prosecution needed the jury to be sure of all three to prove its case.

The defendant said he acted to defend his father and lawful defence is not a crime. If the jury did not believe the prosecution's case of GBH, it should then consider:

1 — Did the defendant believe he needed to defend his father because he was under attack or about to be attacked?

2 — Whether the force used was reasonable, which is proportionate to the threat posed. If it went beyond that it is good evidence he acted unlawfully.

The judge said: "If the jury concludes the defendant merely pushed the claimant, but did so deliberately you may be able to convict him of a lesser charge of actual bodily harm. But first of all, you must consider the charge of GBH."

The judge told the jury to examine the evidence of Hilda Brookes "with special care." She never gave a statement to the police, only what she told a police officer at the scene, so that is hearsay. It could not be tested in court to see if what she said stands up "so only consider it if you believe it is reliable."

He added: "Ask yourselves whether anyone is trying to assist the defendant? In the case of each witness consider whether they have been primed to help you and how reliable it [their evidence] would be."

Regarding discrepancies in identification of what the defendant was wearing, the jury should consider how long the witnesses had the defendant under observation in a fast-moving incident.

30

VIHAAN JAMAL: Grievous bodily harm

THE JURORS did not know they were replacements as the original 12 had been discharged after the judge ruled that the claimant needed a translator.

Biplop Rajah was from Kerala in Southern India and his first language was Malayalam. While he had been in England for 20 years and spoke decent English, he could not understand some of the Crown's questions. The judge agreed; a Malayalam interpreter was found overnight and the trial was re-started with a new jury and the prosecution cross-examining Rajah again. This time the claimant had a little help from his interpreter.

The judge had hinted very strongly that the evidence to the police officer by Hilda Brookes should be treated very carefully, given that it went against just about everything other witnesses cross-examined in court had said.

Had I been a juror I would have asked myself whether such horrendous injuries could have been caused by a shove or a push. My answer would have been 'no' and the jury agreed, finding Vihaan guilty of grievous bodily harm; his father Abdul had already entered a guilty plea.

Father and son appeared together for sentencing — an ignominious GBH family double. I doubt whether Rajah believed the punishment fitted the crime given the injuries he suffered. The judge sentenced both Abdul and Vihaan to 18 months' imprisonment suspended for 18 months; Abdul was given 150 hours of unpaid work. Vihaan was given 200 hours. Vihaan also had to pay Rajah £2,100 in compensation.

THE JUDGE gave Abdul fewer hours of unpaid work because of his early guilty plea. In most cases, if the accused pleads guilty to an offence, they will be given a lesser sentence than if they are found guilty by a jury after a trial. Depending on the stage the case has reached when the guilty plea is entered, a discount of up to one third off the sentence can be given. This applies not only to sentences of imprisonment, but also community orders and fines.

The benefits behind an early guilty plea are obvious. Guilty pleas spare claimants and witnesses the stress of a trial and free up police, prosecutors plus courts for other cases. They also save public money. The earlier the guilty plea, the larger the discount.

31

GARETH COOK: Arson; stalking

A COOK, STOLEN KEYS AND A FIRE

GARETH COOK had an unusual way of showing his love for Miss M. He gained entry to her house and put red roses on the kitchen floor to spell "marry me."

He also had unusual shopping habits — he drove 150 miles to Birmingham's Bull Ring to buy a pair of shoes.

Cook was charged with arson and stalking… accused of setting fire to his ex-partner's house after stalking her. He had previously pleaded guilty to breaking a restraining order to protect Miss M, but denied the other two counts.

Much of the evidence the jury heard was circumstantial. How much credibility could it attach to evidence that had no witnesses or concrete proof?

It was a trial that became increasingly intriguing with almost each piece of evidence.

MISS M and Gareth Cook began a relationship in 2013. Like many friendships, it had its ups and downs and in early 2019 Miss M decided to split from Cook. To paraphrase the song, breaking up can indeed be hard to do.

Miss M told the jury she had bought a house in July 2016 where she lived with her daughter. Cook stayed there occasionally at the weekend.

"Was it a smooth relationship?" the prosecution asked Miss M.

"No. It was very on and off."

"Was there a moment when the relationship changed?"

"It wasn't as clear cut as this. We tried to see if we could reconcile, but when he didn't join us [my family] for Christmas and New Year, that was a turning point. In the January [2019] I called time on it. I told him 'enough is enough.' It was not what I wanted and it was not making me happy."

"What happened between January and June?"

"Gareth would come round on Sunday mornings with takeaway coffee. This wasn't arranged, he'd just turn up."

"Did you like him coming round?"

"At first it wasn't an issue. Around April, I told him to stop coming round."

"Did he accept that?"

"I thought he had."

In June, Miss M was at Royal Ascot for Ladies Day with some friends. She had been warned by a neighbour that Cook was in her home, having gained entry through the garage.

He was in the kitchen and on the floor were red roses arranged to spell out "marry me." He also had an engagement ring.

Miss M continued: "I did not want to marry him, but turning someone down is not a nice thing to do given the courage it takes to ask. He was upset. He'd proposed to me two, maybe two and a half years prior to that, but then changed his mind and did not want to get married."

"How unhappy was he?"

"I'd never seen him more upset. For me it was emotional, too. It's not nice to see someone else in such pain."

"Would there be any misunderstanding in the defendant's mind about the future?"

"I made it very clear I no longer wanted a relationship."

"Did he contact you after that?"

"At the end of July, he sent me an email asking me to send him some photos from the Maldives where I was on holiday with my sister. We may no longer have been in a relationship, but when you have [been] for so long you can still care about the person."

"Did you receive any other emails?"

"Soon after I got back, he said he had booked up a weekend in Hamburg, where we had been before, for my birthday. He hoped I'd turn up at the airport. I told him I wouldn't be there."

"Did something happen on August 14 ?"

"I was on a conference call working from home when I heard my daughter shout: 'Gareth's in the back garden.' He then appeared at the front door. I did not want him in the house so I said we'd go for a coffee. We drove, to somewhere nearby. Gareth bought the coffees which we drank in the car. I said I'd drop him back at his car which he said was in a BP garage."

"Was it?"

"No. He then said it was at the top of a hill nearby."

"Was this true?"

"No. It was somewhere else, in like a dead-end."

"What happened then?"

"I stopped the car and he grabbed the keys from the ignition. He locked the doors and put his hand over my mouth and said I was going to listen to him."

"Could you escape?"

"No. He had a firm grip on my face and pushed it into the head-rest. I was in such a state of shock I can't remember what he said. The car had movement sensors and because he'd locked the car the alarm went off. He put the key back to turn it off and relocked it. Two people were jogging past so I banged on the windscreen to tell them I needed help. They came to the car, Gareth got out and his mannerism changed immediately. He was smiling, relaxed and told them I was being dramatic."

"What happened then?"

"The joggers walked home with me."

"Did Gareth follow you?"

"No."

"Did you report this?"

"Yes. I phoned the police. I said I didn't want any further action. I just wanted it to be on file that it had taken place."

"What about your car?"

"I had a spare key and got the car back [home]. He kept the other key for about 10 days before putting it through the letter box. He originally said he'd thrown it away."

Miss M was so concerned about Cook's behaviour she would sleep with her bedroom curtains open to give him the impression she was not at home should he come round. She believed the defendant had driven past her house because of the distinctive sound of his high-performance car, but had no proof.

She was asked if there had ever been any mention of a fire.

"Yes. He had previously threatened to set fire to the house. We were talking on the phone and I did not take it seriously. When two people are arguing then things are said. I didn't pay too much attention to it. This was a house he'd spent so much time on, doing plumbing and tiling."

On September 13, Miss M was at home working on her computer. Her daughter had gone to the gym. On the screen there was a reflection — it was Cook.

"He pulled me onto a sofa and sat on me. Initially he had his hand over my mouth because he did not want me to scream. He took it away when he was satisfied I wouldn't scream. He then had hold of my wrists, twisting them."

"Did this hurt?"

"My wrists were damaged to the extent it was difficult to write or pick things up for several weeks."

"What did he want?"

"He asked me who I had been out with, what I was doing. He then gave me two alternatives — either get back with him or he would make my life hell. He said I should text my dad and ask him to come to dinner with us so the family could see we were together again. I had to send the text to his phone as proof of the reconciliation. I also had a spare ticket for a rugby game and had to text him asking him to come with me."

"What next?"

"He told me to collect all the keys for the house and garage. He followed me round as I did this. I had to meet him at a service station where he'd follow me to his flat and I'd post the keys through his letterbox. This would have been caught on the CCTV where he lives."

"What did you do?"

"He took my phone off me. I drove to the garage and I asked the attendant to call the police. He gave me a phone and I called them."

The police went to her house to ensure Cook was not there. Miss M stayed with a neighbour most of the evening until her daughter came home.

"I had left the lights on so we would not go into a dark house. As I was walking down the drive the security light did not go on which it does when the sensor beam is broken. We returned to the neighbour's house and phoned the police. They found the wires from the security light had been pulled away."

It was also discovered the locks had been filled with silicone sealer.

GARETH COOK was charged with burglary and held in custody from September 13 to 30. He pleaded guilty and was handed a suspended sentence. The judge also invoked a restraining order to protect Miss M, banning Cook from communicating with her by any means and he must not go to her address or where she was working. He was also banned from publishing anything threatening on social media about her.

However, pushing the restraining order to the limit, Cook wrote on Facebook: "I do very bad things and I do them very well… home is where the heart is if you have a home" with a photo of burnt-out flowers in the shape of a heart.

While Cook was in custody Miss M's brother, who was doing some work in the garden, discovered a can of petrol on the other side of the back fence. It was put in the garage and the police alerted.

The prosecution asked Miss M: "Were extra security measures put in place?"

"The fire brigade installed a fire-proof letter box."

The police put movement sensors by doors and windows in the house while Miss M was given a panic alarm. She also installed CCTV cameras at the front and back of the house plus the kitchen. These could be activated by an app on her phone.

ON THE DAY of the fire, Miss M received a call from a neighbour and upon returning home there was significant fire damage to rooms upstairs. Someone had poured petrol on the floor and on her bed, setting light to them.

The police checked the Automatic Number Plate Registration system and found Gareth Cook's car was in the next road to where Miss M lived about the time the fire started. He was arrested the following day.

Upon being told by Miss M that she suspected Cook had been following her, the police checked her car and found a tracking device. The plot thickened — it was almost solid by now — when Miss M recalled stopping at a service station on the M6. The prosecution called it "a coincidence beyond belief" that the ANPR system showed Cook's car in the area at the same time.

The Crown suggested that while Miss M was inside the service station Cook opened her car. It was further alleged he had a copy made during the 10-day period he was in possession of the car keys. When Cook opened the car it was claimed he took her house keys that she kept in the glove compartment and which, at the time, Miss M assumed she had either forgotten or mislaid. The house keys would have allowed Cook entry to her home without setting off the alarms on the windows.

THE DEFENCE began its cross-examination of Gareth Cook by asking him about his shopping trip to Birmingham.

"Good place to go, is it?"

"The Bull Ring, yes."

"What did you buy?"

"Shoes."

"Where?"

"Timberland."

"Whereabouts? We can find evidence from the shop."

"Not know exactly, just in the Bull Ring."

"You pay by credit card?"

"No, cash."

"Did you follow Miss M?"

"No."

"Why did it seem you followed her?"

"Pure coincidence."

"You go to Birmingham often?"

"Four, five times a year to meet friends."

"You accept you were going out of the city as Miss M was on the M6 southbound?"

"I was going to Manchester to continue shopping. The traffic was so bad I came off at Stafford and came home on cross-country roads."

GARETH COOK, who had accused Miss M of giving him a sexually transmitted disease, said in his police interview that on the day of the fire he had driven from his Surrey home to Ashford, and then to Gravesend.

In court he admitted this was wrong "because I was tired, hadn't slept for 39 hours and didn't really know what I was saying." He said he had spent the night before the fire with Zoe who lived in the centre of London.

The following morning — when there was a fire at the claimant's house — Cook said he left Zoe's flat at 06.45 "to beat the congestion charge" [which is payable from 07.00].

"Where did you go then?"

"Home [to Surrey] where I changed clothes and left about 8.15."

"Where did you go?"

"Ashford. My car had been in the garage and had not been driven. The engine needed to be blown out to clear the problems."

"You went straight to Ashford."

"The traffic was bad on the A23, I think it is, so I decided to go a different way. I stopped two or three roads from Miss M's to let the traffic go down. I got going again about nine."

"Then to Ashford."

"I'd been advised I was in Maidstone, but I thought I was in Ashford, which was the last sign I'd seen. The traffic was still bad. I got to Ashford about 11.15 and went for a coffee."

"So it was now 11.45. Where next?"

"Heading back to London, but the traffic was bad and I couldn't get all the way to London. I meandered around… roadworks on the M25. I went to get something to eat and realised I did not have my wallet."

"What time was this and where were you?"

"About half one. I was just outside the M25. Between the A22 and A21. I thought: 'Do I go back to Ashford for my wallet or go to Gravesend where my friend Patrick lives?' I went to Gravesend."

"How long did that take?"

"Hour… hour and 20 ."

"So you arrived about three. Was he in?"

"No, he got back about four."

"Did you stay at Patrick's that night?"

"I used his car, a Renault, went home and got some clothes, then drove to Zoe's."

THE PROSECUTION began its cross-examination of Gareth Cook

by asking the defendant: "Did you have a previous partner before Miss M called Deborah?"

"Yes, Debbie."

"Did you plead guilty to harassing her?"

"I was just fed up."

"And you also pleaded guilty to intimidating a witness."

"I didn't do it."

"That's an unusual way to behave, to plead guilty to things you didn't do."

"The way you stated it, yes. Do I agree? No."

"Are you sure you're not guilty?"

"I attempted to speak to her [Debbie] three times."

"A restraining order had been placed on you."

"If you attempt to speak to someone three times then it's harassment, so technically I was guilty, I was told."

"Did you confess to Miss M that you had a restraining order against a previous girlfriend?"

"She asked what it was about and I told her."

"Would you say you have difficulties with people who split up with you?"

"No."

WHATEVER the jury may have thought about Gareth Cook, the issue it had to decide upon was whether he was guilty of arson and stalking Miss M. There were no witnesses to the fire at Miss M's house. The evidence put forward by the prosecution was circumstantial or indirect rather than first-hand.

The jury had to be sure that Cook was the person who started the fire in Miss M's property. The only "evidence" the Crown had was remnants of expellant on Cook's phone which he claimed was from when he had filled a car up with petrol and called a friend.

The judge told the jury: "Direct evidence is not always available. The Crown can rely on circumstantial evidence which, taken together, may prove the defendant committed the crime. This must lead to a sure conclusion of guilt even if some loose threads are left over."

Were the ANPR, the phone data, Cook's evidence and not least his unusual shopping destination plus his bad luck with traffic enough for the jury to return a guilty verdict on one or both of the indictments?

The judge explained there were two types of arson. One is to destroy or damage property intending thereby to endanger the life of another; the second is being reckless as to whether the life of another would thereby be endangered.

If the jury decided the defendant was guilty of arson, it then had to decide which type it was.

31

GARETH COOK: Arson; stalking

THE impression was that Gareth Cook believed he had committed a perfect crime (or two). The trouble was, his evidence was pure fantasy and how he thought a jury would be gullible enough to believe him beggared belief.

His geography was poor, to say the least. "I'd been advised I was in Maidstone, but I thought I was in Ashford, which was the last sign I'd seen," he told the jury. Who advised him? Mark Thatcher? Ashford is 20 miles from Maidstone and further south, so how Ashford was the last sign he'd seen is mysterious. In fact, impossible.

The shopping trip to Birmingham to buy shoes was almost comical. There can only be so many "pure coincidences" to use Cook's words regarding his close proximity to the claimant and for me, there would have been sufficient circumstantial evidence to find the defendant guilty

Cook was a cold-hearted ex-partner who appeared hell bent on making Miss M's life a misery.

There were no other suspects for the arson, just Cook. He was either as innocent as he claimed or rather, he had covered his tracks superbly or he was lying through his teeth.

Miss M was brave enough to sit in the public gallery as her private life continued to be exposed. She was no doubt delighted when the foreman of the jury returned two guilty verdicts against Cook who was sentenced to eight years in prison.

32

MATTHEW SWEENEY: Nine counts of indecent assault; attempted buggery

THE DARK SECRETS OF
INCHMORE HOUSE

INCHMORE HOUSE, a care home for "difficult" teenagers, held no happy memories for Mr D, who cannot be named for legal reasons. He claimed he was attacked, beaten, sexually assaulted and raped by deputy superintendent Matthew Sweeney over a three-year period during the mid-1970s starting when he was 14. To add to this, Mr D said he was a prisoner at the home, not allowed out of the establishment which he compared to Fort Knox

In 2018 Mr D wanted closure on what he called his "nightmares" which saw Sweeney charged with a 10-count indictment, the dates between July 16 1974 and September 21 1977:

1 — Indecent assault on a male person under 16 to cause him to perform oral sex on you

2 — Indecent assault on a male person under 16 by touching his penis

3 - As above (different time span)

4 — Attempted buggery

5 — Indecent assault on a male person under 16 on multiple occasions causing him to perform anal sex on you

6 — As above (different time scale)

7 — Indecent assault on multiple occasions causing him to masturbate you

8 — Indecent assault on multiple occasions causing you to masturbate him

9 — Indecent assault on multiple occasions causing you to perform oral sex on him

10 — Indecent assault on multiple occasions causing him to perform oral sex on you.

THIS WAS a trial that veered between the numbing tedium of legal arguments, which the jury did not hear (and therefore neither will you) and continuing revelations that may have altered its opinions one way or another as the case unfolded.

Mr D was sent to Inchmore House because, in his own words, he was "an out-of-control teenager." Opening the case, the Crown said Matthew Sweeney abused Mr D at, among other places, his mother's house when she was away.

"Once, in a remote country lane, he was forced to perform oral sex upon Mr Sweeney until he ejaculated in his mouth," said the Crown. "That kind of abuse became a regular occurrence, more or less every other night. Once, he [Sweeney] tried to bugger Mr D, even using his own saliva to help his penis into Mr D.

"Though Mr D said he reported this to social workers at the time, their reaction was one of disbelief because they wanted to avoid a scandal."

Unsurprisingly, finding any sort of records from a care home that had long since closed down was difficult. Eventually, diaries maintained by teachers on a daily basis were discovered while it was revealed Mr D was 14, not 13 as he thought when he was placed into the care home.

THE PROSECUTION asked Mr D about Inchmore House.

"I was at Inchmore House for two and a half years," he said. "During that time, I was sexually assaulted and abused. I was made to feel a liar by social services and have kept it to myself until now."

There was a short break because Mr D began crying.

He continued: "At that age I was afraid. I was away from my family. Other boys were abused, too. We reported it to social workers who physically stopped us going to the police. They said we were lying and it didn't happen. They told us we were young tearaways and that sort of thing."

Mr D was asked about the first time anything happened.

"Sweeney would take me out in his car to the country and his mother's house. She was never there. The first time he abused me was on a trip to Ashford. He pulled over and started touching me. I tried to say 'no' but he hit me. He made me perform oral sex on him and I had to swallow.

"Once at his mother's house he made me perform anal sex on him. He had tried to do it on me, but it wouldn't happen so he guided me in him. I didn't know what I was doing. I just looked out the window. I was disgusted with it. I feel dirty even now. I had no one to turn to who would believe me."

THE DEFENCE began what turned out to be a marathon cross-examination of Mr D that lasted four days (including multi legal arguments).

"You said you were abused by Matthew Sweeney over a two-and-a-half-year period."

"Yes."

"The abuse started a month after you arrived."

"I didn't keep notes of the times. I have to rely on my memory. I am trying to remember what I can. I am trying to put a time on it. I was abused and sexually assaulted and it seemed to go on forever. They are the time scales in my mind."

"The children went home every holiday."

"I was kept in the home, whatever the papers may indicate."

"You said you were beaten black and blue and had cigarette burns. Not one social worker was asked to see the bruises."

"I said I was being touched. They never believed me."

"You spoke to social workers and never told them about the beatings."

"They said I was lying and seeking attention so I gave up."

"Why did you not tell the social workers you were beaten up?"

"Because I was petrified. The beatings became worse after I tried to tell them."

"Why did you not tell the teachers at Chesterhouse School [where the claimant went after Inchmore House]?"

"Why would anyone believe me?"

The defence turned to the times spent at a local swimming pool where those at Inchmore House were taken.

"You remember going swimming while you were at Inchmore House?"

"No."

"Never?"

"Not that I can remember. Not according to my memory."

"You said you were never allowed to see a doctor."

"Correct."

"You did not report it to anyone else that you were a prisoner. Did the police ever come to the home?"

"If the police came, I never saw them."

The jury was handed a copy of a diary filled in by staff on a daily basis, detailing what the children were doing between October 20 1974 and December 6 1974.

The defence said: "For October 21 it says you and others were taken swimming."

"I do not remember being taken."

"Two members of staff took you and others boys swimming and you do not remember?"

"No."

"It says you were taken to sea cadets."

"I don't remember being a cadet."

"There are references of you going swimming and to cadets. Do you still maintain you were a prisoner?"

"I was not allowed out."

"An entry for October 26 says at 3 p.m. Mr Sweeney took boys, including you, out in a van with a view to going walking. It says you took a bus in the wrong direction and you went to a police station. The police phoned the home."

"I do not have any memory of this, to be honest."

"You said it was like Fort Knox."

"If I wanted to go out, I was not allowed so it was like a prison."

"You don't remember going on a bus, getting lost and going to the police?"

"I don't remember it. The memories I retain are only of abuse."

"The diary says on November 27 you had a bad back and saw a doctor. You said you never saw a doctor."

"I don't remember that."

"Do you accept it happened?"

"Possible. I don't know. The book is not official."

"It [another book] says on January 13 1975 at 10.30 you returned from your weekend at home."

"I have no recollection."

"You say you were deprived of contact with the outside world."

"My perception of it, yes."

"You said 'the doors were locked during the day, we were like prisoners'."

"Yes.

"You were not allowed home every weekend or went for a holiday or camping."

"No."

"You said you were taken to the premiere of Towering Inferno on December 10, 1974. Google said the premiere was on December 12 . The diary says you and other kids were taken swimming. All the kids were in bed by 10.30."

"The premiere could have been over two days."

"Not a premiere, no."

"Maybe he didn't take me on the tenth, but he took me to see the film."

"Do you remember Mr Sweeney taking you rowing?"

"No."

"But you always went [to his mother's] in a white Ford Anglia."

"That is my memory."

"He changed it for a green van in 1975. Were you abused in that?"

"No."

"The diary says on February 7, 1975 you went to Brighton. I suppose you don't remember that."

"No."

"On February 10 it says you arrived back just before lunch. You were thrown out of class, something to do with fags."

"I can't remember that."

"On February 19, the diary says you and other boys left for a camping weekend in Norfolk."

265

"I do not remember."

"Each boy took a turn at the wheel of a boat. There was a barbecue on the beach. The boys went to a funfair. The diary concludes 'it was a very active weekend'."

"I have no recollection of this. I don't remember it."

"Mr Sweeney took you to his mother's house. How many times?"

"I cannot recall how many times, the actual number."

"How long did it take you to get there?"

"Ninety minutes."

"It was pre-M25. I suggest nearer two and a half hours [driving through London] on a good day."

"Could be. It felt like 90 minutes."

"You did the journey on numerous occasions yet you cannot remember how long it took."

"I did not have a watch."

"How long did you stay there?"

"An hour, hour and a half."

"So that means you were absent [from the home] for at least four hours, but more like six or seven."

"I don't know."

"Did you Google earth the house?"

"No."

"You gave the police details of the house. You remember balustrades, which ones were square-shaped. There were trees when you looked out of the window so you could not see other houses."

"I focused on things."

"But you cannot remember a camping trip."

"I focused on things to take my mind off it."

"You cannot remember swimming, camping trips or the fun fair, but you can describe the house."

"Because I was abused there."

"I suggest what you describe quite accurately is 4, Litton Avenue where Mr Sweeney was arrested."

"I did not know the address."

"In 1974 to 1975 Mrs Sweeney lived in number 41. The house you described was number 4. I repeat my suggestion: you looked on the internet to discover where Mr Sweeney lived. Is it just a coincidence that the house you described bears similarities with your description of her current house and you had not realised she'd moved?"

"Maybe I Googled to find out if Sweeney was still alive."

"What did you Google?"

"His name and the town."

"What address came up?"

"About six came up."

The defence asked Mr D about the time Sweeney attempted buggery.

"What happened when he tried?"

"He could not enter [me] so he spat on his fingers. It was too painful so I had to do it to him."

"Are you sure you put your penis in his bottom?"

"I was beaten to do that. It's abhorrent, disgusting."

"You told the police on one occasion it was too painful [for Sweeney to do it to Mr D] so you had to do it to him. Now you are saying there were other occasions."

"They were token attempts."

The defence decided, in an effort to ascertain as accurately as possible when Mr D and Sweeney were away from the home together, that the jurors should each have a copy of every page of the diaries — 362 pages of entries. The barrister went through each page to see if or when the pair were absent from entries together which took two days. There was nothing in the occurrence books where Sweeney and Mr D were said to be absent together for the sort of time scale needed for them to drive to and from his mother's house.

MATTHEW SWEENEY was cross-examined by the defence.

"Were the children residents allowed home weekends?"

"Yes, if social services agreed."

"The records show Mr D went home every weekend."

"If social services agreed, yes."

"The occurrence books were your idea."

"They started in August 1973. In those days they were called incident books. Each member of staff had to fill in details which reflected their work at the home. From 1976 I tried to get a unified approach rather than just filling it in. Every child would be mentioned in each report, even if absent."

The books had been retrieved by Sweeney in January 1977 when Inchmore House, which is now an Indian restaurant, relocated. Despite being on leave, Sweeney was asked to supervise the move and noticed the books were in a skip. He took them as a memento of his time there and put them in the loft.

"Were you alone with the children?"

"Yes."

"So this was not unusual."

"No."

"There was no rule about being alone with a child."

"No."

"And staff members made a note of this."

"Yes. Back then it was for the activities of the children."

Returning to the occurrence books, the defence put it to Sweeney: "There is no doubt on 19 occasions Mr D was taken swimming."

"That's right."

"So he was not a prisoner, then."

"No."

"How far did your mother live from the home?"

"Forty-five to 50 miles, two hours' drive at least."

"So a minimum of four to five hours."

"Minimum, yes."

"If you were absent for five hours, would it be noted by the staff?"

"I would hope so, yes. Every movement would be noted. For fire reasons we had to keep a note of who was in and out of the home at all times."

"Mr D said he did not see his family while in residence at Inchmore House."

"In the record books he had the most regular home visits of anyone."

"What was the situation with school holidays?"

"He went home."

"Half-term?"

"Yes. He went home, as agreed with the social services."

MATTHEW SWEENEY admitted to the jury he was homosexual, but had kept his sexuality secret while at the home. He claimed Mr D effectively started to blackmail him because of this.

"On three occasions you allowed Mr D to have sex with you. How did this come about?"

"Throughout he wanted domination, to be in charge."

"The anal sex before Christmas in 1976?"

"I went round to see his mother who wasn't in and it went from there. He got quite distressed because I was leaving. He said he needed me. I am a gay man, but did not want it exposed. If it would keep him quiet…" [Sweeney was given a short break due to his emotional state].

[Resuming] "It was the fear of being exposed. I had no defence. I just did not want him to tell the police."

"So you allowed it to happen."

"Yes."

"How long did it take?"

"Two or three minutes."

"Did he ejaculate?"

"No idea."

"Anything else happen?"

"Once more in the van in May 1977. He was on the way to see a girlfriend and wanted me to drive him."

"Why did you agree [to the sex]?"

"The threat was always there. It was quite clear what he wanted."

"You allowed it?"

"I did."

"Any other occasion?"

"I had a phone call out of the blue in 1978 from him. He was joining the Army and wanted to see me. He gave me his address."

"What happened?"

"Same thing. He made his demands and I… I went in, had a cup of tea and did the same procedure again."

"Did you attempt to bugger him?"

"No."

"How long did it last?"

"The cup of tea took longer."

"But why?"

"I felt hunted… trapped. The threats were there. You cannot

understand if you are not a gay man."

"Did you see him again?"

"He turned up at my house later that year in his Army uniform. I was not best pleased. He wanted a lift to the Army base."

"So four times in total."

"Yes."

"You saw him again."

"I did. He phoned me and I saw him."

"What took place?"

"Nothing. On advice from my mother, I stood up to him. I made it clear I'd take such action to stop him if he tried sexual contact. I felt so wonderful. If he'd demanded money, I'd still be paying, but I never heard from him again until this."

THE PROSECUTION cross-examined Matthew Sweeney about the occurrence books.

"Why did you not tell the police about them?"

"They never went into the loft and I was not sure if I should give them an advantage."

"They missed them."

"Yes."

"You did not say: 'I can help you in this'?"

"I certainly didn't. If they were going to be important, they were going to be important to me. It did not seem sensible to lose control of anything that might help me. The police weren't exactly my friends at the time."

"You misled them."

"No. I just didn't tell them and they did not go into the loft."

IN ITS summing up the Crown told the jury: "If you had the terrible misfortune of sexual abuse, it is something that would never leave you. Those who are victims are scarred as few other victims are.

"The defendant painted the claimant as something of a bounty hunter. Mr D simply wants justice. He is not the first and certainly won't be the last to come forward in the post-Savile period. If he did not give a complete account, what Mr D spoke about could not be a totally manufactured event."

THE DEFENCE admitted that Matthew Sweeney "should have

known better" than to become involved with Mr D, even though by then he was over the age of 16 so no offence was committed.

"At 16… 17… you can be straight or gay and at that age maybe you are more sexually active than older people. Mr D said he needed to tell someone, but never had the chance. Wrong. He said the doors [to Inchmore House] were locked day and night. He does have a memory, just a selective one."

THE TRIAL went into a third week. The evidence the jury had heard was intense, contradictory and, at times, probably confusing.

The defendant did not deny engaging in sexual activity with Mr D, but only when he was past the age of consent and with his consent. Matthew Sweeney denied any sexual contact while the claimant was under-age at Inchmore House.

Sweeney had a previous historical charge of sexual assault against him.

How much emphasis would the jury put on that, even though it was almost 40 years ago, as it began its deliberation?

32

MATTHEW SWEENEY: Nine counts of indecent assault; attempted buggery

THE JURY was unaware of several factors. This was not so much a retrial as a second trial. A jury was never sworn in at the first trial a year earlier. Then, the judge had ruled that it would be unfair on Matthew Sweeney to stand trial as key witnesses who could have spoken on his behalf were either dead or could not be traced.

The Crown took the matter to the Court of Appeal who overturned the original ruling and a new trial was set.

Second time round the trial was plagued by delays. The first jury was sworn in on a Monday, but dismissed towards the end of a week of legal arguments that effectively delayed the start of the second trial.

At the end of the second week, it was decided it would not be in anyone's interest for the jury to hear the summing up of the Crown and the defence and then go home for the weekend without starting deliberation. The summing-up could not be done on the Monday as one of the barristers was unwell.

The trial had to be moved to a different court on the Tuesday and it took 90 minutes to ferry the Amazonian rain forest of paper evidence to the new court.

The jury finally began its deliberation 16 days after the trial, originally scheduled to last three to four days, had started. After almost two days in retirement the foreman told the judge that the jury had reached a verdict on which it all agreed for seven counts. They had found Sweeney not guilty on counts 2, 3, 4, 7, 8, 9 and 10.

The judge told the jury he would accept a majority verdict on the three remaining counts. After a further hour's deliberation, the foreman said the jury had also found Sweeney not guilty on count six.

The foreman told the judge the jurors were "at breaking point" after two days of intensive deliberating. The court was not sitting the following day, a Friday. The good news for the jurors was they could have three full days away from the pressures of reaching a conclusion on the two outstanding counts.

The jury asked the judge to remind it of the points of law it should be considering regarding counts 1 and 5 with which Sweeney was charged — 1: Indecent assault on a male person under 16 to cause him to perform oral sex on you. 5 — Indecent assault on a male person under 16 on multiple occasions causing him to perform anal sex on you.

The judge said that with count 5, the jury had to be sure the defendant's behaviour forced the indecent assault; that the claimant was forced to do it. In this case, the Crown had to prove there was an assault and then that it was indecent. A sexual assault is causing another person to indulge in a sexual manner.

The counts involved a person under 16, who is considered too young to consent. Whether Mr D consented was immaterial. Was he forced to have oral sex and anal sex with Sweeney?

After several hours' further deliberating, the jury was unable to reach a decision. The judge thanked the jury and dismissed it.

The Crown Prosecution Service decided Sweeney should face yet another trial for the two counts on which the jury could not reach a decision.

1 — Indecent assault on a male person under 16 to cause him to perform oral sex on you

5 — Indecent assault on a male person under 16 on multiple occasions causing him to perform anal sex on you.

Six months later Sweeney returned to court, not for another trial, but to hear the Crown say it was offering no evidence for the two outstanding counts. Four and a half years after Sweeney's initial arrest he left court cleared of all charges.

33

MORGAN SAUNDERS: Grievous bodily harm with intent; unlawful wounding; aggravated vehicle taking; possession of an offensive weapon

GAS METER PETER AND SHINE MY LINE

IT WAS never going to be a run of the mill trial after it was revealed the defendant's drug dealer pal was known as Gas Meter Peter (sadly, no reason was ever given for this). The nickname of the West Indian van driver who was attacked — Black — was easier, if not particularly PC, to understand. Morgan Saunders also said he had been threatened by a drugs gang which called itself Shine My Line.

Gas Meter Peter, Black and Shine My Line were an intoxicating cocktail of names as Saunders was charged with four counts.

Count one: wounding with intent — unlawfully and maliciously wounding Luther Miller with intent to inflict upon him grievous bodily harm. Count two: unlawful wounding of the same person, but without intent. Count three: aggravated vehicle taking — taking a vehicle without the consent of the owner and driving it dangerously. Count four: possession of an offensive weapon in a public place.

What was not in doubt was that there was a particularly nasty fight involving a knife and, inevitably, blood spilled with significant injuries to the van driver. How this happened and who was responsible was a matter for the jury to decide.

THE INCIDENT happened in Neville Road, Norwich. The prosecution called two witnesses, the first Henry Peters who was washing his car when the fight occurred.

"What time was this?"

"About half past four."

"What alerted you?"

"I heard a commotion. I didn't think too much of it at first, but I went to have a look."

"What did you see?"

"I saw two white men in a van. They both had knives. I saw a black male on the driver's side banging on the window."

"How far away were you?"

"About two metres."

"What kind of knives were they?"

"Like bread knives, maybe 10 to 12 inches long."

"What were the two white males doing?"

"The driver was trying to start the van to get away. The other ran away. Then a silver BMW pulled up behind the van."

"How many people were in it?"

"Just the driver."

"What about the black male?"

"He was bleeding from his left ribs area, quite bad. Blood was dripping through his hands. He walked up the road. I went to a garage nearby and called an ambulance. I asked them for a first aid kit, but by the time I got out he was gone."

"Did you see him again?"

"No."

"You said in a second statement to the police two months later you wanted to withdraw your original statement [made to them] because you did not want to be involved."

The witness had a change of mind and gave evidence in court.

THE DEFENCE asked Henry Peters what he saw as he broke off from washing his car.

"Two white men in a van, one black man."

"The white male who drove off in the van, what was he wearing?"

"A red hoodie."

"I suggest it could have been a grey top. Could that have been the case?"

"I don't think so, no."

THE PROSECUTION called Richard McKay whose office overlooked the incident.

"How far were you from the incident?"

"About 60 metres."

"What did you first see?"

"Two white males sitting on a wall."

"What were they wearing?"

"The first male had a red top, the second a grey top."

"Was there any reason you were looking out of the window?"

"I didn't have too much to do that day. Also, there had been a lot of theft and drug dealing in the area which is a business park. It makes it easy for drug dealing."

"Did you notice anything about the two males?"

"They were just loitering. Their body language gave me the impression they may not be up to any good."

"Then?"

"A van drew up. Male two went to the driver's side, male one to the passenger side. I saw the passenger door close. The van was shaking so something was going on, probably some sort of scuffle."

"Was the [black male] driver still there?"

"Yes. Male two pulled him out of his seat onto the ground and then got into the van. The driver managed to get up and was fighting with the man now in the driver's seat."

"What could you see?"

"Flailing arms. The black male slumped back. It looked like he was in pain."

"Could you see anything in anyone's hand?"

"No. I was about 60 metres away."

"Could you see his injuries?"

"Not at that stage, no."

"Then?"

"The van sped off with two white males inside it."

"What did you do?"

"Me and a colleague ran out. The black male was stumbling around covered in blood. He had quite a few gash wounds."

"You called the police."

"Yes."

The black driver had been taken in by a neighbour by the time the police arrived. The injured male would only provide officers with his first name — Luther. He was eventually taken to hospital.

THE VAN had a tracker and was traced to a spot 20 miles from the incident, with police vehicles and a helicopter in pursuit. PC Boxall told the jury: "My colleague and I found the van in a dead-end. It turned around and we allowed it to pass us because we knew back-up vehicles were blocking the road. I ran towards the van and shouted: 'Police — show me your hands now'."

Morgan Saunders was eventually hand-cuffed, arrested and cautioned. Upon being searched the officer found three rocks of crack cocaine and one packet of white powder in the defendant's pocket. He was also arrested for that. Saunders was taken to a police station, interviewed and eventually charged.

His police interview was read to the jury and was to provide some significant contradictions to what Saunders said in court.

THE DEFENCE asked Morgan Saunders if he was guilty of any of the four charges.

"No."

"Let's go back to the day of the incident. Tell us what you did."

"I was walking to catch a train and bumped into a guy called Gas Meter Peter."

"What did he look like?"

"Tall, six-foot, darkish skin, dark hair."

"How did you know him?"

"I met him through taking drugs."

"What did he say?"

"He asked me if I wanted to score. I had been clean for four years, but because of something that happened I had relapsed earlier that year, taking heroin and crack cocaine. He went round the corner and phoned a dealer called Black. He told Black where I was and I was told to meet him in Neville Road which was five minutes' walk away. Gas Meter Peter said someone would show up in a white van."

"How much money did you have on you?"

"About £30 or £40."

"Then what?"

"Me and Gas Meter Peter went there [Neville Road] and we sat on a wall, waiting for the van to show up. It pulled up with a black man driving. He gave me the nod and signalled to come over. Gas Meter stayed on the wall."

"What were you wearing?"

"A blue bomber jacket and a canvas blue hat."

"Any hood?"

"No."

"And Peter?"

"A grey hoodie top."

"So you went to the van."

"Yes, the passenger side. I opened the door and got in."

"How many people were in the van?"

"Two — me and the black guy."

"Was anything in your hand?"

"No."

"Him?"

"Not that I can recall."

"What did you say?"

"I asked for two white and a dark."

"He gave them to you?"

"Yes."

"What did you do with them?"

"Put them in my coat pocket."

"Did you pay him?"

"Yes, £30."

"Was the door open or shut?"

"Shut. I had closed it."

"And Peter?"

"Sitting on the wall opposite."

"Next?"

"The black guy called me a pussy-hole informer. He pulled out a knife and told me I'd grassed his mate up."

"Who?"

"Five months earlier I had a row with a young black guy. I was threatened, they were going to come round and rob me. I was in my car, car pulled up beside me, three black guys tried to get in my back door.

There was 13 of them. I was stabbed, nicked a main artery and had my head kicked in. The incident was filmed by some Asian guy so he had video evidence of it. I told the police, but they never responded. In fact, I was arrested for withholding evidence."

"Do you know who they were?"

"A gang called Shine My Line."

THE DEFENCE returned to the day of the incident.

"So you got in the van."

"Yes. Sat in the passenger seat and shut the door. I gave him [the black guy] the money. He produced a big knife and tried to lunge at me. I put my hand up to defend myself. The knife went through my hand. It all happened so quickly. I don't know where he produced a knife from."

"Which hand was the knife in?"

"Must have been his right. There was blood everywhere and pain shooting up my arm. I grabbed the knife and was struggling with him. I got punched a couple of times in the face. I braced myself against the passenger door and kicked him. My glasses were busted trying to defend myself. The driver's door flew open, maybe because I was overpowering him. He was half out the door, then he's out of the van."

"What happened to the knife?"

"Don't know. It all happened so quickly."

"Did you have a knife?"

"No. I got stabbed. I got attacked."

"What happened then?"

"Pete, Gas Meter we call him... seconds after Black let go of me, he's scuffling with Gas Meter. They had a bit of a to-do. I saw a silver BMW with two or three black guys in it. I panicked even more. I thought I'd been set up for being an alleged informer."

"There was more than one person in the BMW."

"I'm 100 per cent sure I saw more than one guy, certainly there was another on the passenger seat. Gas Meter had a knife, not sure if it was the same one as the black driver had. He said: 'Let's fucking get out of here, sorry to swear, there's loads of them.' As I'm trying to start the van the door's opened, the black driver's trying to grab something."

"Did you see his injuries?"

"No. All I was concerned about was me, my own injuries and to get out without being injured worse. I was scared. I managed to start the van. I pulled out on to the road. Gas Meter was telling me what to do. My hand was slipping off the [steering] wheel because of the blood. The BMW was chasing me."

"How did you consider your driving to be?"

"Erratic. I was trying to get away from people chasing me."

"When you arrived at your location, what did you decide to do?"

"Gas Meter was telling me he'd helped me… he'd saved me. Me, I'm in a nicked van, blood all over it, I've lost my coat, lost my phone."

"Where did they [phone and coat] go?"

"I can't remember."

"Where was the BMW?"

"No idea. I lost it."

"What happened to Peter?"

"Gas Meter found some rags to patch up my hand. He got out the car, said he was going to phone someone. He disappeared. I never saw him after that."

The defence asked the defendant about his police interview.

"Is it accurate?"

"No, but it's mostly accurate. I made some things up because I'd relapsed on drugs. I was doing voluntary work, mentoring other damaged people. I did not want to say I'd relapsed."

"You told the police in your interview that a van pulled over and the driver asked you for directions. Is this true?"

"Mostly, only that I was not pushed in the van. I did not want to say I was scoring drugs."

THE PROSECUTION questioned Morgan Saunders about the driver of the silver BMW.

"Had you seen the car before?"

"Yes."

"It happened to have a black person in it — was this not paranoia?"

"No."

"He was just a member of the public."

"He followed me. He phoned the police [about the black driver] to cover his own arse."

"Gas Meter Peter — is he a friend of yours?"

"Not a friend. I knew him through drug culture."

"You could have helped the police by telling them about him."

"And get stabbed again… my family's house burned down?"

"He'd never threatened you before."

"He had no reason."

"If the black driver had intended to attack you, why go through with the facade of a drugs deal?"

"It was a honey trap. Drugs were used to get me in the van."

"It was two against one. There was no suggestion in the phone call about trouble. How could it have been planned when the van arrived so quickly?"

"I wouldn't have got in the van if I thought there would be violence."

"You said he was punching you, so he could not have had a knife."

"He pushed me and he had a knife."

"You had a knife, didn't you?"

"No."

"What was the first violence?"

"He lunged at me with a knife."

"You told the police he punched you."

"I was wrecked [when I gave the interview]."

"How many lies were in your statement? Let's have a look. You said you were walking along the road and the passenger door opened. False?"

"Yes."

"You said you were pushed in the van. A lie?"

"Yes."

"You said the first violence was a punch. Now you are saying it was a knife. He could not have punched you if he had a knife in his hand."

"I was trying to protect myself with the drugs thing and Gas Meter Peter."

"You said to the police that someone wielded a knife. Someone?"

"It was my vocabulary."

"He [the black driver] had no reason to accuse you."

"Lots of black guys attacked me. He could have been among them."

"You said they were young black guys. He was 35."

"I am 47. He's younger than me."

"You said the BMW pulled up with 'loads of black kids'."

"It was the wrong wording. There was more than one."

"No one got out of the car."

"I can't remember, not 100 per cent certain."

"Did you hit a Toyota driving away?"

"Don't think I did. I drove erratically because I was being chased, not followed, chased. Gas Meter said we were being chased. I just wanted to get away. I was panicking."

"Did Pete get out of the van?"

"When we pulled up in the woods, but the police never found him."

"How could the police helicopter not see him?"

"Don't know."

"Did he get out earlier?"

"No."

"You've made all this up, haven't you?"

"No."

"It didn't happen."

"It did."

"You set the black male driver up."

"No."

"He had no reason to seek revenge."

"He stabbed me."

"You stabbed him."

"No."

IN ITS summing up, the prosecution told the jury: "This was not just a drugs deal. It was a set-up. The defendant's motive was to steal drugs and the van. There was no motive for the driver to attack the defendant. We say Morgan Saunders attacked the driver, not the other way round. The defendant had relatively few injuries, while the driver suffered many wounds.

"He [Saunders] told lie after lie again and again."

THE DEFENCE said the jury should consider the fact that Luther Miller, the black driver, had refused to give evidence. "It's like a one-sided football match. The driver has not been cross-examined or his evidence tested. Not one person produced [in court] said the defendant had a knife.

"What we know is a man was stabbed. The issue is by whom and how. The two witnesses were at loggerheads with some of their evidence. We know the defendant drove off and Peter Gas Meter or Gas Meter Peter whatever he's called gets out and… who knows? Is it important? What is important is whether Morgan Saunders stabbed the van driver."

MORGAN SAUNDERS was no stranger to a Crown Court and the jury was made aware of five previous drugs-related convictions. On the defendant's bad character, the judge said: "The jury is entitled to know the character of the man making allegations against the van driver. Because he took drugs does not mean he had a propensity to violence. You decide, but don't convict because he had a bad past."

The judge told the jury that a wound is "a breakage in the continuity of the skin" while grievous bodily harm was "inflicting really serious injuries." Intent, the jury was told "can be decided in a split second, not necessarily planned."

If the jury decided Saunders was guilty of count one then count two would be ignored. If it decided he was not guilty of count one then the jury should consider the lesser count two of unlawful wounding, but without the intent — acting recklessly which is being aware of the risk of your actions yet still going through with them.

On the charge of aggravated vehicle taking and driving dangerously, the judge said: "He admitted taking the vehicle for his own use and driving dangerously which is in a manner far below what would be expected of a careful driver. Was the defendant fearing death or physical injuries? Would a reasonable person have done this? If you believe this to be the case you will find him not guilty. The prosecution says he just took the van and drugs."

If the jury found the defendant guilty of either of the first two counts then count four would be ignored with the judge directing the foreman of the jury to return a directed not guilty verdict.

Regarding the defendant's admitted lies, the judge said: "The mere fact he lied is not an admission of guilt. Sometimes people lie to protect themselves or panic. You must consider if his lies supported the case against him."

33

MORGAN SAUNDERS: Grievous bodily harm with intent; unlawful wounding; aggravated vehicle taking; possession of an offensive weapon

WHERE to start with Morgan Saunders? When he was arrested for the incidents involving Luther Miller, he was on bail awaiting sentencing after pleading guilty to possessing a disguised firearm — a taser in the form of a mobile phone.

The jury was unaware of this outstanding matter, but it was told about some of Saunders' previous convictions relating to drugs offences.

Inevitably defendants (and claimants) lie in court and for some it can work, but Saunders took this dark art to new heights — or perhaps depths. His entire fantasy story had little credibility and if he deserves any praise — tongue firmly in cheek as this is written — it is for giving us the most memorable nickname of his drugs associate which we can dine out on — Gas Meter Peter.

Admitting that you lied to the police will always raise doubts in a jury's collective mind, but more than anything Saunders' attempt to convince the jurors that he was the victim was as pathetic as it was ineffectual. "The jury saw through your lies," the judge told him as sentencing began.

Saunders is a nasty, violent serial criminal — incredibly he even kept a straight face for his "I'm a pacifist" remark.

Three and a half hours after the jury started its deliberation and returned to the court, when the foreman said "not guilty" to count one Saunders must have thought he had won the legal equivalent of a lottery rollover.

Any joy was short lived as the foreman then announced "guilty" to charges two and three — unlawful wounding and aggravated vehicle taking with count four unnecessary.

In effect, the jury could not be sure he intended to cause Miller grievous bodily harm which I found surprising bordering on astonishing. It was difficult to understand how the jury had concluded Saunders had not intended malicious wounding, but perhaps the absence of any knife being found and whether he had taken a bladed object with him could not make it sure of count one.

Saunders' roll of dishonour had started aged 16 when he appeared at a juvenile court for possession of an offensive weapon. In all he had 29 convictions for 75 offences which had now become 31 for 77.

While searching Saunders' property for drugs, the police found a stun gun disguised as a mobile phone in a kitchen drawer. The defendant said he thought it was "a crap old phone" someone had left at his home. It was fully charged and if used could have caused temporary incapacitation to the victim. The judge rejected his claim that he was unaware of what it was and believed, with Saunders' record, it was likely to be used when he took the law into his own hands.

Unless there are exceptional circumstances the law is inflexible on sentencing for this offence and carries a mandatory five-year sentence. The judge saw no reason not to hand Saunders a five-year prison term. As he changed his plea to guilty during the trial, he lost any discount.

The judge was, however, mindful of totality when considering the sentencing for the other two offences of unlawful wounding and aggravated vehicle taking. With this in mind Saunders was told "considerably reduced terms" would be given.

He was sentenced to 18 months for unlawful wounding and six months for aggravated vehicle taking, these sentences to run not concurrently but consecutively with the disguised firearm offence, making a total of six and a half years. Saunders would serve half of this sentence in prison and half on licence. He had been in custody for seven months so that was deducted from his total. He was also given a 12-month driving ban to start upon his release from jail.

34

TYLER CHARTER: Sexual assault

WHO WOULD WIN
THE EX FACTOR?

"I DIDN'T do it and she is making it all up."

That was Tyler Charter's response to the police when he was arrested for allegedly sexually assaulting his ex-partner contrary to section 3 of the Sexual Offences Act 2003, knowing she did not consent and not reasonably believing she consented.

The prosecution told the jury Charter and Miss T had been in a relationship, but they had been separated for about a year. The defendant still contacted her in an effort to get back. One day the claimant went to the home of the defendant's mother, with whom she maintained a good relationship, to talk about him.

Miss T was not willing to go to court to give evidence, not even to be in a room elsewhere in the building and be cross-examined via video link. The judge gave permission for the necessary equipment to be installed in Miss T's house to "put her at ease." A police officer who supervised the process was the only other person in the room with the claimant as she gave evidence to the jury.

The prosecution asked Miss T about her relationship with the defendant.

"We met some time in 2018 and by the middle or later that year we were in a relationship. We separated about a year ago. I can't remember exactly when."

"Can you tell us what happened on April 7?"

"I went to see his mum, about three or half past. I was still friends with her."

"What happened when you went there?"

"Her partner opened the door. I went upstairs to her bedroom and we [with Charter's mother] had a cigarette. Tyler came up and sat on the bed. I didn't know he was there."

"How did you feel?"

"I was OK, but a bit uncomfortable at the same time."

"What did he say?"

"Just 'hello'."

"And you?"

"Can't remember."

"Did you chat to him?"

"A little bit, I can't remember that much. I left the bedroom to put my phone on charge downstairs. I sat on the sofa in the living room."

"What happened then?"

"He came down, sat next to me and gave me a hug. I said: 'What are you doing'?"

"What was his behaviour like?"

"Offish. He was looking annoyed, but happy. He just looked at me, didn't say anything."

"How did you feel when he cuddled you?"

"Very uncomfortable. I asked him what he was doing. He laughed. That's when everything started."

"The next thing?"

"He got up, picked me up and threw me down [on the sofa]. He held me down, with his left arm, I think. He kept trying to touch me downstairs and stuff."

"What were you wearing?"

"Tracksuit bottoms and a jumper."

"What did he try to do to the trousers?"

"Pull them down with his right hand, I think. I tried to push him off, but he kept trying to get them down. He did get his hand down there trying to do stuff."

"Which part of your body?"

"At some time, he had his hand on my vagina inside my knickers. He kept trying to go in, but he didn't."

"What were you saying?"

287

"Get away."

"Were you able to stop him?"

"I kept trying to knock his arm away, but was not able to do it properly."

"How many times did he touch your vagina?"

"Four, maybe five."

"How did this make you feel?"

"Really dirty, horrible. I did not want him near me. He then had his hand under my jumper and was trying to touch my breast, but did not touch my breast, only over my bra. I think it was his left hand."

"How hard did he squeeze?"

"He really squeezed hard, but I only felt a little bit because the bra was really padded."

"What did you do?"

"Just tried to get him off, but he was too heavy. He then touched my bum and tried to pull the trousers down again. He heard a noise in the kitchen so stopped. I grabbed my shoes and phone and ran upstairs."

"How long did the incident last?"

"Not sure, probably an hour, hour and a half. Could have been longer."

"Why did you run upstairs?"

"To get away from him."

"Did you have any injuries?"

"A bite mark on the side of my belly. I think he did it when he was trying to get at my breast."

"Why did you not say anything to his mum?"

"She'd kick-off and I didn't want a fight. She could tell something was not right, but I didn't tell her."

"How were you feeling?"

"Upset, dirty, useless… everything."

"What happened next?"

"Tyler said he would walk me home, but I didn't want him to after what happened. I just wanted to be with my mum. I ran out the door. A few minutes later I heard footsteps."

"How did you feel?"

"Scared. I know what he's like when he's angry and doesn't get what he wants. I shouted to him to leave me alone. He kept grabbing my arm, trying to stop me. He called me a muggy cunt."

"How did that make you feel?"

"I'm used to him calling me that. He used to do it all the time."

"And then?"

"He asked me if he could drink from my bottle of fizz to take a tablet. He took it, had a drink and threw it back at me. It hit me in the belly. I tried to cross the road. He almost got hit by a car trying to follow me."

"He punched you in the stomach."

"Yes. Not a full punch, not full weight. He then put his hand against my throat. I could hardly breathe. I had a panic attack."

"Did he say anything?"

"He said something about hurting me and putting me in a coma."

"After that what happened?"

"He said: 'Oh, not fucking talking to me now?' I told him to fuck off."

"Then?"

"He kept following me, shouting things out."

"Was there anyone else around?"

"It was dark and I was not really paying attention."

"What time was this?"

"Not too sure. I don't think I got home until eight or half eight."

"What did you do when you got home?"

"I was on my bed crying. I couldn't breathe properly."

"Who was at home?"

"My mum, my sister. They saw me crying. I didn't want to involve the police, but they called them. I don't like courts or talking to people I don't know."

"How do you feel about Tyler Charter?"

"I don't like him."

THE DEFENCE cross-examined Miss T.

"Your relationship with the defendant was on and off."

"Yes."

"You'd get together, argue and split."

"Yes, we'd argue. Then he'd threaten me and ask me to kill myself."

"That's not true, is it?"

"Yes, it is."

"The Tuesday before the incident, you remember that?"

"No."

"You were speaking to him on Facebook."

"That was a few days before. He was talking all nice to me so I thought I'd go [to his mother's] because I didn't want an argument."

"Are you agreeing you were, at some stage, at the defendant's mother's house?"

"I left late afternoon because I don't like walking in the dark."

"How long does it take to walk home?"

"About an hour because I have arthritis."

"In your police statement you said: 'I was going to see his mum. I still get on well with her and wanted to talk to her about Tyler's behaviour over the past year. He contacted me to get back. Tyler came into her bedroom and sat on the bed.' You didn't go there to talk about him contacting you over the last year, did you? Only the past few days. You'd been out of the relationship for a year."

"Yes."

"It was no surprise to see Tyler on the day of the alleged incident as you told the court you'd been there on the Tuesday and he was there."

"I'd been told he was staying with some girl in Liverpool or somewhere. It didn't bother me as I could get on with my life."

"In between the Tuesday and Thursday, you and Tyler had another argument."

"We had loads of arguments."

"He left voice messages and you ignored them. I suggest the relationship was 'on' on the Tuesday but 'off' on the Thursday."

"It was off before Thursday."

"You went to his mother's bedroom. She spends a lot of time there. It's all set up for her to eat and sleep."

"Almost all day."

"You could not charge your phone in her room?"

"She was charging two phones, a tablet and something else. So I went downstairs."

"Why did you have to sit in the room with the phone charging?"

"In case my mum phoned. She worries."

"Fact is you did not go downstairs alone."

"Yes."

"You followed Tyler."

"No."

"You had a smoke with him. There was no reason to feel uncomfortable."

"Yes, there was because of what he'd been saying."

"You'd been speaking to him… 10 minutes of chit-chat."

"How can that be if he tried to rape me?"

"Let's discuss the allegation. You say he held you down with his left hand."

"Yes."

"In your [police] statement you said it was his right [hand]. What was he doing with his other hand?"

"Pulling my trousers down."

"Front or back?"

"Front."

"When he touched your vagina, how did he do it?"

"He put his hands down my trousers."

"Front or back?"

"Front."

"And they happened to touch, to use your word, your bum?"

"His hand had slipped from where it was."

"Slipped from your vagina?"

"Yes."

"In your [police] statement you said: 'He put his hands under my bum and his finger touched my vagina.' You're saying he came from your bottom to your front?"

"I told him [the police officer] it was front first."

"An error by the police officer?"

"Yes."

"You said he went front first."

"One time from the front and then the back."

"I suggest he did not do either."

"I would not say it if he didn't. I would not feel suicidal if he hadn't."

"In your statement you say: 'He managed to get his hand under my bra, touching my breast.' Why did you say under your bra to the police and today you said over your bra?"

"I told the guy 'over the bra.' I said 'on the bra' not 'under'."

"He [the defendant] didn't squeeze your breast at all."

"He did. I would not say he had if he hadn't."

"Why did you not mention squeezing in your statement?"

"I did."

"It's not in your statement."

"I told the guy that."

"You told the jury it [the alleged assault] ended because he heard a noise in the kitchen."

"Yes."

"In your statement you said: 'After I kicked him, he got off. I got up and ran upstairs'."

"I said his mum's boyfriend was making a coffee in the kitchen."

"No mention of that in your statement. Another mistake by the police officer?"

"Yes."

"So, you got there at three or half three. You went upstairs with his mum for... how long?"

"Fifteen minutes, maybe more."

"More?"

"Maybe half an hour... 45 minutes... an hour."

"Ten minutes charging your phone?"

"Yes."

"How long did the assault take?"

"An hour. I was not sitting there looking at the clock."

"There was no sexual assault, was there?"

"Yes, there was. Why would I go through all this otherwise?"

VICKY TAYLOR (name changed for legal reasons), the claimant's sister, took to the witness box.

The Crown asked her what time Miss T arrived home.

"About 9.15. "

"How was she?"

"Sobbing, crying, trying to catch her breath... hands around her stomach. Her face was all red and blotchy. I could tell she'd been injured in some way because her arms were crossed on her stomach. She was very emotional and stressed out."

"Your mum asked her what had happened."

"Yes, but she was not able to respond because she was trying to catch her breath. Eventually she told us what had happened. We knew about Tyler. We asked if he'd tried anything on her and she nodded. I went to the phone and called the police. She said Tyler had punched her in the stomach and had tried it on with her in the front room."

DC DAVID ROWLING, who had assumed control of the case, read out the prepared statement Tyler Charter made after his arrest: "I am completely innocent. She has made up the allegation to get me into trouble. It's all lies."

When Charter was interviewed by the police for 27 minutes he answered "no comment" to every question on advice by his solicitor.

The officer told the jury there were no CCTV cameras on the route home Miss T took. In the crime report the address of the defendant's mother was given as "Avenue" rather than "Crescent."

The jury was also told the claimant's clothes had not been sent for forensic testing. Decisions in this respect are made by the forensic borough manager — "the man who controls the purse strings" — based on, among other things, the level of the offence, how much it would cost and whether it would help evidentially in the case.

No swabs were taken from Miss T's bite mark, nor was she examined by a medical practitioner. The defence pointed out that Charter's dental records could have been checked.

Miss T's statement to the police was taken down by an officer in his notebook rather than the claimant giving a video recorded interview. DC Rowling agreed, when asked by the defence, that this is unusual, especially for sexual assault cases. "It is 'should' rather than 'must'," he said, but could not explain why Miss T did not do a video interview.

"The officer would do his best to make a record of what was said, write it down and read it back to the person. Only when that is done will the officer be happy for the claimant to sign it [the statement]."

THE JURY was told that Tyler Charter had been convicted of three previous counts of sexual assault and two of exposure involving girls aged 15 and 18 two years previously.

Charter was cross-examined by the defence who asked him why he had said 'no comment' to every question during his police interview.

"On the advice of my solicitor."

"When did you meet Miss T?"

"Two days after I came out of custody, through my brother Wade. She went with him to begin with."

"Did she know why you had been in prison?"

"Not immediately."

"But you did tell her."

"Yes."

"Do you accept you were guilty of those offences?"

"No."

"Who were the complainants?"

"Friends of the mother of my [two] children."

"Why do you suggest they did it?"

"They made it up between the three of them so I could have no contact with my children."

"So the allegations were made up."

"Entirely false."

"Did the two complainants talk before making the allegations?"

"Yes. It was all in their statement."

"On the Tuesday [two days] before the alleged incident where were you?"

"At my aunt's."

"Was there any contact with the claimant that day?"

"We chatted on Facebook video."

"Could you see where she was?"

"She was at my mum's."

"What did she want?"

"For me to go to my mum's to see her."

"Did you go there?"

"Yes, about three-ish."

"Was anyone else there?"

"Two of her [female] cousins."

"What did you do?"

"Had a smoke with all of them, about half an hour."

"And then?"

"The cousins were making arrangements to see people. We all went to the front garden, two lads turned up and they went off. Me and [claimant's name] went back inside."

"When did the claimant leave?"

"Half nine."

"Was she in good spirits?"

"Yes."

"Your relationship was that you'd be together for a few days, then off for a few days."

"Yes."

"Between her leaving that Tuesday and the Thursday was there any contact?"

"I made numerous texts to her and other attempts to contact her, but she ignored them."

"Before Thursday did you get to talk to her?"

"No."

"Did you leave any messages?"

"Yes, on WhatsApp. Things like 'What have I done now for you not to talk to me?' and 'You must be seeing someone else'."

"Was suicide ever discussed?"

"Once at the start. She was feeling suicidal. I was in a similar position to her, so we'd do it together."

"On the Thursday, you were already at your mother's. What time did the claimant arrive?"

"Three, half three. My mum's partner let her in."

"And she went upstairs to your mum's bedroom."

"Yes."

"Where were you?"

"Front room."

"Did you go upstairs?"

"Yes, 10 or 15 minutes after she arrived. I shared a spliff with her and my mum."

"Where was your mum's partner?"

"Watching TV."

"What was the mood in the room?"

"Good, normal."

"How long were you with them?"

"Twenty minutes. Then I went downstairs."

"Did you see where the claimant's phone was?"

"In mum's room on charge."

"When you went downstairs did anyone follow you?"

"The claimant came down and we shared another spliff. We were together about 20 minutes."

"What was the mood like?"

"OK until I asked her why she was ignoring me. She started getting arsey with me."

"Who left the room?"

"She did. She went back upstairs. "

"Did you touch her bust?"

"No."

"Did you try to touch her bust?"

"No."

"Did you touch her vagina?"

"No."

"Did you try to touch her vagina?"

"No."

"Did anything of a sexual nature occur?"

"No."

"Did you hug her?"

"No."

"How long was she in your mum's room?"

"Ten or 15 minutes. I went upstairs and asked mum for a cigarette. I took it to the toilet to smoke. While I was in there, I heard her say 'bye'."

"Did you follow her?"

"Outside, yes."

"What did you say?"

"I said: 'What the fuck are you doing? You're now fucking about, you might as well go fuck yourself cos you're making me look a cunt'."

"Did you punch her?"

"No."

"Strangle her?"

"No."

"Assault her?"

"No."

"Where did you go after that?"

"Back in mum's until about six, half six. My new girlfriend who lives in Nottingham and her brother collected me. He drove us back there. We gave him money for petrol."

THE PROSECUTION honed straight in on Tyler Carter's previous convictions.

"Convicted for three counts of sexual assault, two counts of exposure."

"Yes."

"Two victims aged 15 and 18."

"Yes."

"Two different women gave evidence against you and the result was you were convicted."

"Yes."

"You gave evidence."

"Yes."

"The jury disbelieved you. I suggest you are a sexual predator towards young women. What do you say?"

"Nothing I can say politely."

"You attacked them."

"No."

"Exposed your penis."

"No."

"The jury found you guilty."

"I didn't do anything."

"On the day [of the alleged assault on Miss T] you were in a relationship."

"No."

"She said she was shocked to see you."

"She knew I was there."

"How did you feel when she didn't respond to your messages?"

"Not know how to feel."

"You followed her downstairs."

"No."

"You sexually assaulted her."

"No."

"You went to hug her."

"No."

"You wanted some sort of sexual connection."

"No."

"You held her down and forced your hand down her trousers."

"No."

"Touched her vagina."

"No."

"Why would she say you did?"

"She is vindictive to me."

"So, three women made up accusations of sexual assault against you."

"Yes. It's the world we live in."

"You bit her."

"No."

"How did she get the mark?"

"Pass."

"You bit her, didn't you?"

"No."

"You're someone who doesn't take no for an answer."

"No."

"Relentless, aren't you?"

"No."

"All the girls are lying, then."

"Yes."

"All invented everything."

"Yes."

"A 15-year-old and an 18-year-old gave evidence in Crown Court as part of a conspiracy to stop you seeing your children."

"Yes."

"What is this claimant's motive?"

"It's all bollocks."

"What was her motive?"

"You'll have to ask her."

"What was it?"

"She has two daughters. She lied who the father was. She said my brother was the father. He wasn't. Because of all this I almost got stabbed."

"You've not told that before."

"Not relevant to the case."

"You're inventing all this, aren't you?"

"No."

"You got her round the throat by a wall."

"No."

"Threw a bottle at her."

"No."

"Why was she so upset when she got home?"

"No idea."

"I'm going to suggest you are lying about the sexual assault."

"No."

"You have a propensity to attack women."

"No."

"You have an underlying disrespect for women."

"No."

IN ITS summing up the prosecution repeated that Tyler Charter was a sexual predator. "It is up to the jury to decide what relevance to put on his previous convictions in respect of this indictment. Why would three different girls make up similar claims against the defendant? He was convicted of touching girls' vaginas and exposing his penis.

"How else did she get the bite mark? Why was she in such an emotional state when he arrived home? Why was she holding her stomach if she had not been punched?"

The jury had to decide on the reliability of the evidence Miss T gave to the police officer who took it down by hand. However, the claimant signed her statement as being a true record of what she said even though she later alleged the officer had made mistakes.

The defence said: "There are a number of inconsistencies in her evidence. In her police statement she said she went to see the defendant's mother to talk about his behaviour over the past year. Yet she asked to see him two days before the alleged incident.

"In her police statement she said: 'He put his finger inside me' but in court she said his hand was only on her vagina. She said in her statement: 'I also realised he managed to get his hand under my bra, he had his hand on my breast.' To the jury she said: 'He put his hand under my jumper and squeezed my bra hard. It hurt.' Also, if someone is squeezing you and hurting you then you don't realise it... you know it.

"She said in her [police] statement the assault stopped: 'After I kicked him, he got off.' In court she said it stopped when he heard a noise in the kitchen. She maintains these were the officer's mistakes. She didn't say she was stressed, blame her memory or say she was in shock. She blamed the police officer for getting it all wrong."

The defence also threw doubt over the claimant's times.

"Giving her the highest level, Miss T claimed she arrived at the defendant's mother at three to half past three, she chatted to his mother for 45 minutes to an hour — now 4.30. Ten minutes charging the phone — 4.40. The incident took an hour — 5.40. Then 15 minutes upstairs — round it off, say 6 p.m. An hour to get home — 7 p.m.

"Her sister said the claimant arrived home at 9.15. The claimant said she got there at 8.30. The police were called at 9.45 and arrived at 10.30."

During its deliberations the jury may also have wondered why Miss T did not shout for help. But crucially, could the jurors dismiss the not particularly likeable Charter's two previous sexual assault convictions as they reached their verdict? And could they ignore the claimant's sister's evidence?

THE JUDGE had an unusual and, for the female jurors, perhaps uncomfortable ruling in law regarding the vagina. "It is not just the vagina. It is also the labia, vulva and clitoris."

34

TYLER CHARTER: Sexual assault

THE JURY knew that Tyler Charter had two previous convictions for sexual assault. What it was unaware of was the reason this trial was halted on the third day for 24 hours. It was because the defendant was in custody after being involved in a knife fight with a neighbour the previous evening. However, Charter was released on bail so he was able to continue the trial the following day.

The fact that Charter had been found guilty of two earlier sexual offences inevitably gave the jury much to ponder as it deliberated on an ignominious possible hat-trick of assaults on young women. The defendant's language to the claimant and her sister would hardly have endeared him to the jurors. Charter was far from a charmer.

Only two people know what — if anything — really happened at the defendant's mother's house. The problem for the Crown was that Miss T's evidence had more holes in it than a colander, which was why it took the jury only 90 minutes to find Charter not guilty — for once.

She said the attack on her lasted at least an hour. So in 60 minutes he failed to pull her trousers down, touched her vagina four or five times and squeezed a breast? It was incredible the police officer interviewing her never queried this time span. And did it never occur to the claimant to shout for help during the "hour" she was being attacked?

The defence highlighted so many contradictions in what she had initially told the police and then the jury that whatever it may have thought of Charter, a not guilty verdict was no surprise on the evidence it had heard.

The defence easily knocked down Miss T's version of events. Rather than be seen to be uncaring to a "victim" the Crown Prosecution Service went ahead with a trial and allowed a claimant with, at times, barely credible evidence, to take her allegations to a Crown Court.

As much as the jury may have disliked the defendant it was not swayed by his past and correctly judged the case only on the evidence heard in court.

35

MOHAMMED HASHEEM: Sexual grooming

INTERNET INTERCEPTORS
INTERCEPTED

MOHAMMED HASHEEM joined a web site to meet a girlfriend. On the face of it, there is nothing wrong with this, except that the "girl" in question he made advances to was 12-years-old.

Hasheem was charged with attempting to meet a child following sexual grooming, having connected with "Gilly" and attempting to meet "Gilly" not reasonably believing she was aged 16 or over and commissioning sexual activity with a child under 13 years.

The inverted commas are because Gilly did not exist. She was a fictitious girl whose profile was put on the web site by self-styled Internet Interceptors, a dedicated team of parents hunting paedophiles and sexual predators across the UK.

Sarah Doherty, a housewife, placed a photo of "Gilly" on a friendship web site to ensnare men (or women) to meet her. The photo was of a young white female with a caption: "aged 18 from UK."

Hasheem replied to "Gilly" and after exchanging messages the pair arranged to meet near a hotel in London. Instead of meeting "Gilly", Hasheem was greeted by Doherty and a male companion.

THE FIRST witness to give evidence was Sarah Doherty who described herself as a "self-motivated paedophile hunter."

What, the prosecution asked, was her motivation?

"To protect children, to see if any men or women spoke to a child with a view to grooming."

"What profile of 'Gilly' did you put up?"

"18, female, UK."

The photograph of "Gilly" was a 12-year-old girl which was shown to the jury.

"On February 25 there was the first communication from Mohammad Hasheem."

"Correct."

"You kept all the conversations and chatlogs."

"Yes."

The details of Hasheem's exchanges with "Gilly" over a period of a week were read to the jury. Hasheem is from Afghanistan and an interpreter sat next to him in the dock.

They started: "Hey dear, can you be my gf?"

"Not know you."

"You can know me and ask anything, where do you live baby?"

"UK."

"Where?"

"London."

"So do I."

"OMG, I'm 12."

"You just 12? OMG, thought you were 18. My name is Malik."

"What work you do?"

"I'm a butcher, I'm 29."

"OMG, dead meat."

"What do you do?"

"Go to school."

"You have bf?"

"Never had one."

"You will be my gf."

"But I'm only 12 LOL. How do I be a gf?"

"We can meet sometime."

"OK, when you thinking of?"

"Tomorrow."

"Have school. Saturday?"

"OK darling. How do I know you are real? You not got a better picture?"

"How long you been in UK? Your English not that good."

"Eight years, from Afghanistan."

"Does my age not bother you?"

"Up to you."

"What would we do?"

"Shopping, kissing."

"Never kissed before."

"I'll show you how."

"Not know how to kiss."

"I'll teach you, just lips to lips."

The next day.

"Hey good evening."

"Hi."

"HRU [how are you] sweetheart?"

"School was OK. Not feel well, can we meet next week?"

"Tuesday. Cinema, sex, shopping…"

"Never done sex."

"You can do it with me."

"Really? Not sure, what about age?"

"If you're not 18 I'll wait until you are 18."

The next day.

"Hey my love, hi. What you up to?"

"Just homework. We meeting Tuesday?"

"Yes. Are you a virgin?"

"Yes."

"So you like I get virginity and no more a virgin. Are you like to sleep with me?"

"Will it hurt?"

"First time it hurt."

"Where meet?"

"Hotel."

"OK."

MOHAMMED HASHEEM went to meet "Gilly." With him he had a rucksack containing Viagra pills, five condoms, 11 silk lubricant sachets and a sex-prolonging delay spray.

Instead, he was confronted by Sarah Doherty and Peter Roswell. The latter wore a body-cam to record what happened which was played to the jury. And what happened was Roswell said to Hasheem: "You're here to meet a 12-year-old girl, Gilly. You could be arrested for this."

"I apologise."

"You know it's wrong. You were going to take a 12-year-old girl to a hotel for sex."

"I said if under 18 I would not touch her."

"I have all the evidence. You know she's 12."

Hasheem said: "I feel guilty. It was a big mistake. Please give me one more chance. I will never do anything like this again."

He also claimed he had not planned to have sex with the girl and said: "I am a Muslim, I never lie."

AT THIS POINT in the trial the defence objected to the video evidence the jury had seen. When a suspect is arrested by the police an officer will read a caution: "You do not have to say anything. But it may harm your defence if you do not mention, when questioned, something which you later rely on in court. Anything you do say may be given in evidence."

Which was a world apart from the Internet Interceptors' approach. Mohammed Hasheem had said things to the Internet Interceptors he would not necessarily have said to the police.

The judge agreed with the defence, dismissed the jury and ordered a retrial.

THE SECOND trial was held at a different Crown Court where the jury heard much of the same evidence as the initial jurors had, apart from not watching the Internet Interceptors' video.

The defence never had the easiest of tasks, but told the jury about the problems with entrapment.

"It may not fall into entrapment if [Internet Interceptors] are just in a chat room and are waiting for somebody to contact them. The problem is, when they start to entice somebody with [paedophilic] tendencies, then that becomes an entrapment," said the defence barrister.

Entrapment isn't a criminal offence, although it can form part of the defence made by a suspect's lawyer.

"Their responses were tempting [the defendant] to express intentions to go further than he is expressing an interest in doing."

What would the jury decide about the way the Internet Interceptors obtained the evidence against Mohammed Hasheem which saw the police arrest the defendant?

35

MOHAMMED HASHEEM: Sexual grooming

"I AM a Muslim, I never lie," Mohammed Hasheem had told the jury.

Really? He had told "Gilly" he was from Afghanistan when in fact he came to Britain from Pakistan eight years previously. There was a clue about his nationality when he asked for an Urdu translator in court. Urdu is the official language of Pakistan. Afghanistan's two official languages are Dari and Pashto.

Hasheem was found guilty of attempting to meet a child following sexual grooming and was sentenced to 18 months in prison while he will be on the Sex Offenders Register for life. No one could doubt the defendant's ambitions were despicable, yet there was still uneasiness about the manner in which Hasheem was coerced and captured.

However well-intentioned the motives of what is, effectively, a vigilante group may be, the police remain uncomfortable with anybody persuading someone to commit a crime.

A spokesperson for the Metropolitan Police Service said: "The MPS does not support activities by individuals to target suspected paedophiles. This type of action could jeopardise or interfere with ongoing investigations. Our advice to anyone who has information about suspected child sexual abuse — online or otherwise — is to contact the police so we can investigate and, where possible, bring people to justice.

"Revealing the identity of a potential suspect could give them the opportunity to destroy evidence before police become involved. It could also lead to individuals taking action in an attempt to evade police.

"This can divert significant policing resources which would be better invested in investigating and, where there is evidence, prosecuting individuals. Most importantly, those undertaking this type of activity cannot fully assess any risk associated to victims and their families."

Chief Superintendent Tom Richards, head of Kent Police's Public

Protection Unit, said: "We do have significant concerns about people taking the law into their own hands and the methods they use, and in some cases acting outside of the law. We would strongly advise against getting involved in, or setting up activities to entrap those suspected of intending to commit offences.

"Although seemingly well-meaning, this can significantly hinder our work, compromise on-going investigations and negate months of investigative work. There is also the risk that it can potentially identify people who are completely innocent and mistakenly associate them with grooming offences."

THIS has not deterred the vigilante groups who continue to trap would-be paedophiles before handing them over to the police who cannot become involved in entrapment. It is considered to be an abuse of court process for agents of the state to lure citizens into committing illegal acts and then seek to prosecute them for doing so.

In July 1992, Rachel Nickell was killed on Wimbledon Common. The police believed Colin Stagg, an unemployed man who walked his dog on the common, was the leading suspect. "Lizzie James", an undercover policewoman from the Metropolitan Police's Special Operations Group, befriended Stagg and over a period of five months she attempted to obtain information from him by feigning a romantic interest.

In August 1993 the Crown Prosecution Service believed there was sufficient evidence for Stagg to be charged with Nickell's murder. When the case reached the Old Bailey, Mr Justice Ognall ruled that the police had shown "excessive zeal" and had tried to incriminate a suspect by "deceptive conduct of the grossest kind".

He excluded the entrapment evidence and the prosecution withdrew its case. It was estimated the pursuit of Stagg had cost the Metropolitan Police Service £3 million. "Lizzie James" quit the police force in 1998, eventually taking early retirement. With the support of the Police Federation, she sued the Metropolitan Police for damages arising from the "honeytrap" investigation. In 2001, shortly before it was due to be heard, her case was settled out of court and she received £125,000.

In August 2008 Stagg was awarded £706,000 compensation. Four months later Robert Napper pleaded guilty to Nickell's manslaughter on the grounds of diminished responsibility.

36

FRANCIS SAMUEL: Six counts of rape against a child under 13; five counts of sexual assault against a child under 13; three counts of incitement against a child under 13

WOULD MOTHER'S COURT
DOCUMENT HELP DEFENDANT?

CHILD B hoped it would not happen again so she did not say anything to her mother even though she had promised to tell her if her private parts were touched by anyone. But according to the 10-year-old, Francis Samuel, her mother's partner and effectively her stepfather, assaulted her over and over again.

Opening the case, the Crown said that eventually Child B wrote a note to her mother about what had happened to her. The mother reported the allegations to the police and Samuel was charged with six counts of rape against a child under 13, penetrating her mouth and anus with his penis; plus, five counts of sexual assault against a child under 13; sexual touching and three counts of incitement of a child under 13.

The prosecution told the jury Samuel had a preference for anal sex which was to form a significant, if uncomfortable, part of the trial.

Melanie (name changed for legal reasons), the mother of Child B, was the partner of the defendant and had changed her name to Samuel though, she said, they did not live together at the time of the alleged offences. The claimant thought of the defendant as "dad" and loved him. Her mother was a security guard and when she worked weekends Samuel would come over to look after Child B who alleged Samuel constantly assaulted her in the bedroom of her "parents" even when her mother was present on one occasion.

THE JURY watched Child B's police interview in which she gave explicit details of the allegations against the defendant.

Among the accusations were that "I had to kiss his doo-dar [penis]… he kissed my hoo-har [vagina]… he put his doo-dar in my bottom. He said he did it to my mum because it would help her lose weight and make going to the toilet easier. He told me it would do the same and would put Vaseline on it [his penis] before he put it in me. It was, like, gooey. I did not want to damage the relationship he had with my mum because I know she loved him. I looked up to him and loved him a lot. At first, I thought it was fun, but then I realised it was weird."

On one occasion Child B claimed she was assaulted while she was in bed with her mother and the defendant as they watched a movie. "Dad was in the centre and I was, like, on the edge. I was wearing a nightie and had nothing underneath. He put his hand on my mini. Mum did not see it as she was falling asleep."

She added: "He kept promising he would not do it again, but he never kept them [the promises]. I tried to sort it out myself, believing every time would be the last time. In the end I had to tell my mum."

When she did, her mother took her daughter to the police station the next day. Francis Samuel was arrested and, the Crown said "completely denied any sexual contact" and that the allegations were "complete and total fabrication."

The prosecution added: "He told the police he used Vaseline with his partner, but had not told the claimant about this. How would the claimant have known about the Vaseline if he had not told her?"

CHILD B was too young to appear in court so she was cross-examined via video-link. The age of the claimant and the nature of the offences presented a challenge to the defence who, while working on behalf of the accused, had to adopt a more softly-softly approach than with an adult witness to effectively attempt to discredit the claimant's evidence.

To help Child B feel more comfortable, the judge and barristers did not wear wigs or gowns as the cross-examination began.

The defence asked her if her mum was her best friend.

"Yes."

"You like being together."

"Yes."

310

"Last year mum and Francis were engaged."

"Yes."

"Did you want them to marry?"

"Yes."

"Your mum taught you about your body."

"Yes."

"Which bits are private."

"Yes."

"Mum said no one should touch your private parts."

"Yes."

"Did she say if anyone did then you must tell her?"

"Yes."

"How many times did she say this?"

"Every time we are alone."

"What did you say?"

"No one's touched me — I'll be careful."

"Did she ever ask if dad touched you?"

"No."

"Did mum buy any treats for Francis?"

"Chocolates and clothes."

"Were you a bit jealous of Francis?"

"No."

"Did you want to get rid of him?"

"No."

"Did you want mum to yourself?"

"No, because I could see she was happy."

"Did mum tell you to say he only stayed weekends?"

"No."

"He was there every day, wasn't he?"

"No."

"Did he ever stay in the week?"

"No."

"Nan looked after you in the week."

"Wednesday nights."

"Francis never kissed your private parts, did he?"

"Yes, he did."

"You've never touched his willy."

"I have."

"He never put it in your mouth."

"He did."

"Or in your bottom."

"He did."

"Did it go inside the hole or just between your cheeks?"

"In the hole where you poo from."

"In what position were your legs?"

"A V-shape."

"Was there ever any blood on the bed?"

"No."

"On your bottom?"

"No."

"Was it painful?"

"Just gooey."

"Have you made everything up about Francis?"

"No."

MELANIE FISHER [name changed to protect identity of her daughter], Child B's mother, was asked by the prosecution if she had reverted to her original name.

"Yes."

"How long had you and Francis been together?"

"Five years."

"Were there plans to marry?"

"There were. We were engaged."

"Did you ever live together?"

"Two years ago, until I moved for work purposes."

"Who looked after your daughter on Wednesday nights when you worked?"

"My mother."

"What was your relationship like with Francis?"

"At the time I thought it was OK."

"You were sexually active."

"Yes."

"Any preference?"

"Anal sex."

"Anything used?"

"No."

"Did you notice any difference in Francis's relationship with your daughter?"

"No."

"Did she have any medical problems?"

"A couple of years ago she had constipation, but some powder sorted that out."

"Was there a time when she said Francis did something?"

"Yes. She said he'd touched her mini in my bedroom."

"Where were you?"

"In the bedroom with her."

"What did you say?"

"I asked her if she wanted me to say something, but she said 'no'."

"As a result of that what did you do?"

"I would regularly ask her if Francis had touched her or vice versa."

"What about the letter?"

"I thought it was going to be something like 'I love you mum.' After I read it I went into the bathroom. When I came back, I asked Francis how he could do this... how he could have hurt my child I thought. I could trust him. He just said it wasn't true and she was lying."

"Where was your daughter at the time?"

"In the bedroom with us."

The following day the police were shown the letter and Francis was arrested.

THE DEFENCE asked Melanie Fisher if she would describe herself as a very protective mother.

"I would."

"Is that because of something that had happened to you?"

"Yes. I was sexually abused as a child."

"The occasion all three of you were play-fighting in bed — were you all fully dressed?"

"Yes."

"Your daughter said Francis touching her might be a mistake."

"Yes."

"Did you make her promise to tell you if anything happened again?"

"Yes."

"Initially you and Francis had regular vaginal sex."

"Yes."

"Sadly, you developed thrush."

"Yes."

"He had a rash on his genital area."

"Yes."

"You told him you had Googled anal sex."

"No."

"Initially he refused."

"No."

"Ultimately he agreed."

"It was his suggestion."

Ms Fisher was asked about when she applied for Francis Samuel to have parental responsibility for her daughter.

"He could not have that without a court order."

"No."

"You gave a statement about Francis's relationship with your daughter."

"Yes."

"When was this?"

"Can't remember."

"Did you tell the [county] court that Francis was not living with you?"

"I can't remember if I said we were living together. Whatever I wrote was what Francis told me to write."

"You told the police he was not living with you."

"Yes."

"In fact, he was living with you seven days a week."

"No, he wasn't."

IT WAS confirmed that Melanie Fisher did, in fact, say on the parental responsibility application that Francis Samuel was living with her. The gas and electricity at the property were in the defendant's name.

The jury was told Samuel was a man of good character with no convictions or criminal record of any sort. When arrested his two mobile phones were examined by the police and no untoward texts or photographs were found. Francis's clothes were seized and tested while swabs from his mouth, nails and penis were sent for DNA analysis. There was nothing of any forensic nature to indicate anything of a sexual nature with Child B.

The police checked the address where Ms Fisher claimed Francis was living during the week and it was confirmed a Polish family had occupied the property for the last four and a half years.

FRANCIS SAMUEL denied all of Child B's allegations when cross-examined.

The defence asked him: "Who were you living with at the time of your arrest?"

"Melanie and her daughter."

"What was your relationship like with them?"

"Fantastic. Good."

"Did you work?"

"No. I home-schooled [said Child B's name] mathematics."

"How did you get along with her?"

"Fine. I got on with all the family."

"Do you have any idea why she might have made the allegations?"

"No."

"She said you did not stay at the house during the week."

"Not true. I did."

"She said you anally raped her."

"No."

"Have you ever made her hold your penis?"

"No."

"Put it in her mouth?"

"No."

"Kissed her vagina?"

"No."

"Bathed with her?"

"No."

"Touched her private parts?"

"No."

"Told her that anal sex could help her lose weight and make going to the toilet easier?"

"No."

"Kissed her on the lips?"

"No."

"Has she ever seen you naked?"

"No."

"Have you ever put cream on your penis?"

"With her mum, but not always."

"For anal sex?"

"Yes."

"Did her daughter ever use it?"

"For a scratch or a rash maybe."

THE EDUCATION Act states parents are responsible for ensuring that their children receive an education suitable for their age, ability and aptitude. No particular qualifications are needed to home-school a child; you do not have to conform to the National Curriculum; children are not required to take examinations or SATs.

IN ITS summing up the Crown concentrated on the Vaseline that Child B said Francis Samuel used while raping her.

"We say the claimant was isolated and vulnerable. She was home-schooled so had no school-friends while her biological father had no interest. The only two people she really had were her mother and the defendant who she looked up to and called dad.

"Would she have fabricated lies which meant he would be out of her life? Why would she do it? Could she have made it all up? How else could she have known about this unless she had witnessed it or been a victim of it?

"That she said he didn't live with them has no bearing on what went on. Her mother said he wanted parental responsibility to help with his immigration status. Have they really put their heads together about where he lived? The lies about the County Court are just a smokescreen.

"The claimant gave details in the innocent way a child would. She spoke about him telling her that anal sex would help her weight and going to the toilet. Are these words made up? When she spoke about his penis being small and then being long and hard — they are the words of a child.

"The defendant used his position of trust to sexually abuse her and

316

you can be sure he is guilty of every indictment."

THE DEFENCE asked the jury to decide whether the lies about the defendant living with the mother and daughter meant other evidence was questionable. The jury was told parental responsibility had no direct bearing on immigration status

"Start your assessment with something that may hold the key. If the defendant is correct and lived with them full-time the consequences flow from that. If he is correct then you have to ask why his partner did not tell the police the truth and she got her daughter to join her?

"You have to approach everything else they said with caution. The defendant gave a very different story about the document — the mother said he only lived there, weekends. When asked, she said 'I can't remember' and 'he made me lie' while her final version was 'he lived there four days a week.'

"If he did only live there two days a week, why would you agree to parental responsibility? If she got her daughter not to tell the truth about where he lived, what else might she have told her to say? Why, if he was there all the week, would he only abuse the child at the weekend? She never once mentioned pain with the anal sex. Would it not have hurt a child?

"There was nothing on his phones, no DNA linking him to the claimant. You may think something about this case is not right and you have to be sure to find him guilty."

THERE WAS MUCH for the jury to consider from both the prosecution and the defence. It would have to deliberate why the claimant might have made up such stories against a man she said she loved. And why, having promised her mother she would tell her if the defendant touched her inappropriately, did she leave it until the 14th alleged incident before informing her?

The judge told the jury it must consider each count separately and each required its own verdict. He said: "You must avoid any emotional response and do not speculate on anything. The defendant has no criminal record which does not mean he did not commit the offences, but it is something you should take into account."

The jury was instructed that if it was not sure the defendant's penis, by any degree, however slight, had not penetrated the claimant's anal passage the defendant could be found guilty of attempted rape if it was thought the activity was intended to be more than just between her buttocks.

A trial that was initially estimated to last three to four days went into its 10th day before the jury finally delivered its verdict.

36

FRANCIS SAMUEL: Six counts of rape against a child under 13; five counts of sexual assault against a child under 13; three counts of incitement

CHILD B was 10 when she gave her evidence about a subject no one of such tender years should have to speak about in private, let alone in a Crown Court.

There was, on the face of it, no reason for her to lie about Francis Samuel who she referred to as her dad. But a jury has to be sure, beyond all reasonable doubt, that a defendant is guilty of the charges. If there is any doubt in a juror's mind, they must not return a guilty verdict. And if just three jurors have doubts, even a majority verdict is impossible.

It can take only one piece of dubious evidence to raise questions in a jury's collective mind and in Samuel's case there were several. Firstly, where was the defendant living at the time of the allegations? Melanie Fisher had either lied to a County Court on the parental responsibility application or to the police and jury about where Samuel resided. Child B had also said in evidence the defendant stayed only at weekends, which contrasted with the full-time details given to the County Court by her mother.

If the jury accepted the County Court evidence and that Samuel lived with mother and daughter all the time, why would he have assaulted Child B only at weekends? A paedophile's vile habits are not confined to Saturday and Sunday.

After a fourth day of deliberation the foreman told the judge there was no chance of an 11–1 or a 10–2 majority verdict, so with a hung jury a retrial was ordered for three months later. This meant, because of the seriousness of the charges, Samuel would have been in prison on remand for eight months as the case against him went into extra-time.

A retrial usually favours the defendant as their barrister has heard the prosecution's case — in football terms it can be easier to defend against a team when you know its tactics.

The retrial proved to be more of the same, but both the prosecution and defence were quick to highlight any perceived inconsistencies in what the mother and defendant had said this time compared with the first trial. In the retrial Melanie Fisher's mother took to the witness stand and was questioned by the defence who it was who had asked her to appear.

"The police," she replied, but under cross-examination it was clear her daughter had asked her to confirm she had looked after her granddaughter every Wednesday.

"So it would be impossible for your granddaughter to mistake you for Francis Samuel," said the defence.

"Yes."

"You were there every single Wednesday for a five-month period."

"Yes."

"Alone?"

"Sometimes my husband came with me."

Melanie Fisher was asked more details about the County Court document and subsequent parental responsibility hearing. She said that Francis Samuel was not at the hearing even though the evidence by the district judge said that he was.

"So the judge is lying?" asked the defence.

"Yes."

FRANCIS SAMUEL was asked some new questions by his barrister at the retrial.

"Homosexuality... sex between two men or two women... is not allowed in Nigeria [his birthplace]. Correct?"

"No, not allowed."

"Anal sex?"

"I do not practise this. It is not allowed."

"Did you ever have anal sex before Melanie?"

"No."

"Ever want to?"

"No."

"But you tried it once [when she had thrush]."

"Yes. I didn't want to, but she did not accept this and because she was not happy, I decided to try. She said it was so painful I stopped doing it. It was the first and last time."

THE DEFENCE ended its evidence with its trump card which was not "played" at the original trial — a letter from Dr David Clark who had acted in 400 sexual assault trials, 50 involving children. Dr Clark's view was that as Child B weighed 90kg (14 stones) she was "grossly obese for a child of her age and height." The level of obesity made it "almost impossible" to have anal sex in the way Child B had described with her legs in a V-shape "as the defendant would have needed to use both hands to support her buttocks."

The doctor was wary of the claimant's view she did not suffer pain because "the penetration of a penis would induce extension of the anus and anal cord" and the "insertion of an adult penis on 10 or 20 occasions" without pain was "surprising." He concluded: "There was no sign of forced anal intercourse and no reliable corroboration between the allegations and the evidence."

Game, set and match. Or was it?

THE Crown Prosecution Service had charged Francis Samuel on the evidence of a 10-year-old child. The allegations were damning, but there was no medical, forensic evidence or indeed any evidence to back up Child B's accusations. The charges were made on the word of a child who had been home-schooled for two years and was obese.

Perhaps these considerations should be irrelevant, but they formed part of a scenario that was worrying with a growing feeling that something significant had not been revealed. Accepting that it would be difficult for the CPS not to charge someone given the seriousness of the allegations, it should only do so if it believes that with the evidence available there is a good chance of a conviction. Of course, this is subjective, but with nothing to back up the prosecution's case apart from Child B's evidence the odds were always stacked against the Crown.

For the retrial, Dr Clark's assertion that there was no sign of forced anal intercourse and no reliable corroboration between the allegations and evidence made it virtually impossible for the jury to be sure Samuel had committed the anal rape crimes he had been accused of.

The jury had deliberated for over 10 hours when the foreman

delivered its verdicts. It found Samuel not guilty of the charges of rape, but the foreman told the judge there was no realistic chance of even a majority verdict regarding the lesser charges, so effectively a second hung jury. There could be no third trial so after eight months in custody Samuel was a free man again.

37

FAH AROMDEE: Conspiracy to smuggle a mobile phone into prison

A KILLER FRIEND... A PHONE...
AND A HUSBAND IN PRISON

THIS SHORT TRIAL was a painstaking exercise in persistence for the prosecutor as he cross-examined the female Thai defendant who spoke through an interpreter. Every question and answer had to be translated, a process that is guaranteed to test patience at the best of times.

Fah Aromdee either genuinely did not understand some questions or tried her best to be evasive, hiding behind the language barrier with some answers incomprehensible. It was the legal equivalent of pulling teeth.

While the trial lasted only one morning, much of it comprised the prosecutor asking Fah the same question over and over again in an effort to get a direct answer. He would admit, no doubt, that he failed more times than he succeeded. There were no witnesses and the defendant was the only person called to the witness box.

Fah's British husband, Robert, was being held in custody for reasons the jury was not told. His friend, John Frizell, who had been given an eight-and-a-half-year sentence for culpable homicide [manslaughter] in Scotland six years previously, wanted to help Robert by arranging for a mobile phone and charger to be smuggled into jail. While it was accepted Fah did not go through with this offence, she was charged with conspiracy to arrange for a prohibited article, namely a mobile phone and charger, to be taken into prison.

Various texts and WhatsApp exchanges were given to the jury which had to decide whether Fah was simply going along with a person who had killed because she feared for her safety, or was she complicit in the potential crime?

FAH AROMDEE had been married to Robert for 10 years and spoke good, though apparently not good enough English for court purposes. The time-consuming translation must have been borderline painful for the jury as the defence began its cross-examination of the defendant.

"When Mr Frizell was sending messages to Robert in prison, you knew."

"Yes."

"Would you have liked to help Robert if you could?"

"Only in how he was feeling."

"If he asked you to do something, would you?"

"If I could."

"You knew you could speak to him on a prison phone."

"Yes."

"You did so."

"Every day."

"He said you must be careful as conversations are recorded."

"Yes."

"Were you aware Robert wanted a phone of his own?"

"Not know."

"Mr Frizell was messaging Robert. What phone did you think Robert was using?"

"John told me he gave a phone to Robert."

"You messaged John to say he will appreciate what I do for you LOL. Who is LOL?"

"It means lots of love."

"Phone language…" responded the barrister with a smile before resuming his cross-examination. "You knew Mr Frizell had killed someone."

"Yes, Robert informed me."

Fah told the jury that Frizell had threatened her with violence and that "I was on my own and did not know what to do." She claimed Frizell wanted her to pay half with a payment for a mobile phone, which she refused. Frizell came to her house, she said, but she would not answer the door so he put a mobile phone, which was in a box, through her letterbox.

THE PROSECUTOR cross-examined Fah Aromdee, though the Crown's barrister could have had little idea this would be so challenging.

"You had an exchange on WhatsApp with Mr Frizell. Did you understand what he wrote in English?"

"Not fully."

"You knew he had killed someone?"

"Yes."

"What did you mean when you said: 'I was scared of him, I did not want to follow what he wanted to do?' Did he threaten you with violence?"

"Yes."

"How did he threaten you?"

"He started to throw stones at my windows and poisoned my dog."

"What violence did he threaten you with?"

"He shouted at me with attitude and body language."

"You said: 'He threatened me with violence.' Or did you mean duress where you are in danger of physical force?"

"I was on my own and did not know what to do."

"What did he threaten you with?"

"I told him I did not want to do what he wanted to do."

"You have not said if he threatened you with violence."

"I was alone in the house."

"Did you not think you were in any physical danger?"

"I did think that he would hurt me."

"But he never did."

"No."

"Why not say at the start that you did not want to do anything illegal?"

"I did not want to get involved."

"On WhatsApp you agreed to do something. What was the something?"

"I understood what John wanted me to do."

"Mr Frizell wanted to help Robert. What was he talking about?"

"He wanted to help Robert, but me as well."

"Mr Frizell sent you a photo of a phone. Why do you think he did this?"

"I have no idea."

"You said: 'The phone is too small.' Why did you say that?"

"No idea."

"Who bought the phone?"

"John. I had no idea about it."

"Why did he tell you?"

"He wanted me to pay half, but I refused."

"What was it for and who?"

"He said he bought it for Robert."

"The next thing you knew it came through your letterbox."

"Yes."

"Did you open the box?"

"No."

"Did you guess what was in the box? What else did you think it could be?"

"I did not want to think about it."

"But it came through your door. You must have thought about what was in it."

"John said he was sending a phone."

"You gave it to a neighbour."

"Yes."

"Why?"

"I did not want to be involved with John, so thought it best to give to a neighbour."

"You gave it to a neighbour because he asked you to."

"He threatened me, said he'd follow me if I didn't do it."

"Mr Frizell told you on WhatsApp: 'Tell him to make sure the phone is between his cheeks, especially before opening time in the morning.' What did you think that meant?"

"I did not understand."

"What are cheeks?"

Defendant pointed to her face.

"Buttocks?"

Defendant pointed her bottom.

"You told Mr Frizell: 'His [Robert's] phone was off.' What did you mean?"

"He could not use it."

"How did you know he'd got a phone?"

"John told me."

"You knew the number."

"John gave it to me."

"Mr Frizell texted you: 'It's only a bit of cable and you won't get caught anyway.' What did that mean?"

"I did not know what to do."

"During the week you were certainly helping Mr Frizell to get the phone to your husband."

"I did not want to help him. I wanted him to leave me alone. I didn't want any trouble."

The defendant said she was driven to the prison by Frizell, but when she got out of the car, she put the phone and charger in a rubbish bin.

FAH AROMDEE went to a police station to report John Frizell. She was asked to leave her mobile phone which was examined. At 04.30 the following morning she was arrested and taken in for questioning regarding conspiracy. On the advice of her solicitor Fah gave a "no comment" interview.

The prosecutor, clearly becoming exasperated, resumed: "Why did you not tell the police you did not intend to help Mr Frizell?"

"I was confused."

"What were you confused about?"

"I did not understand it. I was scared."

"What were you scared of? Did you think the police were going to beat you up? A punch from someone?"

"I asked for help and I was arrested."

"You were accused of trying to get a phone into prison and if innocent why did you not tell the police your story?"

"My lawyer advised me."

"He made it clear it would be your decision."

"I was confused and followed his instruction."

"It was not an instruction, only advice."

"I do not understand."

"Are you seriously saying you did not understand you were helping John Frizell get a phone to your husband in prison?"

"I said I didn't."

"You replied 'no comment' to every question."

"I said 'no comment' after I said I didn't do it."

"Are you pretending to be confused? I'm suggesting you are deliberately trying not to understand. You were told the [police] interview would be recorded and you were asked a lot of questions. You replied 'no comment' to every single one. Would it not have been better to explain your story at the time instead of to a jury?"

"I did not do anything wrong."

If the prosecutor could have thrown in a legal towel he would have done so.

HAVING cross-examined Fah Aromdee, the next step was for the Crown to deliver its closing speech. The prosecutor told the jury: "What her husband may have done is irrelevant and standing by your man may illicit a certain sympathy. A natural reaction is to ask if you would really want to punish this woman.

"Every person in the country is subject to law and if you believe she agreed [to help smuggle the phone into prison] you must not avoid the responsibility of finding her guilty. Her story just does not make sense. It's a very sad case, but she reluctantly agreed to the smuggling of a phone even if this was not completed."

THE DEFENCE said: "To be guilty of conspiracy she must join in the agreement and intend for this to be carried out even if it isn't. She wasn't intending to do anything criminal. She was trying to manage the situation carefully. If she was going to commit a crime, why would she have reported John Frizell, a man capable of killing, to the police? She wanted support and help, instead she was arrested at half past four in the morning. She did her best not to be sucked into the agenda of Mr Frizell."

THE JUDGE told the jury that John Frizell had pleaded guilty to the conspiracy charge, but this was "irrelevant" in their deliberations.

Compared to most trials, where there are witnesses for the prosecution and defence, the jury had relatively little to discuss — the evidence of just one person. Was the defendant going along with Frizell because she was afraid of what might happen to her? Or was she serious, but changed her mind at the last minute which would make her guilty?

37

FAH AROMDEE: Conspiracy to smuggle a mobile phone into prison

HAD the jury known more about John Frizell the deliberations may have been shorter than the two hours it took to reach its verdict. His "previous" would be enough to frighten anybody. He had been handed an eight-and-a-half-year sentence for the "pointless" knife killing of a father-of-three after a press-ups contest in Aberdeen.

He was involved in what was described as "macho banter" and press-ups which turned into a fight with Ian Wilson, 48. Frizell was originally charged with murder, but admitted culpable homicide [manslaughter].

The court heard both men took part in a press-ups contest, but a confrontation broke out and punches were thrown. Frizell picked up a knife and stabbed Wilson in the chest. The judge in the Scottish court said that Frizell had "a lengthy and significant criminal record" which included convictions for possessing an offensive weapon and drugs. He was previously jailed for three months for assaulting the then deputy chief constable of Grampian Police, Pat Shearer, by slamming a car door on his leg in 2005.

Being in possession of a mobile phone in jail is not a new scenario for Frizell. While he was serving his sentence for culpable homicide, Frizell was caught with a mobile after becoming so drunk on prison hooch he left it on and it rang out loud. It was claimed he was so drunk he couldn't find the phone when it started to ring.

The jury in the Fah Aromdee trial knew no details of Frizell's culpable homicide conviction, only that he had killed someone which, of course, is enough to make any right-minded person wary. Fah was not the easiest of defendants to understand in many ways; the majority of her replies — non-answers may be more appropriate — seemed vague, to say the least.

The fact that she did not smuggle the phone and charger into prison did not matter. It was whether she had pulled out at the last minute after having intended to commit the crime or was she was just stringing Frizell along because she was afraid of a violent man.

Given that he was a killer, regardless of the details and what he did subsequently it was difficult for the jury to ignore Frizell's past and Fah was given the benefit of the doubt and it found her not guilty.

38

CHILD J: Theft; two counts of unlawful wounding; two counts of wounding with intent

CHILD A: Two counts of unlawful wounding; two counts of wounding with intent

'AT THE END OF THE DAY PEOPLE GET STABBED UP'

WHEN David Barlow popped into a cycle shop in south-east London, he had no idea what the visit would trigger. His Cipolini bike, worth almost £10,000, was stolen and two men who worked in the shop were stabbed in a violent attack lasting a turbulent 10 seconds after seeing the thief in a nearby park.

The jury was given a crash course in urban street slang and text-speak, neither of which bore any resemblance to the English language as most know it.

All those involved in the assault were aged 14 at the time. Given some of the evidence heard and the way it was presented, no doubt jurors had to continually remind themselves of the defendants' age.

IN LAW you do not actually have to commit the crime to still be culpable. If someone holds the ladder while their accomplice breaks into a property both are guilty of burglary. It is called a joint-enterprise and both are charged with the same offence.

When Simon Jackson and Zbigniew Gorgon were stabbed by Child G, it was deemed that Child J and Child A were also guilty of malicious wounding — grievous bodily harm with intent — because they were part of the gang, according to the Crown. Child G had previously pleaded guilty to the offence, but Child J and Child A pleaded not guilty. Child G also pleaded guilty to theft [of the bike].

DAVID BARLOW had cycled to a cycle shop one Sunday afternoon. There were fellow cyclists sitting outside drinking coffee so he did not lock his Cipolini when he went inside to buy a helmet.

Before he had even tried on the helmet two or three people who worked in the shop, including Zbigniew Gorgon, ran outside because they were aware a male had taken the bike and was riding away. Together with Barlow, they started to give chase, but inevitably the bike, worth between £8,000 and £9,000, gave its rider a huge advantage. They immediately notified the police.

When the shop closed, Gorgon cycled to a nearby park to enjoy the late evening sunshine. Walking his bike through the park he saw a group of four teenagers, one with a bike which he recognised as the stolen Cipolini.

Gorgon remarked that it was "a nice bike" and one of the males asked him if he wanted to buy it for £500. Finding himself in an unexpectedly awkward situation, Gorgon said he only had £300 on him, but would phone someone he knew for the rest. Gorgon called Simon Jackson who worked with him in the shop and lived nearby. After what Jackson thought was an unusual, to say the least, conversation he joined his colleague in the park to find out what was going on and immediately recognised the distinctive Cipolini.

According to Gorgon, he told Jackson he was phoning the police which resulted in a brief but violent assault on the two men by Child G who stabbed the Pole four times and Jackson once. Gorgon suffered internal bleeding and underwent significant emergency surgery. He was in hospital for eight days. Jackson's single injury was a 4cm wound to his chest which resulted in a partially collapsed lung. He was in hospital for three days.

The police arrested Child A later that evening. She was dressed in distinctive camouflage clothing with blood stains and holding a hospital crutch which, it was said, was a fashion accessory. Child G handed himself in to a police station the following day and Child J was arrested a day later. The fourth teenager in the group was not charged as she was deemed not to have played any role in the attacks.

Child J was charged with theft [of the cycle]. He and Child A were each charged with unlawful wounding and wounding with intent. It would be up to the jury to decide if they believed the intention was to cause really serious injury to Gorgon and Jackson.

OPENING the case, the Crown said that Child G and Child J plotted the theft the day before the incident with WhatsApp messages between the pair who used their street names and text abbreviated language.

Snaps (Child J): "Yo get at me ASAP real — got the bolt-cutters."

Smokes (Child G): "Cool man."

After the knifing incident Snaps messaged Smokes: "Girls been bagged [arrested]. Need to get stories sorted, let's go no comment."

Smokes: "They went too far, if I see 'em [them] be on life support. SC [stay cool]. SN [say nothing], GYS [get yourself sorted]."

When interviewed by the police Child J answered "no comment" to every question.

SIMON JACKSON told the jury he was telephoned sometime after six [in the evening] by Zbigniew Gorgon who was in the park.

He said: "I live nearby so I walked there. I saw a couple of bikes leaning against a tree. One belonged to Zbigniew, the other I had seen earlier. Four people were there."

The Crown asked Jackson what happened.

"There was a brief conversation with Zbigniew about the bike that had been stolen from the shop. I said we should call the police. The look on their faces changed as if to say, there's no need to do that. One of the males kicked Zbigniew from behind and he half-collapsed."

"Then?"

"I moved towards the person who'd kicked him, he punched me and I punched him. I felt some pulling on my arms and jacket."

"Did the second male strike you?"

"Not as I'd expected. I thought I'd be punched in the face, but I felt a push to my chest."

"How did it come to a halt?"

"A female hit me over the head with a crutch. They then all left. I grabbed the stolen bike, Zbigniew grabbed his and we left the park. It was only then he realised he'd been stabbed. And so did I."

"Did you see a knife at any point?"

"No. The whole thing lasted only 10 seconds."

The injured pair went to a nearby shop where the police and

ambulance service were called.

ZBIGNIEW GORGON told the jury a similar story about the assaults.

"Simon spotted me and came over. Their demeanour changed when they heard me say it was the stolen bike. I dialled 999, but did not have the chance to talk to them [the police]. I was interrupted by some punches to the face. Simon was then attacked."

The Crown asked: "Were any females involved?"

"I believe one helped a male with some stick or something."

"You left the park."

"I grabbed my bike and pushed it along. I felt some pain. Simon noticed we were bleeding. I saw blood on my trousers."

BEFORE Child J took to the witness stand the jury was told that Child G had pleaded guilty to theft and causing grievous bodily harm with intent when aged 14. He had subsequently been convicted of battery [an unprovoked attack on a male outside a fried chicken shop], theft [of a mobile phone from a 12-year-old], possession of an offensive weapon and possession of cannabis.

Child J's evidence has been reported as it was told, though his heavy "street" accent made understanding everything, indeed anything, a challenge.

His defence barrister asked him what he had done on the day of the incident.

"Kinda woke up late, quarter to one."

"What did you do?"

"Had a smoke."

"Cigarette?"

"Cannabis, three spliffs, two in the morning [after I woke up]."

"You phoned Child A."

"Yeah. He said: 'There's a place I wanna show you.' But at the time I had no idea what he was talking about."

"And when you met up?"

"He was speaking about a bike."

"CCTV shows you walking up and down the road by the bike shop. Why?"

"Had nothing to do, innit."

"Were you casing the joint?"

"No need to, know what I mean?"

"Did you know Child G was going to take the bike?"

"Not know he was going to that day."

"Did you intend to help him steal it?"

"No. Not have to, one man job. Bike was all in his head."

"Did you know what was in his head at the time?"

"No."

"The WhatsApp messages the previous day — one mentioned bolt-cutters and a push bike. Did that relate to the next day?"

"No."

"What did it relate to?"

"Not know, but nothing to do with the bike. Not remember what they would have been about."

"You went home — what happened?"

"He [Child G] called me and said he had sommat to show me. He came round with a nice bike. Didn't say much. Rode it round the estate a bit."

"Did you know where it came from?"

"Yes."

The jury was told Child A and another girl arrived and the four went to the park.

"What happened then?"

"I'm in, like, a walk-up bit, could see the sports centre. Guy was sitting on a bench, like. He was looking at me and I looked back at him. As we got closer, he said: 'Nice bike'."

"What did you say?"

"We spoke about the bike. Started at £700 , he said £500 . He called a friend to lend him some money, saw him coming a bit later. He said sommat about the bike being stolen from his shop and wanted to phone the police."

"When you heard about the police, what happened?"

"I knew the bloke was gonna do sommat, but not know what. Child G did what he did."

"What was that?"

"Had nothing to do with me."

"What did Child A do?"

"Not see no knife, but he had his hand in his pocket."

"The knife was yours. How did he get it?"

"Earlier when we came in the park."

"Why was Child G given the knife?"

"He asked me."

"Why do you carry a knife?"

"Problems I've had in the past. Just a little flick-knife."

"You say you did not see a knife."

"He must have stabbed him. All that was in my mind was the bike. As I went to take it I was punched [by Simon Jackson]. Ain't gonna get punched without punching back. Child G was doing what he was doing, not care about him. He was none of my concern."

"Did you know he was going to stab someone?"

"Not think he would've done it like that."

"Did you intend to help Child G cause really serious harm [to Zbigniew Gorgon and Jackson]?"

"No."

"Encourage him?"

"No."

"To cause some harm?"

"No, no harm at all. What he did was what he did."

"What happened when you got back to your flat?"

"He must have realised he cut his hand, innit. Tried to help him. Got some water and that. Put a plaster on it like, but wasn't gonna stop da bleeding."

"Did you think you did anything wrong?"

"No."

THE CROWN asked Child J how he came to have the knife in the first place.

"Not remember."

"You carried it for protection."

"That was then. In areas I might need it."

"The park?"

"The estate."

"When did you plan to use it?"

"If someone came at me with a knife."

"Let's look at some messages. Why would you need bolt-cutters? For padlocks?"

"I dunno. They break things, not only padlocks. Can be used for other things."

"Were you planning to steal some bikes?"

"Can't remember."

"OK, to the park. You met Mr Gorgon and discussed the sale of a bike. Was it yours to sell?"

"Just helping Child G. At the end of the day the bike was in his possession."

"How did you feel about getting £500?"

"Five hundred's nothing."

"To a 14-year-old schoolboy?"

"What can you buy wiv that?"

"Things have obviously changed since my days. Anyway, the first man [Gorgon] made you angry because you thought you were being set up."

"Not so much angry, more pissed off."

"He was stabbed four times because of a bike."

"All of us knew probably be a fight. At the end of the day people get stabbed up."

"How did you feel about it?"

"Not know what I was thinking. Child G did not do things properly on the day."

"What things?"

"He didn't know, like, who's real and who's not. Who is a good person and who is not a good person."

"He stabbed a bloke four times and another once. That's all right?"

"Not saying it's all right. He knows it was wrong thing to do. Who doesn't?"

Child A was arrested during the evening of the incident after being spotted at a bus stop, holding a hospital crutch, and blood-stained trousers. In her bag was a bandana with what proved to be Child G's blood.

While she never fully explained why she was carrying a medical crutch, Child A said that the six-inch flick-knife belonged to Child J, but he had given it to Child G who was her boyfriend at the time. Child A said that Child G had "jokingly" pretended to stab here with the knife as they entered the park.

"One man tried to hit me," she said. "So I hit him with the crutch. Then Child J stabbed him. Child J stabbed both."

THE CROWN told the jury there can be no doubt Child J and Child A assisted Child G. Child J had given Child G his knife as they entered the park and, the prosecution claimed, was involved in the theft of the bicycle. According to Simon Jackson, he was attacked by Child J.

"All three were in possession of the bike before the explosion of violence took place," said the Crown. "We say it was a group activity, a collective effort to attack the two males. Child A knew full well there was a knife at the scene. She disclosed that Child J said that Child G was 'moist [scared].' She saw Child J give his knife to Child G and there could have been no doubt in her mind what was going to happen.

"Child G used Child J's knife. He provided the weapon that was used. It is up to the jury to decide if this was intent."

THE DEFENCE said that presence alone is not enough to say Child G was assisted or encouraged in any way.

"Child J did not know what Child G was going to do. There was no discussion. The attack took the others by surprise. There is no evidence that Child J intended to assist Child G.

"Child A's only involvement came at the end when she hit Zbigniew Gorgon with a crutch, causing no injury. There was no intent to do serious harm by hitting him with a crutch. Her knowledge of the knife does not amount to intending to help with intent."

THE JURY had to decide whether Child J and Child A intended to help or encourage Child G to stab Zbigniew Gorgon and Simon Jackson. If it believed this was the case, was it unlawful wounding or wounding with intent?

Grievous bodily harm (GBH) is a criminal offence which relates to Section 18 and 20 of the Offences Against the Person Act. While both sections are commonly referred to as GBH, the difference between the two is significant.

Section 18 specifically refers to intentionally inflicted GBH —

wounding with the intent to cause GBH and is considerably more serious than Section 20 due to the level of intent involved.

However, there can be a fine line between Section 18 and 20 assaults and it boils down to what was intended or was going through the mind of the offender at the time when the assault took place. For Section 18 GBH the jury must be satisfied that the hostility to the victim was motivated and that the defendant had full intention to cause GBH. In cases of Section 18 GBH, it is for the prosecution to prove the presence of elements including a repeated or sustained attack; evidence of planning of the attack; deliberate choice of an offensive weapon such as a blade.

38

CHILD J: Theft; two counts of unlawful wounding; two counts of wounding with intent

CHILD A: Two counts of unlawful wounding; two counts of wounding with intent

TRIALS like this make me despair. Fourteen-year-olds involved in the theft of a bike worth almost £10,000 and then a vicious attack on two men who spotted the stolen cycle. According to Child J (a 14-year-old schoolboy, we must remind ourselves) £500 buys you nothing, while at the end of the day everyone gets stabbed.

Do they?

The body language of the defendants a few feet from each other in the dock gave the impression there was now little love lost between Child J and Child A, the pair barely exchanging glances let alone conversation in or out of the dock. The pair stood emotionless when the foreman of the jury delivered its unanimous verdict which probably did not come as a huge surprise to the defendants.

It found Child J guilty of theft — intentionally assisting Child G — who had also previously pleaded guilty to GBH with intent — of stealing the bike. Both Child J and Child A were found guilty of unlawfully wounding Zbigniew Gorgon and Simon Jackson (who Child A had hit with her crutch), but not guilty of the more serious charge of grievous bodily harm with intent. Child J was found guilty of unlawfully wounding Gorgon, but not GBH with intent. Child A was cleared of both charges relating to Gorgon.

A probation report was ordered on both defendants ahead of the sentencing six weeks after the verdicts. The punishment should always fit the crime, but when the perpetrators are 14 this is easier said than done.

The respective defence barristers had the unenviable task of trying to obtain the best (i.e., lightest) sentence for their clients. In the cases of Child J and Child A, their age at the time of the offences — 14 — and the fact that neither had any previous convictions went in their favour.

While Child G had no previous convictions at the time of the incident, he had subsequently been convicted of battery, possession of a bladed object [knife] in a public place and assault [of a police constable]. His defence barrister tried to make a positive about the knife offence — "he has been able to attend a weapons awareness course."

Judges have to take the age of defendants into consideration. Child G, the teenager responsible for what he called "an explosion of violence", was given a three-year custodial sentence.

Child J, whose attitude in court gave me the impression he is destined for the Old Bailey one day, was given an 18-month Youth Rehabilitation Order — a community sentence which includes a knife crime prevention course.

Child A was also given an 18-month Youth Rehabilitation Order with programmes to help her.

39

ROKAS LESCINSKAS & ANDRIUS PANOVAS: Kidnapping; possession of an imitation firearm

BIG DAVE'S MISSION IMPOSSIBLE

WE HAVE seen it many times in movies when someone escapes from a moving car and just misses being hit by another vehicle before escaping. Darvydas Galkauskas claimed that this really happened to him in the Dartford Tunnel when, with his hands tied together, he pressed down the electric window switch, put his hands out of the window and opened the door. He rolled to the side as a lorry advanced before running to what he thought was a police car at the mouth of the tunnel.

Oh, the escapee was 6 feet 9 inches and nicknamed Big Dave.

Adding extra spice to what the jury was told, not that it needed any more, this was a retrial and the two Lithuanian defendants — Rokas Lescinskas and Andrius Panovas — spoke through an interpreter.

It also became obvious soon after a fascinating trial was up and running that the jury was going to be working overtime to separate fantasy from fact with the latter appearing to be in short supply. In its opening speech the Crown told the jury it would hear translations of texts in Lithuanian that appear to suggest Big Dave is heavily involved in drug dealing.

"He has given evidence previously when he was asked to explain about the messages," said the prosecution. "The trial did not get beyond his questioning and the jury was discharged. You must consider, in due course, what you make of this material [the text messages] and whether he is being truthful of whether the messages are incriminating. Whether he is lying about the kidnap or is he telling the truth about this."

LITHUANIAN linguistic experts were called upon by the Crown

and the defence to give their opinions on the meanings of certain words in the texts. In English, it would be the equivalent of "How's Charlie?" Would that be an inquiry about someone's health or slang for cocaine? With no actual words for different drugs could the jury be certain that the Lithuanian equivalent of Charlie was, in fact, a Class A drug?

THERE WAS no dispute that Big Dave was a big builder and after work he enjoyed three or four beers with his boss. The claimant was not in court and gave evidence via a video link from an unspecified location. The Crown asked Big Dave, who spoke excellent English, how the evening ended.

He said: "We worked until the sun went down, maybe about nine. We had three or four beers and I was heading home."

"Did anything happen?

"As I was walking along the road, I was hit very hard to my face. A bunch of three people started punching me. I was hit on the back of the head, the nose and forehead though I cannot recall in which order. I tried to defend my face. I fell on the floor and was hit more. I saw faces and recognised Rokas first, then Zukas [Panovas' nickname]."

"What did the men then do?"

Big Dave told the jury he could only remember "snapshots" of what happened after being hit. "The next thing I remember for certain was standing next to the car, with my hands bound behind my back. It was a blue car, a Volkswagen, and I was told to get in the back seat. Someone said to me that I knew too much and I had to disappear. Someone else said: 'This is not a game.' I was also told: 'You are dead meat' and 'this is a dead-end for you'."

Big Dave claimed his hands were bound with thick, brown tape and that as the car was driven along the A2 into the Medway area of Kent, Lescinskas threatened him with a gun and a knife.

The claimant said: "Rokas [Lescinskas] was holding the knife next to my neck and then next to my chest, scaring me with it. He was shouting: 'I'm going to knife you.' Panovas said: 'Not here, we will go where it's quiet and there's nobody around.' While the car was still driving, I saw Rokas load a gun. He put it next to my head and then next to my leg as well. I was in shock. I thought 'this is going to be it for me'."

When questioned by the prosecution about what kind of gun it was,

Big Dave said he recognised the weapon as an automatic handgun from his time in the Lithuanian military.

Big Dave then told the jury how the car stopped for around 10 minutes on a residential street in Medway before the men began to drive him back towards the Dartford Tunnel. He said he saw what he thought was a police car and as the vehicle he was in approached the mouth of the tunnel he decided to try to escape.

"I thought about breaking the window with my head or elbow. I touched one of the window buttons and felt it open. I was shouting, offering to give them money to cover the sound of the window opening. My back was by the door and when the window was open, I got my hands out and unlocked the door. I jumped out. I remember a lorry coming from behind, but I just wanted to get to the police van. I got my hands free of the tape. I cannot remember exactly how. I ran along the hard shoulder to the tunnel enforcement officer."

The jury saw CCTV from inside the tunnel which did not show conclusively how Big Dave exited the car, but he was seen running against the traffic on the hard shoulder. Breathtaking stuff and no doubt Tom Cruise would have approved.

As Big Dave ran towards what he thought was a police car, he discovered it was a Highways England (HE) car and asked the HE representative to call 999.

Big Dave was taken to hospital with bruised ribs and injuries to his face, nose, shoulders and buttocks, of which the jury were shown photos. He claimed that while the shoulders and buttock injuries were the result of him landing on the road as he left the car, the facial injuries and rib bruising were caused by "constant beating." However, the jury would have to decide how each injury was caused.

From hospital, Big Dave was taken to a police station where he was interviewed. At two separate identity presentations Big Dave identified Rokas and Zukas. He claimed he had not seen the third assailant again after the day of the incident.

THE NUMBER PLATE of the car from which Big Dave escaped was put on the Automatic Number Plate Recognition system which allows police to trace vehicles. The vehicle was intercepted on its way to Portsmouth. The three occupants were arrested, though the female was released. The two males, Rokas Lescinskas and Andrius Panovas, were interviewed by the police, but they exercised their right to remain silent, answering "no comment" to every question.

They were both charged with kidnapping Darvydas Galkauskas — they unlawfully and by force took him against his will. Also, for possession of an imitation firearm, an item that appeared to look like a handgun which was not fired or recovered by the police, but which the claimant believed to be real and unlawful violence would be used against him.

Both defendants denied everything. They did not kidnap him, they were friends, they did not threaten him with anything and they had no idea why he suddenly jumped out of the car. Basically, the pair said they had no idea what Big Dave was talking about.

An unusual, putting it mildly, case for the jury to decide.

39

ROKAS LESCINSKAS & ANDRIUS PANOVAS: Kidnapping; possession of an imitation firearm

BIG DAVE, aka Darvydas Galkauskas, told a wonderful story, but that's what the jury thought it was… fantasy rather than fact. There were no witnesses to any kidnapping and no evidence of any firearm, real or imitation.

Why Big Dave decided to leave the vehicle in such an unorthodox manner we shall never know, but there was, presumably, insufficient evidence for the jury to be sure Rokas Lescinskas and Andrius Panovas were guilty of the charges.

However, the suspicion remains that the three Lithuanians would meet up again for a little chat and probably more.

40

DERRICK BRANTER: Three counts of sexual assault; two counts of assault by beating; witness intimidation; criminal damage

A VILE AND VIOLENT MAN OR THE VICTIM OF DRUNKEN LIES?

DERRICK BRANTER'S relationship with Miss R was as far from Mills and Boon as is possible. Depending on which you believe, Branter was a violent partner with a liking for a most unnatural form of pleasure or Miss R was an alcoholic who simply made up the allegations against the defendant.

This was a most uncomfortable trial with Miss R giving evidence almost continually in tears. Given what she spoke about this was understandable, but was it a figment of alcoholic excess or the truth? Branter claimed Miss R had made up all of the allegations against him and he was the calming influence in a stormy relationship.

Branter was charged with seven indictments; three of sexual assault, two of assault by beating, one of witness intimidation and one of criminal damage. The evidence of the defendant and claimant were polar opposites with both alleging to be the victim of a controlling partner. The jury was to hear things it had almost certainly (and hopefully) never heard before or would hear again.

THE PROSECUTION asked Miss R how she met Derrick Branter.

"In a club, three and a half years ago. We started a relationship straight away."

"What was he like then?"

"Nice. He made me feel good and happy."

"Did you stay happy?"

"For a little while, a few months."

"What changed?"

"Derrick changed."

"How did the change begin?"

"He would contact me more, phone me all day. He would ask where I was and what I was doing. All my time was spent with him, even though we both had our own homes. I did not see my friends as it might upset Derrick. I didn't want to hurt his feelings."

"Did anything change about you?"

"He stopped me wearing make-up. He said it didn't suit me and I didn't need it. I dressed down. He said I was better in track-suits. He made me feel ugly."

"What happened if you dressed the way you liked?"

"I didn't. He'd shout at me, make me feel small."

"Anything else?"

"I put a lock on my phone, but he broke it. If anyone phoned me, he'd question me about it. He had keys cut for my house and without my knowing he'd be there waiting for me."

"Did you want to leave him?"

"Yes, but I was scared."

"Was there anything apart from the shouting?"

"He'd hit me across the face if he couldn't get his own way or if I didn't give the right answer according to him."

"Was it only one time he hit you?"

"No. I lost count of how many times."

"Was he a drinker?"

"Yes, vodka. It made him horrible... worse."

"How often did he drink?"

"Every day. He'd start in the morning. I'd find an empty bottle later."

"Did you drink?"

"Yes. Not that much, but it increased because I wanted to block everything out. He punched me a lot on my head, on the top so no one could see the injuries."

"What was your sex life like?"

"He used to like me licking his arse and pooing in my mouth, not by accident. He'd laugh. He once broke my phone and pooed on it."

"Why do you think the poo came out?"

348

"Because he was excited."

"Why did you lick his anus?"

"He asked me to. I didn't want to."

"Were the police ever called?"

"Yes, because of the violence."

"How often can you recall calling them?"

"About 150 times."

"Would he know you were calling the police?"

"Yes. Once he threw the house phone in water and then said 'I'm sorry, I'm sorry'."

"What would happen?"

"The police would arrive and I'd say I was OK because I was scared of what he might do... get more angry, and hit me more. Once he was removed from my house and came back to say he loved me and was sorry. I'd drop the case because I was so scared."

"Was there an incident at his mother's on May 13?"

"He'd been drinking vodka. He pulled my hair, I don't know why. He dragged me to the hallway. I wanted to leave, but he wouldn't let me. He cracked my phone when I tried to call the police. He pulled down his trousers and pooed on me on the upstairs landing. It was on my back and all over my dress. The police turned up and Derrick told me to hide in a cupboard. I did because I was scared."

"What happened next?"

"He threatened to kill me. He dragged me across the room by my hair, my head hit the TV. He pooed on me again. I phoned the police again. The police returned, but I had to hide in a cupboard again. This time I came down and told them what happened."

"Did you withdraw the statement?"

"Yes."

"You said you were not placed in fear to withdraw the statement. Was this true?"

"I can't remember, so much happened."

"What happened on June 8?"

"I was round Derrick's. We were in bed. He told me to shut the fuck up and open my mouth."

"Then?"

"He pulled down his shorts, squatted on top of me and pooed in my mouth. He laughed and told me to swallow it. He grabbed my mouth and made me."

"Then?"

"He head-butted me. I ran to the toilet and was sick."

THE LAST time Miss R saw Derrick Branter was on June 9. Tehran Lewis, a friend, was at her home. Branter asked a neighbour to attract her attention through the letter box. When the door was opened by Lewis, the claimant said: "Derrick came flying in shouting: 'Where is she?' He went straight upstairs and I called the police. He punched me on my face, on the left side."

THE DEFENCE honed in on Miss R's excessive drinking, continually suggesting she was so drunk she either fabricated allegations or was so inebriated she could not remember what she had done.

"The first time you slept with him after meeting him, it was a one-night stand."

"No."

"You did not see him for 12 months after that."

"No."

"You met again in the same pub and it became a regular relationship."

"Yes."

"It'd be an on-off relationship."

"Yes."

"During the whole time between 2016 and 2018 you both had your own accommodation and did not rely on him financially."

"Yes."

"Initially he was a delivery driver for a store and then worked on a construction site."

"No. He never worked at the beginning, only 2017."

"You have read your statement. Have you had difficulty remembering things?"

"So many things happened."

"I accept you have difficulty in remembering. Is it because you were consuming large amounts of alcohol?"

"No."

"Or that the incidents did not happen as you told them?"

"They did. Some of the incidents I don't want to remember."

"You made out he was the aggressor."

"Yes."

"Is it not the case you became violent yourself when you consumed alcohol?"

"No."

"You tried to create things that were just false?"

"No."

"You would hit him."

"Not that I can remember."

"You are saying you did not hit him at all?"

"Only two incidents."

"In August 2016 police had been called to Terminal 5 at Heathrow. You and Branter were returning from a week's holiday in Spain. You paid for it."

"Yes."

"By Costa Coffee you hit him over the head at 13.00 with a vodka bottle."

"Yes."

"The police found the bottle in your bag with blood on it."

"Yes."

"Lot of people around."

"Yes."

"You were given a police caution."

"Yes."

"Why did you hit him?"

"He upset me. I pleaded guilty."

"In September 2016 police were called to your address by an anonymous person who reported fighting in the street while there was blood on the floor in the house."

"Yes."

"Branter had a head injury. He said he'd fallen and banged his head. In fact, you picked up a piece of wood and hit him over the head."

"No."

"In October 2016 you were arrested for assaulting him in the car

351

park at Thorpe Park. It was captured on CCTV."

"Yes."

"You used the palm of your hand and struck him on the forehead."

"Yes."

"You hit him many times."

"No."

"On May 13, 2017, you hit him."

"No."

"He suggested to calm you down he would take you to the nail bar."

"Yes, we went together."

"On the way you purchased a bottle of vodka."

"Yes."

"And a tropical mixture for him."

"Yes."

"You were both drinking vodka."

"Yes."

"Then a fry-up."

"Yes."

"You had an argument."

"Yes. He was insulting my children."

"You did not go home. You went to his house."

"He followed me."

"He asked you to leave, but you wanted to stay."

"No."

"One condition of his bail was not to see you, but you kept turning up. That's why you hid in a cupboard,"

"No."

"You say he defecated on you. Why did you not call the police?"

"Out of fear."

"You could have just walked out. Called a friend to get you."

"I'd had no credit on my phone for six years."

"You stayed in his house because you wanted to be there. Is it not a case that you were obsessed by him?"

"Not at all."

"On June 8 you stayed in his house all day drinking alcohol. When he came home [from work] you asked him why he was late."

"No."

"He mentioned something about Amanda Holden on TV. You became jealous. You hit him with his construction helmet."

"No."

"Threatened to smash his TV."

"No."

"You said in your statement you had not been sexually assaulted or penetrated at any stage. You told the police you'd been hurt 'down below'."

"I don't remember suggesting that."

"It's recorded. Why did you say 'hurt below' if nothing of the like occurred? Was it not a case of the drink talking and you said the first thing that came to mind?"

"No."

"You have attended Alcoholics Anonymous in the past. On June eighth you told the police Branter had bloodied your mouth. Was it the drink talking?"

"No."

WHILE she made reference to Derrick Branter's defecation when cross-examined by the prosecution, Miss R's police statement, made on June 9, told more details of the defendant's apparent liking for an act that clearly made the jury baffled and horrified.

She said: "I was in Derrick's room and had been drinking alcohol all day. He returned home at 8.30. I did not know what was happening, but I awoke at about 11. When I woke up I was naked and Derrick had undressed me. He said to me: 'Open your mouth and shut the fuck up.' Derrick then pulled down his boxer shorts and squatted over me while I was on the bed. I knew what he was going to do because he has previously defecated into my mouth. This has been reported to the police. I shouted: 'No, it's disgusting.'

"I am scared of Derrick and I am petrified what he might do to me. I was very scared. It was a liquid texture and it squirted into my mouth. I would guess about one quarter of a pint went into my mouth. Derrick then grabbed my mouth and forced me to swallow the faeces.

"I said to Derrick: 'I am going to call the police.' He got very angry. He then head-butted me on the side of my forehead. I then had to run to the toilet to be sick. The taste of the faeces was disgusting. I felt awful and degraded. I feel ashamed. When the police arrived, I provided one mouth swab and one mouth wash."

The defence continued: "On June 12 Branter came round at 7 a.m. You did not answer the door. He shouted through the letterbox because he wanted his CSCS card for work. You had a male friend [Tehran Lewis] with you who shouted: 'What do you want?' Lewis and Branter were pushing each other, having a bit of a scuffle and you barged into."

"No."

"He did not strike you."

"He did."

THE JUDGE asked the prosecutor: "Any re-examination?"

She played a recording of the last 999 call the claimant made to the police on June 12. The jury heard a frantic Miss R sobbing and saying: "Please get them here quickly… he's assaulting me."

In the background you could hear Branter shouting, swearing… things going crash, bang all over the place. Miss R's TV was smashed. The call lasted for two minutes.

When the recording ended the prosecutor said to the jury: "Making it all up, is she?" And then to the judge: "Nothing more Your Honour."

DERRICK BRANTER took to the witness stand to give the jury his version of events with the defence barrister.

He said: "After going to the nail bar I went to the cafe for something to eat, but she [Miss R] did not come with me. She'd got the hump and left the nail place before me. We'd had an argument. I was on the phone to customer service and because I wasn't all nice and chatty to her, she got angry.

"I stayed to finish my food. I had no idea where she was going. I went to the bookies to do my football accumulator and then went to my mother's. I arrived about 15 minutes later and she was in my room. I was a bit upset about the way she'd left me. She'd embarrassed me and I didn't expect her to be at my mother's.

"I said she should go and I asked her to leave immediately. She put two nines on her phone screen and said she had nowhere to go. If she left, she'd press a third nine. I was on bail at the time for allegations she'd made against me and if the police had come, I'd be automatically recalled. I was desperate to get her out, but she was making all sorts of threats.

"The police arrived and I told them Miss R was not there. The police searched the property. I wasn't sure where she was. I didn't tell her to hide in a cupboard. I was desperate for her to go. When the police left, she was on the floor on the landing, acting injured. I was so nervous I defecated next to her. I was wearing shorts and T-shirt at the time. She didn't even know I'd done it."

The defence asked: "How many times did you do it?"

"Only once."

"Did it work?"

"She got up."

"The police came a second time and again she claimed she hid in a cupboard. How did she get it over her clothes?"

"She rolled over into it. I didn't put faeces on her. That would be disgusting."

"Have you ever pooed on her?"

"No."

"She said you asked her to lick your anus."

"That's ludicrous. I don't do that sort of thing."

"The police arrived a second time."

"Yes, but I did not tell her to hide either time."

"You were arrested. What happened when the police came?"

"I wanted to put my trousers on. I had a tag on my ankle and didn't want the neighbours to see it."

"On May 31 she stayed at your house. Why let her stay?"

"I felt quite bad. She was going through a lot."

"She'd got you arrested."

"She told me there'd be no action as she was withdrawing her statement."

"She stayed at your house until June 8. What was it like for that period?"

"Everything was OK until June 8. I got home from work about 7.45 and Miss R arrived about eight o'clock. She seemed OK-ish. She was a bit sluggish. She'd been drinking and came into my room with a glass of cider. She was niggled because I hadn't said goodbye to her at 6.30 that morning. My mother came to the door and asked who the judge was on Britain's Got Talent. I said it was Amanda Holden. Miss R kept going on about it and hit me with my hard hat and stepped on my Play Station. I just blocked her off and told her to calm down."

"Miss R alleged you squatted over her and pooed in her mouth."

"It did not happen."

"Any issue with faeces?"

"No. The first time I heard about it was at the police station. I've never pooed in her mouth."

"Did you head-butt her?"

"No. She was very creative. I was concerned about my well-being and went to stay with a friend."

"June 9 — did you phone her?"

"No."

"June 10?"

"I called her twice from a phone box. There was no answer the first time."

"What about June 12 when Tehran Lewis was at her house?"

"I did not hit her. He thought I was going for her. We were tussling and pushing each other because she'd dialled 999. I left and walked away."

The defence asked Branter about previous convictions.

"The two occasions you were arrested, were they the only occasions with the claimant?"

"No."

"Any convictions when she was the victim?"

"No."

"Really?"

"There was no case to answer."

"Let me ask you about Jane Keane."

"Two cautions and a non-molestation order."

"From 2010 to 2015 did you have any other relationships?"

"Yes, with the mother of one of my children who lives in north London."

"Were you the aggressor?"

"No."

"The controller?"

"No."

"Violent?"

"No."

THE PROSECUTION cross-examined Derrick Branter — and how.

"Would it be fair to say your evidence is all ad-libbed?"

"No."

"What was your role in all this?"

"I kept going back to her."

"So all Miss R's fault, not yours."

"Apart from pooing on the landing."

"You had a reason for that. It's a crap reason, but a reason. Anyway, how often did you see her initially?"

"After the second time, she stayed at my place the weekend and I didn't see her until the Friday."

"You say she was jealous."

"Yes."

"Controlling."

"Yes."

"Quick to fly off the handle and make false allegations."

"Yes. She's a nice girl when she's not drinking. She was my friend, not my girlfriend. I made that clear."

"So not your partner."

"No. An on and off fixture."

"On for how long?"

"A day here, a day there."

"So when were you properly together?"

"Before the holiday in August 2016. Only then did I introduce her to my kids as my girlfriend."

"Why not a relationship earlier?"

"She had a lot of issues and problems, things going on."

"Were these still going on when it became a relationship?"

"She calmed down."

"Because of you?"

"I was there for her. I was everything to her. So was my mother."

"The same mum you hit on the head?"

"Yes, nine years ago. We had an altercation."

"So you were everything to her [Miss R]?"

"Yes."

"Was that why you put up with her controlling behaviour?"

"I'm only a guy, there's only so much I can put up with."

"I suggest you were into her."

"I found her quite attractive, yes."

"She was vulnerable and you took advantage of that."

"No way."

"You were possessive of her."

"No. She had her life. I don't want to put her down, but she didn't have much [sic] friends, just family who lived in Grays... strict Sikhs... not allowed to drink."

"You controlled how she dressed."

"No."

"Her drinking increased."

"No."

"You drank vodka."

"Socially."

"If she was with Alcoholics Anonymous, how did you support her by taking her drinking?"

"I didn't know the severity of it."

"The clue is in 'Alcoholics'."

"I'm quite naive like that."

"So you took her to AA, but didn't know the severity of it."

"I did not know the extent of the problem. I should have been a bit cleverer."

"You drink a lot?"

"I'm never all over the place."

"You can control it."

"I know when enough is enough."

"Was it a coincidence she hit you with a vodka bottle, the drink of your choice?"

"We both drank it."

"You get worked up over nothing when drunk."

"No."

"You want to lash out at her."

"No."

"You did not tell police she'd hit you out of embarrassment."

"She got a caution for the vodka bottle. I wanted a restraining order."

"She got a caution because she admitted what happened. You never admitted anything with her."

"Not done it."

"She made all the incidents up?"

"Yes."

"Why would she make up all the incidents?"

"To control me and make me stay around."

"A controlling mechanism."

"Yes."

"When you were with your ex, Karen McDonald, in 2008 — you hit her with a crutch, put her in a headlock and got a caution for common assault. Was she controlling?"

"No."

"You were the calm one in that relationship?"

"No... yes... it was quite a long time ago."

"But it happened."

"Yes. It was at the lower end of assault."

"Does that make it all right?"

"No."

"Jane Keane — you were guilty of harassment."

"She's the mother of my child."

"Who took out a non-molestation order against you. Was she controlling?"

"No."

"She wanted to keep you from her."

"Yes."

"So, your mum and two ex-girlfriends..."

"It's in the past. I was young and no angel."

"Now, serious allegations. Is it a coincidence or do you just like hitting women?"

"No."

"Sure?"

"Yes."

"You called her [Miss R] on June 12. A girl who had caused you nothing but trouble. Why?"

"Wanted to see if she was OK."

"The person who had caused you nothing but grief."

"Yes."

"But why? She's causing you so much harm."

"I was in a relationship with her."

"The relationship you didn't call a relationship."

"We both had to calm down."

"But you wanted to get away from her."

"I wanted my CSCS card."

"You shouted through the letter box."

"Yes."

"There was a man there, at 7 a.m. You'd been replaced already."

"I was a bit upset."

"The male voice bothered you."

"A little bit. Ego, you know."

"You went back a second time to see who the male was."

"Could have been anyone. Even her brother."

"You got someone else to shout out because they wouldn't answer the door to you."

"No."

"You went past Miss R and up to the bedroom."

"I didn't care."

"She phoned the police. We heard the police call."

"I don't remember the conversation."

"Remember when the male said: 'Don't put your hands on a woman'?"

"No."

"You initially took it out on the TV."

"An accident. I stumbled into it."

"You punched her in the face."

"I was never that close to her."

That was the end of the cross-examinations from the prosecution and the defence.

THE JUDGE'S summing up instructed the jury to be wary of Miss

R's demeanour in the witness box. He said: "She claimed he had hurt her 'down below' but she said to the police there was no penetration. Is that inconsistency? She had to refresh her memory [by referring to her police statement] on a number of occasions. The defence says that if it had happened you would not need to refresh. You have to decide whether inconsistency means not truthful.

"Sometimes people who are traumatised... the way in which trauma affects a person varies considerably. Recall is not always consistent. Inconsistent accounts may be an indication the whole evidence is untrue.

"You must decide whether Miss R provided you with a truthful account. What you make of her demeanour... it is up to you to make that assessment. Who is to say how anyone who has been through an emotional experience is affected? Some show distress, some cope with it. Demeanour in court is not necessarily something to count towards the witness's honesty"

On Derrick Branter lying to the police that Miss R was not at the house, the judge said: "He admitted he lied and it was deliberate. There is no issue there. He said it was because he was in breach of his bail. A lie in itself never proves guilt, only part of the evidence."

While the jury would decide the verdicts, the judge directed them on law. He said: "On counts 1, 3 and 5 — sexual assault... you have to decide whether it was intentional touching and if that touching was sexual... that the complainant was not consenting and the defendant had no reasonable belief she was consenting.

"The defence argues there was no touching and certainly no sexual touching. The prosecution argues the touching was pooing which was sexual because the defendant gained sexual gratification from it... having his anus licked and any intentional defecation. If you do not consider the assault was of a sexual nature, you must then consider whether it was just assault."

On count 10, criminal damage, the judge said: "The Crown says he pushed the TV to the floor and stamped on it. Was it intentional? The defendant said he made accidental contact only."

The jury was in retirement for 15 hours before it returned with its verdicts.

40

DERRICK BRANTER: Three counts of sexual assault; two counts of assault by beating; witness intimidation; criminal damage

I AM unsure how much the jury would have been influenced by the judge's summing-up which seemed designed to undermine Miss R and her evidence. Had I been a juror my first thought would be — yes, girls can make revenge lies about an ex out of spite. Mostly that would be rape because it is "easy." But would anyone even be able to THINK of defecating in someone's mouth if it did not happen let alone make an accusation? He raped me, yes. He hit me, yes. But pooing? No... it had to be true, surely. And as revolting as it may sound, some people — well, one — find it a turn-on.

It would also have weighed heavily on my mind that Derrick Branter had convictions for violence against three people, including his mother. His mother, for heaven's sake. Plus, the significant re-examination of the Crown in playing the 999 call — "so, making it all up, is she?"

Also, being an alcoholic does not make you a liar. They can be clever and deceitful, yes, but such dependence on alcohol does not make you an automatic liar.

DERRICK BRANTER was found guilty of five counts of common assault. He was found not guilty of criminal damage, the jury believing that he did not intentionally smash the TV, but did accidentally stumble into it. As you do.

He was also found not guilty of witness intimidation. The phone call where he allegedly said he would kill Miss R unless she dropped the charges. Maybe, just maybe, I'll give way to this one. It was one person's word against the other.

But the common assault charges... two were assault by beating when Branter head-butted Miss R and when he punched her after the defendant went round to find Tehran Lewis at the house.

The other three assault charges he was found guilty of were

originally sexual assault. The judge ruled that the jury had to be sure the touching was intentional, that it was sexual, the complainant did not consent and the defendant had no reasonable belief she was consenting.

The defence argued there was no touching and certainly no sexual touching.

The judge ruled that sexual touching, by its nature, the person doing the touching was seeking pleasure... gratification. The prosecution claimed the touching was when the defendant was pooing, that it was sexual and Branter gained some form of gratification in having his anus licked plus any intentional defecation [in her mouth].

However, the judge ruled that if the jury did not believe the defecation was for sexual gratification it must consider an alternative charge of "just" assault. The jury decided that yes, Branter did defecate in Miss R's mouth, but no, it was not for sexual gratification.

It is not a subject anyone (maybe apart from Branter) would want to talk about. Trying to play the devil's advocate, perhaps the jury thought that as such an act is so vile, so horrific, so unnatural, so unimaginable... it could not possibly understand how anyone could get a sexual kick out of it. There is some logic in that (if that was the belief) and while it seemed likely that Branter gained pleasure from such a despicable act (I am prepared to believe Miss R when she said he laughed), could the jury be sure it was sexual or just humiliation?

However, if this was the jury's train of thought, the act of defecating in another person's mouth as an assault should surely be worth more than six months? In law, it is not. It comes under common assault like a punch on the mouth and is a summary offence, meaning that if it was dealt with at a magistrates' court, as common assault is, then the maximum punishment is 26 weeks. Summary offences, in law, must run concurrently, so even if he had done it 100 times, the sentence would still only have been 26 weeks.

The judge ruled that as Branter had been in custody for 10 months, which was four months longer than the sentence he received, he should be released.

Ten months is the equivalent of a 20-month prison sentence as prisoners are released on licence after serving half such a sentence. The 26-week sentence for common assault would have meant Branter being in jail for three months and three on licence, so Branter had effectively been in jail for more than three times his sentence.

The jury was never aware of Branter's full crime sheet. Over the past 10 years he had (before this trial) 42 convictions for 119 offences, including a restraining order from an ex-partner. The new total is 43 and 124 with Miss R granted a restraining order. It says much for the way the police viewed Branter that Miss R was also given a panic alarm… just in case.

In fact, Miss R had to use the alarm 48 hours after Branter was released. Despite the restraining order he went round Miss R's house and forced his way in. She pressed the silent alarm and the police arrived within minutes. When he became aware of this Branter hid, unsuccessfully, in a cupboard — talk about a role reversal.

He was taken to a police station and spent the night in a cell before appearing at a magistrates' court the next day where a district judge handed him a 26-week sentence, asking: "How on earth are you walking the streets?"

This meant that for offences regarding Miss R, Branter had spent at least 13 months in prison — the equivalent of a two years and two months sentence — plus time on licence. Slowly, the punishment was starting to fit the crime.

But this was far from the end of Miss R and Branter. Incredibly, three days after he came out of prison again Miss R telephoned him. Despite the restraining order on Branter, she went to his house and stayed for three days. Eventually, he'd had enough and left. Miss R was so worried about Branter she contacted the police who promptly put him back in prison for breaking the restraining order.

Branter, with some justification, said it was Miss R who had been the instigator. Jailing him for six months suspended for six months, the judge told Branter that he should have slammed the door and not let her in.

The end? If only. Despite being assaulted and allegedly defecated on by Branter, Miss R still loved him. She wrote a letter to the court to ask for the restraining order on him to be revoked "as he is the only man for me."

41

JACKIE GOGGINS: Eight counts of sexual assault

GIRLS ALLOWED?

WHEN the eight-count indictment of sexual assault was read to the jury it was understandable that one juror winced. The claimant, Miss H, was now 15 but was 11 when the sexual assault allegedly began. The charges against Jackie Goggins (a female) were:

1… Assaulting a child under 13, penetrating her vagina with your fingers on at least three occasions [later changed to two]

2… Assaulting a child under 13, penetrating her vagina with your fingers on at least three occasions

3… Assaulting a child under 13 and the touching was sexual on at least three occasions

4… Assaulting a child under 13, penetrating her vagina with your fingers on at least five occasions at a Shopping Centre's toilets [later changed to three]

5… Assaulting a child under 13, intentionally touching her and the touching was sexual on at least five occasions at a fast-food restaurant's toilets [later changed to three]

6… Inciting a child under 13 to engage in sexual activity on at least five occasions

7… Assaulting a child under 13, intentionally touching her vagina in the bathroom at a friend's party

8… Sexual activity in front of a child under 13; intentionally engaging in sexual activity — masturbation — at a church

THE defendant was 26-year-old Jackie Goggins; females charged with sexual assault are very much in the minority.

Opening the trial, the prosecutor told the jury: "The claimant played football with Miss N, who was Miss H's younger sister, and they became friends. In August 2015, Miss H had a row at home and left. She did not take her mobile phone and in her daughter's absence her mother looked through her messages. She was concerned to find one from Goggins asking her daughter to send her a photo of 'her mini' and spoke of her love for the younger girl. When the claimant returned home, no further action was taken, but she was 'advised' to keep away from Jackie."

Things blew up again later that year when a message "you are the love of my life" was seen on the claimant's phone. In January 2016, Miss H was taken to the police station by her parents, but said nothing untoward had happened.

Goggins was arrested and her phone seized, but it was not given great priority by the police

Later in the year the contents were belatedly made available to the arresting officer, the timing coinciding with the claimant's mother receiving a bill of £300 for her daughter's phone — all for calls to Goggins.

At that stage the claimant disclosed more of what had happened. Initially she had shared a bed with Miss N on a stopover and when Miss N was asleep Goggins climbed in the bed and touched Miss H's vagina, though she claimed it was a result of "a dream about a boy called Tommy" and any touching was accidental.

Soon a bigger story unfolded.

The prosecutor told the jury: "You will hear details of sexual abuse over a long period. It is not a comfortable case, but the claimant's contact with Goggins was a two-way relationship. There are explicit references to fisting both ways, with the claimant saying how excited she was, exchanges of details about masturbation and exchanges of mutual love."

The following day the jury watched the claimant's two police interviews and then Miss H took to the witness box.

THE PROSECUTION started the cross-examination by explaining that Miss H was a friend of Miss N, Jackie Goggins' younger sister.

Miss H was asked: "How many times did you stay over there?"

"Ten times."

"How many times did Jackie penetrate your vagina with her finger?"

"Eight."

Miss H's parents eventually stopped their daughter staying there. The claimant said that the defendant also touched "my private parts" at a toilet in a shopping centre and a fast-food restaurant.

"Was there an incident at a church yard?"

"Yes. Jackie texted me to meet her there. I was with a friend and told her I was going to see my sister. Jackie pushed me against a wall and fingered me."

"What happened at a party for one of the football team?"

"Jackie texted me asking me to go to the bathroom. I did and she pushed me against the door. She started kissing me and wanted me to touch her breasts. She put her hand inside my jeans and touched my vagina from outside of my knickers. Denise [one of the mothers] knocked on the door and then pushed it open. Jackie told me to put my head down the toilet to make out I was ill. I told Denise I was OK."

"How often were you in contact by social media?"

"Every day."

"What sort of things would she ask you to do?"

"Put my fist inside my vagina and different objects. I said it would hurt me. She sent me images of herself naked on Facetime having a shower and masturbating. She asked me to do the same."

"Did she say she had the keys to a friend's flat?"

"Yes. She wanted me to go there for a bondage session."

THE DEFENCE barrister, who had been instructed by the judge to ask age-appropriate questions, took over cross-examination of Miss H.

"When text messages were shown to you by a police officer for the first time today you said you could not remember sending messages like that. Did you ever place your fist inside your vagina when you were told to?"

"Yes."

"What objects did you put inside your vagina?"

"I don't remember."

"Did you say you loved each other?"

"Yes."

"You wanted to be girlfriends."

"Yes."

"Was there role play text talk?"

"Yes."

"You were happy to engage."

"Yes."

"You took the lead to speak dirty."

"Yes."

"Told her how to do things."

"Yes."

The jury was later given a folder of text messages between claimant and defendant.

"Some things you were asked to do were anatomically impossible?"

"Yes."

"Once when you were asked to fist yourself you said: 'Can you beat me up instead?' Why?"

"My vagina was sore."

"Did she say: 'I don't care, put your fist in'?"

"Yes."

"What did you say?"

"OK."

"She asked: 'Does it hurt'?"

"Yes."

"She said: 'Good, keep it there'."

"Yes."

"She said: 'Good, keep it there until three o'clock'." [which would have been 58 minutes later].

"Yes."

"Did you?"

"No."

At this point the judge told the jury the prosecution did not have to prove the claimant did anything against her will.

The defence continued: "I suggest that the texts from your relationship... you made them real to get Jackie into trouble."

"No."

"There are no references to you being sexually abused."

"No."

"In your police statement about the church incident it does not say she kissed or touched you."

"You do not realise how hard it is."

"Why did you retain all the pix?"

"I was a girl aged 11 to 13. I did not think anything of it."

"I suggest Jackie would not have been able to get into bed with you while Miss N was asleep."

"She did."

"It was an old carpet in the bedroom. Did the floor not creak?"

"No."

"Why did you not wake Miss N to stop Jackie?"

"I was 12 and not know what was going on."

"You never told Jackie to stop it."

"No."

"You did not tell your mother."

"Same answer."

"But why did you keep going back?"

"I was young and not know how serious it was."

"You knew it was wrong, didn't you?"

"No, I didn't."

"Nothing happened, did it?"

"It did.

"It did not happen. It's a figment of your imagination, isn't it?"

"Disagree."

"Did you do anything to stop it?"

"No."

"In your statement [to the police] about the party bathroom incident you said Jackie closed the door. There is no suggestion she tried to kiss you."

"I don't know."

"Nothing about touching her breasts."

"Dunno."

"No reference to her fingering you."

"Not remember saying that."

NEXT in the witness box was Denise Haden, mother of one of the girls at the party. She brought a few smiles to the jury with her reply to "how long were you outside the door waiting to go to the toilet?" — "I waited for a wee while."

She told the jury: "Miss H was crying when I went in. She was really upset. I asked her if she was OK, but she didn't say anything."

Which was a little different from Miss H's evidence.

Denise concluded her short stay in the witness box: "I spoke to Nicola [Miss H's mother] who did not seem concerned."

JACKIE GOGGINS insisted the exchanges with the claimant were no more than fantasy role play and denied any sexual touching. Given the claimant's age, consent was never an issue because nobody under 16 can consent to sexual activity.

What had appeared a straightforward deliberation for the jury became far more complicated.

41

JACKIE GOGGINS: Eight counts of sexual assault

BEFORE the trial opened, the jury was unaware of what had gone on behind the scenes.

The judge had told Jackie Goggins: "I am surprised this case is still being contested. The Crown's evidence is extremely strong, supported by a number of texts and messages. It is very likely you will be found guilty and that will be worse for you because the claimant will have had to relive what happened.

"You still have the opportunity to get some discount and stop the claimant giving evidence. I am willing to go further than 10 per cent because it will mean you have shown remorse."

Goggins was given two hours to think it over, to effectively take the judge's advice or put herself at risk for a harsh sentencing should she be found guilty after a trial. The defendant had been self-harming and was heard speaking to a friend on the phone saying she was going to self-harm again "tonight."

Returning to court, to the surprise and bewilderment of most, Goggins maintained her not guilty pleas. Surely a late guilty plea with the offer of maybe 15 per cent off the sentence would have been the only sensible way forward?

Yes and no. The jury found her not guilty of counts one, two, three, four and five, but guilty of six, seven and eight.

The jury obviously could not be sure of most of the sexual assaults. The video sent by Goggins to Miss H was damaging for the defendant, though she may feel a sense of relief in some respects when the verdicts were announced by the jury foreman — guilty of "only" three out of eight charges.

Miss H was not a shy, retiring rose, despite her age. Some of her evidence was contradictory while not being able to remember what she allegedly put in her vagina was difficult to take on board. She was also a willing partner to a large extent, but given Miss H's age Goggins should have kept a safe distance.

The judge ordered a pre-sentence report from the Probation Service. Goggins was eventually given a three-year sentence.

42

PATRICK MOLLOY: Attempted murder; controlling and coercive behaviour; criminal damage.

'A MURKY WORLD OF LACK OF
RESPECT FOR LAW'

THIS WAS a trial in which the jury did not so much have to decide who was telling the truth; rather was *anyone* telling the truth?

The prosecution witnesses were: Prescilla Ackleton junior (claimant), Prescilla Ackleton senior (mother), George Ackleton (father), Bridget Saunders (George's twin sister), Lisa James (fellow traveller).

This is how the BBC reported the incident at the time — May 13, 2018:

A man has appeared in court charged with attempted murder after a woman was hit by a car in Gravesend.

She was seriously injured in Dering Way at about 10:05 BST on Sunday, Kent Police said.

Less than 10 minutes later a car was found on fire in the same road near the Denton Caravan Site.

The claimant and prosecution witnesses did not turn up for the original trial date in December, saying that as travellers they did not receive mail at their site and what's more, they could not read or write. The judge sentenced them all to four days in prison — Belmarsh (male) and Bronzfield (female) — for contempt of court.

They were subsequently given a 10 p.m. to 7 a.m. curfew and had to sign on at a local police station every day before the trial six weeks later. The impression was that this was not going to be a straightforward case which, as it turned out, was putting it mildly.

All the prosecution witnesses' original statements were withdrawn almost a month later. Offered as a script for a television show, this would have been rejected as being ridiculous fantasy. However, what you will read is all true — well, it was what the jury heard. It was up to the jurors to decide what, if anything, was actually true.

In Prescilla Ackleton junior's original statement to the police she claimed Patrick Molloy, 28, reversed over her a number of times. She had a broken wrist, head injuries and severe skin abrasions. She claimed it was his "grand finale" having "beaten the shit out of me" during their time together.

"I saw who it was driving," she had said. "It was Patrick Molloy. No doubt about it."

Prescilla Ackleton senior was treated as a hostile witness by the prosecutor because she, like the claimant and other witnesses, all withdrew their original statements.

"You'd had an argument with Patrick Molloy previously. In your statement you said he called you an English snail."

"I can't remember what I told the police."

"What does 'snail' mean?"

"In the travelling community this is very insulting. Like, you are very slow."

"You also told the police he said [of your daughter]: 'If it takes me 20 years, I am going to have your girl. She will never have anyone else. I'll kill her.' How did you feel?"

"I was very scared."

"How was Molloy at the time?"

"Drunk and upset."

"Moving on to May 13, 2018… where were you at 10 a.m.?"

"In bed asleep."

"Anything happen?"

"I heard shouting outside. I didn't take too much notice at first as it's noisy where we live. My husband George said: 'It's starting… he's starting'."

"Did he say who?"

"He said it was Paddy."

"How was George at the time?"

"Very drunk. He has a drink and drugs problem, has done for 25 years. He hides his beer so I won't find it. He was slurring his words. [Daughter] Prescilla went out, I followed her. She said: 'Help me.' There were so many people. I grabbed her. There was a lot of blood."

"Did you see the driver of the car?"

"No."

"In your statement you said you saw a silver car and Patrick was in the driver's seat. Did you?"

"No."

"How far away were you?"

"About six feet."

"In your statement you said: 'I could clearly see Patrick driving the car.' Is that true?"

"No."

"How did it find its way into your statement?"

"At the time I was traumatised. In shock. People were saying 'it's Paddy' and 'Paddy's done this.' I assumed it was him. It's wrong to assume it. I'll never assume anything again in my life."

"Why did you assume it was Patrick?"

"Don't know."

"You said in your statement you saw Patrick in the driver's seat and saw him clearly in the car by himself. So you provided the police with inaccurate information."

"Yes."

"About the attempted murder of your daughter."

"Yes."

"You misled the police who may have then looked for four people instead of one."

"Yes."

"You said: 'The back of the car hit her. I was paralysed with fear. It went back over her two more times.' Is that what happened?"

"No."

"What did you think you were saying?"

"Not know."

"There was an attack on a family member, your daughter, right?"

"Yes."

"You said 'The back of the car hit her'."

"I was in shock."

"Did it hit her a second time?"

"Don't know."

"So why did you put it in your statement?"

"People were shouting: 'Paddy's killed her'."

"Who exactly?"

"Someone standing on the road."

"You said in your statement: 'The tyre marks were on her arm and back. There was a lot of blood. It will stay in my mind for the rest of my life.' You seem to have forgotten quite a lot. How could you forget?"

"I haven't forgotten."

"You had your statement read over to you."

"Yes."

"Why did you not say there were inaccuracies?"

"Not know."

"You said: 'I make this statement while it's fresh in my mind. There is no doubt Patrick tried to kill her'."

"I could not think of anyone else who'd want to kill her so I assumed it was him. I should not have assumed this."

"Your second statement was made over three weeks later. Had you discussed this with your daughter, the prospect of changing your statement?"

"No."

"Did you give her any advice about changing hers?"

"No."

"Anyone put you under pressure?"

"No."

"Offer you money?"

"No."

"Sure you never discussed this with your daughter?"

"I might have because I'm a Christian. I cannot tell a lie. I do not know if he did it. I didn't see him."

"How long before you changed your statement was this?"

"Not know."

"You, your husband George and daughter Prescilla all went to Gravesend Police Station at the same time."

"Roughly."

"What did you think they were doing there?"

"George cannot take a lot in so he could not be left by himself. If he was there, he came with me. If she was there then she either came with me or someone else."

"Why was Prescilla there?"

"To amend her statement."

"Did she tell you?"

"I think so."

"You went to the police to clarify your account."

"Yes."

"Today in court you said when George woke you up, he said it was Paddy. Why in clarification did you not say it was wrong?"

"Not know."

"You were there to get it right."

"Not know."

"You said: 'I want everything I said to be discounted. I cannot live with myself.' You originally stated Patrick put his car in reverse and knocked Prescilla to the ground."

"I don't know who was in the car."

"You said it was fresh in your mind. You had no doubt Patrick was in the car."

"Not correct. Not know why I said it."

"Did you want the person who did this to be caught?"

"Yes."

"You realise your information was used in the investigation by the police to catch whoever. You gave them the wrong information. That makes it less likely they'll get the right person."

"The only thing I was thinking of was 'Paddy done it'."

"Were you able to comment to the police, OK?"

"Think so."

"In control of yourself?"

"Think so."

"Spoke to the police willingly?"

"Not know."

"In your second statement you said you were not willing to attend court. Why not?"

"I didn't think I'd have to."

"Why were you not willing?"

"I thought I'd have a choice."

"You know what 'willing' means?"

"Not know."

"You said: 'I do not want to be seen as a liar.' How do you know Patrick was not the driver?"

"I don't. I want someone put in prison, but not the wrong person. The person who did it. I don't want the person who did it walking around."

"In your second statement you said you had no recollection of speaking to the police at the time of the incident. Is that true?"

"Yes."

"Did you lie?"

"No. I just told them what I'd heard from other people."

"You had said: 'I saw Patrick'. Why not: 'What people told me'?"

"Not know."

"Why change your statement?"

"I did not come here to lie. If he done it, he done it. If not, I want the person found."

"Do you think they said his name because of his reputation?"

"Could have been. He's not well liked."

BODY WORN footage was shown to the jury who heard Prescilla Ackleton senior tell police officers: "He put his car over her three times. He runned (sic) her over. Runned (sic) her over again. It was not an accident."

She was asked: "Which car?"

"The one he set alight. It's Patrick Molloy. I saw him run over her, reversing. He tried to kill her, reversing on her over and over. He said: 'I run Gravesend'."

"Is that an account of what you saw?"

"I was full of adrenaline."

"If the people who saw what happened and you didn't, why did you not put them in front of the police officers?"

"Not know."

BRIDGET SAUNDERS took to the witness box.

"What were you doing before the incident?" asked the prosecutor.

"Making the kids breakfast."

"And then?"

"I heard some shouting. I went outside to see what was happening."

"Did you see who was shouting?"

"One man. But there were a lot of people on the site."

"Had you seen him before?"

"Not sure."

"How would you describe him?"

"A white male."

"Just a white male. Hair?"

"Gingerish. Five feet something tall."

"Where was he?"

"He was sitting in a silver car, I think."

"Ever seen him before?"

"Not know."

"Did he get out of the car?"

"Yes. I asked him what he was doing here."

"Why?"

"I thought it might be Patrick Molloy or Malone."

"Why did you ask him?"

"He'd had a row with Prescilla [senior]."

"How did he respond?"

"He jumped out of the car and shouted at me. Said he was going to beat me. That my other half was in prison and he was a dead man."

"What did you do?"

"I told him to fuck off. He got back in his car and drove it at me. He stopped just before it hit me. He put it in reverse and Prescilla got run over. I did not see the motor hit her. He then went forward, back and drove off."

"Who else was there?"

"George."

"Where was he?"

"By the back of the car."

"Do you remember the statement you made to the police?"

379

"Yes and no. Kind of."

"Did you describe what happened that morning?"

"Yes."

"You said in your statement: 'I heard him say to George 'if I can't have her no one can.' Did you hear him say this?"

"No."

"Do you remember telling the police who was driving the car?"

"Not remember."

"Who did you tell them it was?"

"Patrick Molloy."

"You said: 'I saw Patrick in the car with a bottle of vodka between his legs.' Did you?"

"No."

"Why was it in your statement?"

"It was something I heard everyone saying."

NEXT UP for a memorable cross-examination by the Crown was George Ackleton.

"What were you doing on the morning of May 13, 2018?"

"I went to the shop to get some fags and then went home."

"Which side of the road were the shops on?"

"Either the left or right."

"From which direction do you enter the site?"

"In."

"What happened then?"

"Someone with a car or van arrived. Not know who. We had a few words or an argument."

"What sort of car was it?"

"Parked."

"Colour?"

"I'm colour blind."

"Anyone in the car?"

"Not at the time."

"Were you near the car?"

"Yes."

"Where was the man?"

"Next to the driver's side."

"Describe him."

"To the best of my recollection, I can't remember."

"Was it a man?"

"Yes."

"Colour?"

"White."

"Hair?"

"Not sure. I'm not backward, but I can't remember."

"Did you speak to him?"

"Yes."

"His accent?"

"Irish."

"What did you say?"

"A few words, can't remember."

"Seen him before?"

"Not personally, but I might have seen him before."

"What happened then?"

"As I was walking home my daughter came out and the bloke I've just described. I remember a car reversing over her. I panicked."

"How far away were you?"

[He measured in court and said he would have been six feet away].

"In your statement to the police on the day, did you tell them what happened?"

"I think so."

"You said: 'I saw a man I know as Paddy Patrick, that's what I always called him. I think he's Patrick Molloy, but I refer to him as Paddy Patrick'."

"I do not know if he was the bloke there."

"How about: 'He was in a silver car on his own.' Does that help you?"

"I know it was a car, but I can't remember what happened yesterday."

"You said: 'He shouted 'you fucking English pig'."

"Not denying he called me that. I just can't remember."

"Were you telling the police the truth?"

"What I remember, but not know what I was saying."

"Did you know, on May 13, that it was Patrick Molloy?"

"Yes."

"Met him before?"

"Yes."

"Heard his voice?"

"Yes."

"Why did you tell the police the car was silver?"

"Not know."

"Was it him in the car?"

"It was a man."

"Your statement said: 'I've known him a year or so. He'd previously courted my daughter.' That right?"

"Yes."

"Describe Patrick Molloy."

"What I can remember… a big bloke, curlish hair."

"How tall?"

"I don't understand heighth [yes, he said that]."

"In your statement you said: 'Slim, ginger hair, five feet six inches.' How did you manage to describe him to the police?"

"Not know."

"You said he had ginger hair."

"I wasn't with it."

"You said: 'I had to walk past Paddy in his silver car'."

"I assumed it was someone like him."

"Why assume it was Patrick Molloy?"

"Don't know."

"You lying?"

"No."

"He shouted: 'English gypsy'."

"Not remember that."

"It's fairly specific."

"Just a name."

"Would an English traveller say that?"

"Not think so."

"You said: 'I said fuck off, don't want to speak'."

"Not remember. I'm trying the best I can."

"You said: 'He reversed over her as she lay on the floor, then a second time'."

"Think it did. Not sure if my daughter was run over once or twice. Could even have been four."

"You remember an air ambulance arriving?"

"Not really."

"Is this true? 'I saw him up close, we were within a few feet of each other.' True?"

"Yes."

"How about: 'I have known him for a couple of years. As soon as I saw him, I knew it was Paddy Patrick'."

"People were talking. I know I told the police something. I don't know what I put in the statement."

"It was read back to you and you said it was accurate."

"Might have been."

"Before your further statement almost a month later… before this did you speak to anyone?"

"Not remember. I don't know what a statement is."

"Did your wife speak to you about changing her statement?"

"Not know."

"Your daughter?"

"No."

"Twin sister Bridget?"

"No."

"Why did you make a second statement?"

"A lot of questions… didn't want to make any more statements, so I went to the police."

"Why go to the police?"

"I was not sure what I was saying. If I said something wrong, I should not have made first statement."

"You said: 'We are honest people and just want to get on with our lives. I am doing this because I now realise it was not Patrick Molloy.' Are you lying to the jury?"

"No."

"In court you said you could not remember if it was Patrick Molloy. In your new statement you said: 'It was not Patrick Molloy.' Why the difference?"

"Not know. I am trying to put all my brain into answering."

"In your statement you said: 'I'm not a Christian. I'm Church of England. I am now telling the truth about what happened'."

"I don't know what I'm saying. I'm not with it today, just trying to help. I was hit by a car 20 years ago and my brain moved."

"You said: 'I now realise it wasn't Patrick Molloy. I was confused.' If you didn't know what colour hair he had, how could you tell it was ginger?"

"Not know."

"You told the police the car reversed over her twice."

"I have to be taught how to dress and walk to the toilet. I can't remember what I'm saying now. I'm not backward. I just need help."

THE JURY was shown further body worn footage from when police officers arrived at the caravan park.

George Ackleton was initially bare-chested — "I don't wear a lot of clothes in the morning."

He said: "It's Patrick Malone." His wife corrected him: "Molloy."

Ackleton continued: "He tried to kill her mate, that's an offence and he's got to be locked up. He's out of his nut. Ran her over twice. This is when he'd tried to kill her. I hope the police don't arrest my daughter."

The Crown put it to him: "You were capable of giving the police a very clear description."

"I don't know what happened."

"Why did you not tell the police you did not remember?"

"Not remember."

PATRICK MOLLOY has seven brothers and three sisters. Cross-examined by the defence barrister, he said had been married "on and off" for five years. He was now with Kelly and they had a five-month-old daughter. He said he had never heard the expression "English snail" and had "no problems" with the English.

He claimed he met Prescilla junior on Facebook, even though she said she cannot read or write. He was "still married" when they met, but his wife had gone to live in Ireland. The relationship with Prescilla junior blossomed while he was in HMP Elmley on the Isle of Sheppey where he was serving a three-year sentence for actual bodily harm after spraying bleach in someone's face.

Prescilla junior would visit him "even though it is a two-hour drive each way" said Molloy, but "I never asked her to come." They spoke "every day" on the phone — "I phoned her." He would receive "three or four love letters" a week, but did not have the letters now.

"When I came out of prison, I had no need for them."

"Did you ever threaten Prescilla?"

"No."

"Hit her?"

"No."

"Slap her?"

"No."

"Control her?"

"No."

"Harm her in any way?"

"No."

"What was your relationship with her?"

"She was very jealous. Even when we were not together, she told me not to see anyone."

"George?"

"He's an alcoholic."

"What makes you think that?"

"He was always drunk. I've never seen him sober."

"Where were you on May 13 ?"

"In the morning I took Amy [a girl he had been with the previous night] home. I was with Alex, a Romanian who I worked with. We stopped at the Lion garage in Northfleet for breakfast at 05.55."

"Did you see anyone while you were there?"

"George."

"What was he doing?"

"Buying beer."

"You say anything?"

"He said: 'Hello.' I said nothing."

"And then?"

"I took Amy home. Had a coffee there. I had a call from John Jarvis, Lisa James's son. It was about a bulldog puppy and a black cat. He wanted a swap deal, but the dog was £500."

"How did you have a bulldog puppy?"

"I had the mother and she had five pups. The swap was a non-starter. I wanted the dog back. We had some heated words."

"Then what?"

"I went to Lisa James's house. She told me to fuck off, excuse my language."

"She said you had a hammer."

"The hammer was on the ground."

"Did you hold it to her face?"

"No."

"How long were you there?"

"About 30 seconds."

"Then?"

"We [Alex was still on the scene] drove to my friend Tammy in Northfleet."

"Then?"

"Danny, one of Lisa James's brothers who lived ten doors along, ran towards me. Danny was joined by his sister... they had weapons... poles. They attacked the vehicle with the poles. They smashed the driver's window, the windscreen and a passenger window. We drove off to my place."

"Where did you go?"

"To the Lion garage where we met two of my brothers."

"Then?"

"As we both drove off my brother was pulled in by the police. I did a U-turn."

"Where exactly were you, around 10 a.m. on May 13?"

"At my sister's."

"How long were you there?"

"An hour and a half. Certainly, over an hour."

"Did you at any time go to the Denton caravan site?"

"No."

"Did you drive a silver Peugeot?"

"No."

"We heard evidence from witnesses who said you were at the Denton caravan site."

"Yes."

"Why do you think they said it was you there?"

"They don't like me because I dumped their daughter."

"When you were arrested the officers concluded you were drunk and mouthy."

"I was terrified."

"You declined to undergo a breathalyser test."

"I just thought the police were out to get me. Still do."

"How did you feel when you were charged with attempted murder?"

"I thought it was a joke."

"Why did you say nothing in your police interview?"

"I was advised so by my solicitor and I took his advice."

THE PROSECUTION took over cross-examination of Patrick Molloy.

"When you were arrested you told the police: 'I'll fuck youse all up'."

"I was frightened."

"At the pre-trial hearing you were ordered to serve a defence statement drafted by your lawyers. This was what you were saying about the allegations, after you had seen the statements the prosecution were relying upon. You would have approved this."

"Yes."

"You would not have approved it if it was wrong."

"No."

"You made a mention of Lisa James's brothers when it was her sons. Did you not notice this mistake at the time?"

"No."

"You made a statement to your legal team."

"My words look different in writing."

"Your statement said: 'The defendant did not damage any ornaments or the wall at Lisa James's property'."

"I pleaded guilty to the wall."

"You didn't."

"The statement said you didn't damage any ornament. Did you?"

"Yes."

387

"So that's a lie in your defence statement."

"No. Just a mistake."

"You have been deceiving the CPS."

"I'm a Catholic and I do not tell lies."

"When your statement was read to you that you did not damage any ornament, what did you do?"

"I don't really recall it, but if I had recalled it I would have said something."

"You must have told them lies."

"I told them my recollections. There are mistakes, but more in the prosecution's."

"You said: 'The damage was already present.' Another mistake?"

"Yes. If this was read back to me, I would have noticed. My solicitor made some minor mistakes."

"Like whether you were guilty or not."

"Minor mistakes."

"You said you did not attend the Denton caravan site on May 13. How did your solicitor know?"

"I told them."

"You said it was two hours' drive to the Isle of Sheppey. It's 30 miles."

"That's what I was told."

"Your statement said the family fabricated lies against you because you slighted Miss Ackleton."

"What does 'slight' mean?"

"That they were angry with you."

"They were angry with me."

"The first time you mentioned that you were with your sister at the time of the incident was in court. Why did you not say this in your defence statement?"

"I wasn't asked."

"How long were you with her?"

"About a quarter of an hour."

THE PROSECUTION'S application for bad character against the defendant was granted by the judge who explained to the jury: "Patrick Molloy has said in the witness box that nine or 10 women could give positive character references for him.

"He basically said he is a man of good character. He is not and had he not been challenged then the jury could have been left with a false impression. The impression Patrick Molloy gave about that needed to be corrected. You now have an accurate impression rather than an inaccurate one."

Molloy's previous convictions started in October 2014 with two counts of criminal damage. There followed possession of a knife, threatening behaviour, theft, sexual assault, ABH, affray and another knife possession. The defendant had trouble remembering the sexual assault conviction for which he was imprisoned. "I had a hip operation," he said. "It may have affected my memory."

The judge said: "These convictions do not show a propensity for attempted murder and cannot by themselves prove his guilt. The critical evidence is that which you heard."

The jury was also told that the average journey from Northfleet to the Isle of Sheppey was 41 minutes.

THE JUDGE gave the jury the directions in law which it must consider when reaching its verdict.

"First of all, are you sure Patrick Molloy was the driver of the car and that it was deliberately driven at Prescilla Ackleton junior? Are you sure that when he drove over her, he was trying to kill her? If not, then you can consider grievous bodily harm with intent which is causing really serious harm as opposed to some harm.

"Consider the evidence of the witnesses. How long did they observe him for? Take into account the distance and the light. The actual description they used on the bodycam — did they have any reason to say what happened? Was it spontaneous and genuine, or might they have made a mistake?

"How much emphasis you put on what was said closer to the incident in police statements is your choice. Was there any difference in what the witnesses subsequently said and if so, what emphasis do you place on this?

"Your task is to judge the credibility of each witness overall. You can accept some and reject some of the evidence you heard. What part, if any, are you sure of? If you believe they were truthful at any stage you can accept this.

"Patrick Molloy has given three different time accounts of how long he was with his sister at the time of the incident. An hour and a half, over an hour and a quarter of an hour. Whether you believe this is because he was genuinely confused or forgetful or was lying is for you to decide."

THE CROWN'S summing up was unusual as it challenged the honesty of its claimant and the prosecution witnesses.

"With a warped association of the truth, Patrick Molloy admitted to the criminal damage, which is different to pleading guilty," said the prosecutor. "Regarding the controlling and coercive behaviour, the evidence is there for you. It shone a true light on his character. The claimant said the relationship was mentally and physically abusive. There were threats to kill.

"Prescilla Ackleton junior said it was a deliberate act. Bridget Saunders said he [Molloy] had a bottle of vodka between his legs. When he was arrested, he declined a breath test at 10 a.m. Why would he do that?

"The witnesses changed their evidence because they have been manipulated by the defendant. The truth has held no value for the participants in this trial which has descended into a murky world of lack of respect for law.

"There is no lack of evidence of Patrick Molloy's dishonesty and bare faced lies."

THE DEFENCE made the point that Patrick Molloy chose to give evidence in court, which he was not obliged to. "I have no idea what you think about travellers and their way of life," said the defence barrister to the jury. "The prosecution said witnesses all perjured themselves to tell lies. That's a dangerous starting point."

The jury had to decide whether to believe the initial statements and evidence of the prosecution witnesses or if their subsequent withdrawals were more credible.

42

PATRICK MOLLOY: Attempted murder; controlling and coercive behaviour; criminal damage.

THE TRIAL became almost addictive in a bizarre way, if only because it was obvious everyone, except perhaps Bridget Saunders, who gave evidence in court was lying. Oaths or affirmations were innocent bystanders as the jury heard contradictions and withdrawals from all prosecution parties. Their evidence made "the dog ate my homework" credible.

But the old adage of always taking your chance with a jury rang true for Patrick Molloy. His guilt could barely have been in doubt, but what was he guilty of?

The jury decided that despite the witnesses belatedly claiming they could not positively identify the driver of the car, it was sure it was Molloy. However, the jury did not consider the defendant reversing over his former partner at least twice to be attempted murder, only grievous bodily harm with intent.

The jurors could also not be sure Molloy was controlling and coercive towards Prescilla Ackleton junior during their time together. As the defendant admitted to criminal damage of Lisa James's ornament and wall, he was found guilty of that charge, though it would make no difference to the overall sentencing.

The police had to take the pragmatic view which was that the defendant was convicted despite (or perhaps, because) the prosecution witnesses claimed they were not sure Molloy was the driver. The jury did not buy into their collective withdrawal of evidence.

We shall never know exactly why the witnesses did an about turn with their statements. Molloy was in custody before he had a chance to speak to anyone, so draw your own conclusion — the judge did. The prosecution merely said the witnesses had been "manipulated."

The judge asked for a pre-sentence report from probation to assess the level of dangerousness Molloy posed to the public.

AT THE sentencing of Patrick Molloy there were seven armed police officers. Molloy's defence barrister had the unenviable task of trying to ensure the lightest possible sentence for her client.

Defence: "It is possible that when he ran over Prescilla Ackleton junior it was all in one movement." Judge: "I do not accept that at all. It was not just once, it was repeated."

Molloy's barrister tried to convince the judge the defendant had nothing to do with the victim and witnesses changing their statements a month after their original ones. "There is no evidence he had any part in the withdrawal of the [original] statements. Whatever action the family may have taken, it does not mean Patrick Molloy was involved. He was sitting in custody, unable to control the actions of those on the outside."

The judge interrupted her: "Given the extent of the pressure, it is an irresistible inference he was involved. It is perfectly reasonable [to believe] he was."

Why Molloy might have turned out to be a serial criminal, his barrister explained: "His parents separated when he was young."

Saving the best till last, she said: "He's lost weight in prison. He heard a fellow prisoner say he had a bladed object and he told a prison officer about it."

So he's a thin grass, then.

Some details of Molloy's previous convictions were read out, including an incident for which he was given three years' imprisonment. He had an argument with a mechanic about his car and became so angry he punched the mechanic and then threw bleach in his face. The next day he telephoned the mechanic and apologised, saying he had now calmed down.

Some consolation for the poor mechanic who, thankfully, did not lose his sight.

Molloy wrote (or, more likely, someone wrote it on his behalf) a letter to the judge in which he expressed his remorse about running over his ex-partner. It didn't work. Judge: "I heard the way he conducted himself giving evidence. The letter amounts to crocodile tears."

Molloy was given 10 years plus two extended for his level of dangerousness.

43

ROGER OATLEY: Coercive and controlling behaviour

GROUNDED AND CONTROLLED
...OR WAS SHE?

THE OFFENCE of controlling or coercive behaviour in a relationship is relatively new, coming into effect on December 29, 2015. England and Wales were the first countries to criminalise the offence which carries a maximum of five years' imprisonment. Some think the police should not become involved in what is just a bad relationship without violence, but the law was introduced to prevent extremes of control. The belief was that threats, humiliation, monitoring and isolation from friends and family can be as damaging as physical violence.

Controlling or coercive behaviour is that which causes someone to fear violence will be used against them on at least two occasions; or causes them serious alarm or distress which has a substantial adverse effect on their usual day-to-day activities. It does not relate to a single incident. It is a purposeful pattern of behaviour which takes place over time in order for one individual to exert power, control or coercion over another.

Broken down in law, controlling behaviour is a range of acts designed to make a person subordinate and/or dependent by isolating them from sources of support, exploiting their resources and capacities for personal gain, depriving them of the means needed for independence, resistance and escape and regulating their everyday behaviour.

Coercive behaviour is a continuing act or a pattern of acts of assault, threats, humiliation and intimidation or other abuse that is used to harm, punish, or frighten their victim.

Joanna Dalton, who was 17 when she met the defendant, believed

Roger Oatley controlled her life.

THE PROSECUTION had no further questions for the claimant whose police interview had been watched by the jury. The defence opened the cross-examination of Joanna Dalton.

"You met Roger in 2018 when you had a part-time job."

"Yes. In Domino's. I was studying."

"You met him on a bus."

"No, in a store. He approached me to ask if I smoked weed. I gave him my number and we started dating."

"When did he meet your parents?"

"After a couple of weeks."

"You were living at home."

"Yes. He was homeless, staying with friends and with me from time to time."

"You fell pregnant after three months."

"Yes. He wanted to live elsewhere because he did not like my parents. There were a lot of arguments. I preferred to stay with my parents."

"What did he do?"

"He found a room, but it was not appropriate for a baby. There were people smoking and a lot of drugs."

"He did not force you to leave."

"Yes, he did. He made me choose between him and my parents. He had my money etc. so I had to go with him. I was intimidated and scared of him. When our daughter was born, he was homeless again."

"He moved back to your parents' house."

"Yes. We agreed he should not be homeless when the baby arrived."

"It was your choice."

"Well, yes, but I had no real say because I was so scared. He threatened to kill my parents."

"He put pressure on you to keep the baby."

"Yes. I didn't think I was ready to have my first child aged 17 under all the circumstances."

"You went on a family holiday after a couple of months so he was not controlling."

"I received abusive messages, asking what I was wearing. I did not know what to do. I'd never been in this situation before. I was scared. My parents saw the messages."

"What was it like when he moved in with your parents?"

"There were arguments in the family house and the police were called by my mother who'd confronted Roger after what he had said to me. He was shouting in her face and pushed her on to a door. The police were told the father was trying to leave with the child. Social Services attended, but it was classed as a minor altercation with no injuries."

"What happened next?"

"I went to my aunt's house. It was the only option I had. All three of us went there. I was forced to do that."

"Why did you not tell the police?"

"I had never had anything to do with the police. I did not know what to say."

"You declared yourself homeless to the council which is a requirement to get a house. They provided a studio flat for you and you had a set of keys between you. You say he took the keys so you could not go out. He never locked you in, did he?"

"I never went out. I was scared. I wasn't allowed to shop."

"He used your money for family food, milk, baby wipes etc. The weekly shop."

"No. Once a month if I was lucky."

"The rest of the time he did not have possession of your card."

"He did."

"You said in your ABE [achieving best evidence — her police interview that was recorded] that during your time together it was used to get the £500 deposit for the room. You gave him permission."

"He had the card so it didn't matter. He'd do it anyway. He said: 'I'm going to use money from your card' and if I said 'OK' it was because he would do it regardless. I cannot remember him ever asking me if he could use the card. He just told me he was going to do it. If I ever said 'yes' it was to prevent an argument as I was scared. The £500 was originally for a room for the three of us. When he left after a couple of weeks the landlord wouldn't give him back the deposit, or so he said."

"The £728 transferred to Roger was money to be spent on the family for Christmas."

"No. It was child benefit money and he transferred it for his drugs money, for his friends, or rather his customers."

"I suggest you made the transfer."

"No. He did it. I remember, I was breast-feeding the baby. Do you think I'd let him transfer all that money for Christmas presents in early September? That's a long time before Christmas so it doesn't make sense."

"Why didn't you go to the bank?"

"I didn't have any money to go anywhere. I didn't have a phone either."

THE DEFENCE moved on to Jim Stafford, Joanna Dalton's new partner.

It was put to the claimant: "Your plan was to leave Roger for Stafford."

"No."

"You were in a relationship with him."

"Not then. Later."

"This is the second time this trial has been listed."

"Yes."

"Was Mr Stafford in court that day?"

"Yes."

"It was adjourned because of his behaviour."

"Both of their behaviour."

"He threatened Roger. Taunted him."

"I don't think so. I did not see or hear anything."

THE PROSECUTION cross-examined Roger Oatley.

"When arrested you did a no comment interview. Why?"

"It was what my solicitor advised."

"But your choice."

"Yes."

"What happened last September?"

"It was outside the court [room]. Jim [Stafford] looked at me. I'd never seen him before. He provoked me. I did not say anything to him."

"Why do you think Joanna Dalton has made these allegations?"

"Because she does not want to be with me. She wanted to be with Jim, but no idea why she made these allegations."

"You controlled and coerced her."

"I do not accept I behaved in that manner."

"Would you agree controlling and coercive behaviour is not normal?"

"Yes."

"Where did you learn your skills of relationships with the opposite sex?"

"No one taught me. Just picked them up."

"Your relationship with the claimant ended with her phoning the police."

"Yes."

"That's not normal."

"No."

"Why did she need help?"

"She didn't. She could've just left [me]."

"Your relationship with her parents was not a success. Why?"

"There was a lot of stress. It was a stressful situation."

"How did you get on with her aunty?"

"Very well."

"The pattern I am getting at is you rub everyone up the wrong way and it ends in social disaster."

"Not true."

"You left care at 18. Did you have a lump sum for a flat?"

"I never had it."

"Why were you an exception?"

"It was their mistake. I'm trying to sort it out."

"Initially how was your relationship with her parents?"

"Good."

"They were welcoming."

"Very."

"They saw you as son-in-law material."

"I like to think so. We shared quality time together."

"But it all ended in tears. What led to the police being called?"

"About me taking the baby."

"You just grabbed the baby in a fit of pique and stormed off."

"No."

"Tell me about the £500."

"We were looking for a house. A place to live."

"But it was not appropriate. People smoking and that."

"Yes. I wanted a no smoking house. The landlord kept the deposit when I left."

"You ended in a place in Catford. An attic conversion. Barely big enough for two people."

"Not true."

"A loft conversion with windows looking up. All you could see were birds flying."

"Not true."

"She could not call to anyone if she was in danger."

"Not true."

"You effectively had her locked up in it."

"Not true."

"Who came to visit her?"

"Couple of her friends, I think."

"Her mum and sister not come?"

"She stopped talking to them."

"Only one set of keys."

"One of us should have done it. It was never an issue."

"I suggest it was extraordinary."

"Now… maybe a bit silly."

"You can get a key cut for a fiver."

"Don't know."

"It was your father who eventually had another cut."

"A spur of the moment thing."

"You serious? It was controlling behaviour."

"No."

"Why did you have her bank card?"

"I never had it."

"Again, why did you have her bank card?"

"No idea."

"You isolated her so much she was totally reliant on you."

"No."

"The transfer of £728. No one has ever said to me: 'Can I borrow

£728?' It's an odd sum."

"Yes."

"You wiped her out."

"No."

"The only money coming in was tax credits and benefits."

"Not true."

THE PROSECUTOR produced Joanna Dalton's bank statement from July 14 to September 9.

"There are 35 transactions to R. Oatley. Yet there is no money from you."

"No."

"You do not have to search the statement. You never paid her a bean."

"Not know that."

"The money coming in was child tax credits and money from DWP. What you got are £35 transactions to you. The last wiped her out — £728, leaving her 59 pence. Is that not controlling behaviour?"

"No."

"There are lots of fast-food payments. McDonald's, Hungry Horse, Burger King — that's you, isn't it?"

"No, her."

"Did anyone else have use of the card?"

"Not as far as I know."

"Who went to TK Maxx in Watford?"

"Don't know."

"Well, if it wasn't you, it must have been her. How did she get there with a young baby? Taxi or public transport?"

"Not know."

"Cabs are expensive especially if there is no money coming in. Lot of Uber payments. Cabs every day. I couldn't afford it."

"You and me are not the same."

"You're dead right there. Did she have a motorbike?"

"No."

"August 18 — £150 for motorbike spares. That's you."

"I guess, yes."

"What I'm suggesting is you controlled her account."

"Not true."

THE JUDGE directed the jury it had to be sure that the defendant knew his behaviour was controlling or coercive and he was aware that it would have had an effect on Joanna Dalton's day-to-day activities and cause her distress.

Did Roger Oatley make her suffer or was it her own choice? If he was only guilty of not being the perfect partner, the judge told the jury it must find the defendant not guilty. If it was sure the defendant knowingly made the claimant suffer and acted in a manner that a reasonable person would have known was controlling or coercive then he must be found guilty.

The jury asked only one question during its deliberations — why did the aunt not give evidence? The judge told the jury it should not speculate on the reason as it came to its verdict which took two hours to reach.

43

ROGER OATLEY: Controlling and coercive behaviour

THE DIFFICULTY for the jury would probably have been to imagine how Joanna Dalton — or, indeed, anyone — could allow themselves to be dominated in such a manner, especially so quickly. Could she really have let herself be controlled in this way, remembering there was no evidence of violence?

It would be natural for each juror to ask whether it could happen to them with the likely answer of "no." Yet, as we know, people of all ages can fall victim to initially sweet-talkers with an agenda. Just because it could not happen to you, it would be wrong to assume it could not happen to someone else because it does.

As with so many trials, it effectively boiled down to one person's word against the other. However, Roger Oatley must have thought he had been smiled upon from above when the foreman of the jury announced: "Not guilty."

For me it was an unbelievable verdict... unfathomable... ridiculous... and surely completely wrong.

The prosecution's evidence could hardly have been stronger. The bank statements; the 35 transactions to the defendant's bank account with none going the other way; the defendant having "no idea" why he had the claimant's bank card; the motor bike spares — the evidence against Oatley was surely as strong as it gets. But apparently not.

Only 12 people know why they did not believe Oatley controlled and coerced the life of Joanna Dalton and why the evidence they heard was insufficient for them to be sure of this and return a guilty verdict.

File under baffled.

HOW A JUDGE SENTENCES GUILTY DEFENDANTS

A JURY is not obliged to sit in on the sentencing of defendants and it was understandable that none of the 12 who found the five accused guilty in this gang-war trial wanted to re-live the evidence they had heard over a seven-week trial.

If anyone wondered about the depth of feeling, violence and revenge killings between rival gangs then the sentencing remarks of Mr Justice Spencer will leave you in no doubt. This is how His Honour sentenced the five young murderers.

It will show you how much time, work and background research the judge put into his sentencing. How his hands are tied, to some extent, by the Sentencing Council guidelines. And how he has to determine totality whereby, unlike in the United States, 60- or 80-years' imprisonment is not a reality in England and Wales.

You may be puzzled how law differentiates the intention to kill as opposed to just causing serious bodily harm when more than one defendant is involved. Many would feel if someone is stabbed in the chest multiple times there can be only one motive — to take a person's life. Law is not as black and white as that.

The Queen

v

Clayton Barker, Charlie Chandler, Ben Potter, Jamie Chandler and Earl Bevans

Sentencing remarks of Mr Justice Spencer, Luton Crown Court, January 6 2021

1. Clayton Barker, Charlie Chandler, Ben Potter, Jamie Chandler and Earl Bevans, I have to sentence each of you for two offences of murder and two offences of wounding with intent, all committed within the space of a few minutes around midnight on Saturday October 19 2019. Two of your victims were stabbed to death. The other two were

stabbed but survived. It is a dreadfully serious case. You, Earl Bevans, pleaded guilty to all these offences on the first day of the trial, before the jury was sworn. The other four of you were convicted by the jury after a trial lasting seven weeks.

2. The five of you gate-crashed a 17th birthday party at a house in Milton Keynes, armed with knives and machetes, with masks to conceal your identity. You had been tipped off that members of the rival M4 gang were at the party and you travelled there together by taxi. Four of you climbed over the fence into the back garden and burst into the house through the conservatory. The fifth remained outside to intercept anyone who ran out of the house. Ben Gilham-Rice was stabbed to death in the living room whilst the party was in full flow, in the presence of several teenage boys and girls. Two other victims were stabbed in the house but fortunately not fatally. Dom Ansah managed to run out of the house but was chased, eventually cornered and brutally and mercilessly stabbed some 35 times. He died in hospital three hours later.

3. For murder there is only one sentence for an adult: imprisonment for life. That is the sentence which I shall pass upon you, Charlie Chandler and you Earl Bevans. You are both over 21 years of age. Because you, Clayton Barker, are still only 20 years of age, the sentence in your case has to be expressed as custody for life. Because you Ben Potter, and you Jamie Chandler, were under 18 years of age when you committed these murders, the sentence in your case has to be expressed as detention during Her Majesty's pleasure. But make no mistake, the effect of the sentence for each of you will be the same. Each of you will remain in custody for very many years to come until you have served the minimum term which I am obliged by law to fix in the case of each of you; thereafter you will remain in custody until such time as the Parole Board considers it safe to release you. You will then remain on licence for the rest of your life, liable to be recalled to prison if you commit any further offence or breach the conditions of your licence.

4. No sentence I pass can reflect the depth of the grief suffered by the families of the two young men whose lives you took. The families have sat throughout the seven weeks of this trial with enormous dignity as they tried to understand and come to terms with the horrifying brutality of the events of that fateful night. In their moving personal statements

read to the court they have explained the devastating impact of their loss. Ben Gilham-Rice and Dom Ansah were both only 17 years old, with their lives ahead of them. For the families the loss of their beloved sons is in a very real sense a life sentence.

5. The all-too-familiar background to these senseless and tragic killings was rivalry between gangs of young men and the culture of violence and knives, promoted on social media. Sadly, Dom Ansah was himself caught up in that gang culture as a leading member of M4. And it was through his association with Dom Ansah, albeit not to a member of the gang himself, that Ben Gilham-Rice was at the party that night with M4 gang members. But the violence that night escalated way beyond anything that had gone before.

6. You Clayton Barker, Ben Potter and Jamie Chandler were enthusiastic members of the rival B3 gang. You Charlie Chandler and Earl Bevans were not members of B3, but you were closely associated with those who were and willing to lend your support that night in this revenge attack as part of the ongoing feud.

7. In September 2017, you Ben Potter were subjected at the age of 14 to a vicious and degrading assault at the hands of members of the M4 gang, including Dom Ansah. You were beaten and stripped. A video clip of you naked and bloodied was widely shared on social media. I have no doubt that this episode traumatised you deeply and left you with a sense of understandable grievance.

8. In April 2019, just six months before these murders, you Jamie Chandler were the victim of gang violence when you were attacked in broad daylight and stabbed in the lower back. You had no choice but to report the matter to the police, who had already been called to the scene, but you were unable or unwilling to identify your attackers. It is plain that those responsible were members of M4. The widely circulating belief aired on social media was, rightly or wrongly, that Dom Ansah was responsible.

9. I have no doubt that these two incidents fuelled the desire on the part of members of B3 to have their revenge on members of M4 if and when a suitable opportunity arose. That is undoubtedly the background to these horrific offences.

10. In fixing the minimum term which each of you must serve before

you are eligible even to be considered for release by the Parole Board, I am required to take into account the seriousness of these two offences of murder and the two associated offences of wounding with intent. I am required to have regard to the general principles set out in Schedule 21 to the Criminal Justice Act 2003, now re-enacted in Schedule 21 to the Sentencing Act 2020. In your case Earl Bevans, because you were convicted before December 1 2020, the 2003 Act applies. In the case of the other four of you, because you were convicted after that date, the 2020 Act applies. There is no material difference in the provisions of the two statutes.

11. In the case of the three adult defendants, it is common ground that because you have been convicted of two murders committed after you had attained the age of 18, the starting point set by parliament for your minimum term is 30 years, which is the equivalent of a determinate sentence of 60 years. In the case of the two juvenile defendants, the starting point set by parliament for your minimum term irrespective of the number of murders is 12 years, the equivalent of a determinate sentence of 24 years. It is rightly conceded on your behalf that there must be a significant uplift from the starting point of 12 years to reflect the fact that you are being sentenced for two murders.

12. Before turning to the aggravating and mitigating factors requiring departure from the starting points set by parliament, and to the individual circumstances of each of you, it is necessary for me to set out briefly my findings of fact on the evidence.

13. I have no doubt that it was you, Clayton Barker, who received the tip-off that members of M4 were at the party. That message came late in the evening, shortly after 11p.m. You were then at Charlie Chandler's flat, 23 Fitzwilliam Street. Directly or indirectly contact was made with Jamie Chandler and Ben Potter who were at Jamie Chandler's home, where they had been joined by Earl Bevans. At just before 11.15 p.m. Jamie Chandler and Ben Potter were recording a clip of themselves rapping, in which Ben Potter was talking about "boring", which is slang for stabbing and asking Jamie Chandler where his mask was, to which the reply was "in the garage". Jamie Chandler then phoned for a taxi, a seven-seater, to take the three of them to 23 Fitzwilliam Street, to pick up Charlie Chandler and Clayton Barker. I have no doubt that you,

Clayton Barker were taking the lead in this expedition to mount a surprise attack on members of the M4 gang at the party.

14. On the way to the house in Archford Croft where the party was in full swing, the taxi was directed to stop off at some garages in Braybrook Drive for what can only have been the purpose of obtaining weapons or further weapons. You, Charlie Chandler, knew the house in Archford Croft from the outside at least, from previous visits. You stayed outside whilst the other four went over the back gate into the garden and then rushed into the house through the conservatory, armed with weapons and wearing masks.

15. I am quite sure on the evidence that, with the exception of Charlie Chandler, all four of you went into the house and that you did so intending to take part in attacking and inflicting serious injury on any members of M4 who were present. You, Ben Potter, were distinctive not least because of your small stature. On its own, the voice identification by Olivia Burgess might not have been sufficiently reliable, but coupled with the description of your appearance by her and other witnesses inside the house I am quite sure that you spoke to her, asking if she wanted to be stabbed and that you had a large knife which you were trying to conceal in your waistband.

16. Within seconds of you all entering the house, Ben Gilham-Rice was repeatedly stabbed in the living room, in full view of the terrified teenagers. There were six separate sharp force injuries, including four stab wounds. The fatal wound to his chest penetrated to a depth of 20 cm and pierced the heart. There was a second stab wound close by which cut through the sixth rib and penetrated to a depth of 8 cm. There was also a stab wound 17 cm deep to the back of his right thigh. The clear inference is that Ben Gilham-Rice was stabbed by more than one person. He died within minutes from massive blood loss.

17. Ryan Brown was stabbed in the left side of the chest, with sufficient force to fracture a rib. There was a laceration to his spleen and a contusion to his lung. He was standing just outside the front door when he was stabbed; the person who did it clearly recognised him as a member or associate of M4, and said his name "Ryan" immediately before stabbing him. Ryan Brown fled from the house and escaped further attack. Tom Honhold was also stabbed in the house, receiving a

wound to his right arm and a cut above his right hip. He, too, fled from the house and was pursued for some distance but he, too, escaped further attack.

18. Dom Ansah ran out of the house when he realised what was happening. It is entirely possible that he received some of his stab wounds in the house, but when he ran outside, he managed to keep ahead of his pursuers. This part of the incident is clearly shown in the dash cam footage from a taxi parked outside the house. Although there was much discussion and argument during the trial about the identity of the two defendants chasing Dom Ansah and Tom Honhold, I am quite sure on all the evidence that you, Jamie Chandler, were male 3 leading the chase and you, Clayton Barker, were male 4 who joined him and revived Jamie Chandler's interest in the chase when he hesitated momentarily.

19. The dash cam footage shows Dom Ansah running back towards the house a few seconds later, closely pursued by the two of you. He slipped and lost his footing for a moment, thereby enabling the two of you to catch up with him. There followed an appallingly brutal sustained attack on Dom Ansah, close to the house, in which he was repeatedly stabbed and subjected to chopping injuries from a machete. There were some 35 separate sharp force injuries. The number and distribution of those injuries leads to the sure inference that two or more of you joined in the frenzied attack. The fatal injury was a stab wound to the back which penetrated the left lung with a track depth of 15 cm. There was a chop wound to the back of the left shoulder which almost split the bony process of the shoulder blade. There was a classic defence injury to the left hand which split the bone of the little finger. As the pathologist explained, there must have been some hard surface against which the hand was struck, the anvil effect as he called it, and he demonstrated how this would have been caused with the hands protecting the head. There were other defence injuries to the hand where Dom Ansah had tried to grab the knife or knives being used against him. There were stab wounds to the back, to the chest, and to the left thigh.

20. This attack was witnessed in part by a neighbour watching from his window nearby, although his view was somewhat impeded. He described his growing horror at realising that the victim of the attack was being struck repeatedly with a machete brought down on him. What he

saw that night will stay with him forever. He saw at least three people taking part in the attack. I am quite sure on the evidence that you, Clayton Barker, and you, Jamie Chandler, were two of those three.

21. I cannot be sure on all the evidence that it was you, Charlie Chandler, who was wielding the machete. But I am quite sure that you were no mere spectator whilst the attack on Dom Ansah was taking place. You were there close by, ready to lend assistance if necessary and I am sure, as a matter of inference on all the evidence that you were in possession of a weapon of some kind at the scene, in all probability a knife. You were the only defendant to give evidence. You denied that your role was to cover the front door and intercept anyone from M4 who ran out of the house, but I am sure on all the evidence that this was indeed your role. You accepted, in cross-examination, that it would make no sense for anyone playing that role not to be armed. You could give no explanation for what you were doing with your right hand, apparently fiddling with your sleeve, when you walked away from the house and turned to face the camera in the dash cam footage. I am sure you were concealing a weapon. I am sure as well that you had taken a face covering with you, giving the lie to the suggestion that you had no idea of what was afoot until you saw the others put on masks and begin to climb over the fence. I am quite sure that you knew perfectly well from the outset what the plan was and that you were encouraging and supporting the attacks.

22. The five of you stayed together immediately after the attacks. At one stage or another you disposed of the clothing you had been wearing. Some clothing was burnt at Jamie Chandler's home, along with a mobile phone. Only one knife was ever recovered, which was put down a drain by Furzton Lake. That knife must have come from your home, Jamie Chandler, and may well have been taken to the scene by Earl Bevans. I am quite sure that Daniel Freeman was telling the truth in describing how you, Clayton Barker, told him you had disposed of a large knife or "Rambo sword" by Furzton Lake, but had retained the sheath which went with it. With considerable courage and presence of mind, Daniel Freeman made an excuse to leave his flat and summon the police when you confessed to him.

23. I am also quite sure on the evidence that you, Jamie Chandler,

confessed to Chloe Congdon that you had been involved in the stabbings, and showed her the blood staining on your tracksuit bottoms. You, Ben Potter, confessed to her as well. I am sure too that you, Ben Potter, were boasting to Katie Dart that you had taken part in the killings.

24. You Clayton Barker, wrote about the killings and your part in them in the rap lyrics found in your diary. You may have been imitating the style of others more famous, but I have no doubt that you were describing real events and revelling in what you had done. One passage in particular, at tab 16-page F of the jury bundle, describes all too graphically the stabbing of Dom Ansah, whom you said you "kept knifing" as well as Tom Honhold and Ryan Brown. You, Ben Potter, recorded yourself rapping and describing how you had stabbed one of the victims ["drilling"].

25. As well as sentencing each of you for two murders, I have to sentence you for two further offences of wounding with intent. It is common ground that the appropriate course is to reflect the additional criminality of those offences in fixing the minimum term for the offences of murder and to impose concurrent sentences for the offences of wounding. Applying the relevant Sentencing Council guideline, it is common ground that these offences would each be classified as category two, lesser harm but higher culpability, indicating a starting point of six years' custody after trial. The appropriate determinate sentence has to be halved in adding it into the minimum term and the principle of totality must also be observed.

26. There are a number of aggravating factors common to all of you which would justify an increase of the starting points in schedule 21. Some of the factors overlap.

27. First, I am satisfied that there was a significant degree of planning and premeditation. I accept that the opportunity for this ambush attack arose spontaneously on the night, but there was a hastily conceived plan to attend this party armed with weapons and wearing masks in order to take the rival gang members by surprise and inflict serious injury upon them. It is different, for example, from a situation where one gang, out looking for trouble, comes across a rival gang and engages spontaneously in fighting. Here this house was targeted specifically because M4 were there. The attack may not have been long in the planning but it was

planning and premeditation to a significant degree.

28. Second, this was a group attack by five defendants, a classic joint enterprise.

29. Third, the attack and the killings took place at a private house in full view of a large number of young people, causing untold trauma to those who witnessed it as their evidence and demeanour in the witness box demonstrated.

30. Fourth, knives and deadly weapons were carried to the scene. Even for a single offence of murder, the starting point for an adult would have been 25 years on that account alone.

31. Fifth, there was mental and physical suffering inflicted, specifically on Dom Ansah before death. He was chased, running quite literally for his life. There was a prolonged attack during which he was fully conscious, even finding the strength, quite remarkably, to get up and knock on the door of the house before he collapsed in the sitting room. He survived for a further three hours. It is clear from his mother's evidence that at the hospital he was well aware of the seriousness of his injuries and expected to die. He was also greatly distressed by knowledge of the death of his friend Ben Gilham-Rice, whose own suffering was cut short by his swift loss of consciousness.

32. Sixth, successful efforts were made to dispose of clothing and weapons, with the intention of avoiding detection.

33. All these aggravating factors must be reflected in the minimum term for each of you, together with the additional criminality of the separate offences of wounding with intent.

34. The aggravating factors have to be balanced, however, against the mitigating factors. They vary for each of you. There is the additional complication of the gross disparity in starting points as between the two juvenile defendants (12 years) and the three adult defendants (30 years), reflecting the disparity in your ages and the impact of that on your respective culpability. This makes it a particularly difficult case to sentence.

35. I have considered carefully all the authorities referred to in counsel's written and oral submissions. In particular, I have regard to the guidance in the leading case of R v Peters [2005] EWCA Crim 605; [2005] 2 Cr App R (S) 101, and the importance of recognising the need

for flexibility in applying the Schedule 21 starting points to young people for whom there is no step change in the level of maturity and responsibility simply by attaining the age of 18 or 21.

36. It has been submitted by counsel that an important common mitigating factor is the absence of an intention to kill, as opposed to an intention to cause serious bodily harm. I am prepared to accept that because it is impossible to know who inflicted the fatal stab wounds; it is impossible to say which if any of you intended to kill rather than to cause really serious injury. However, where there is such a sustained and frenzied joint attack, as there was on Dom Ansah, the difference between the two intentions pales almost into insignificance.

37. Nor is any real distinction to be drawn, on the facts of this case, between those who physically took part in stabbing the two victims who died and those who may not have stabbed but encouraged the others. By their verdicts, applying and following the Steps to Verdict documents for each of you, the jury must have concluded that each of you fell into one or other of these categories.

38. In the case of each of you the minimum term will run from today and you will have credit for the time already served on remand before trial and following conviction.

39. I bear in mind that the last nine months of the time you have served already has been made more difficult by the restrictions imposed by the Covid-19 pandemic. That is likely to remain the case for several months to come.

40. The surcharge provisions apply to this case and the order can be drawn up accordingly.

41. With those general observations, I turn to consider the individual circumstances of each of you. I have considered carefully all the written and oral submissions made by your counsel.

Clayton Barker

42. I deal first with you, Clayton Barker. You are now 20 years old. At the time of these offences, you were aged 19 years six months. At the age of 15 you were made the subject of a referral order for offences of robbery, but I do not treat that as an aggravating factor. For the reasons I have already explained, I am satisfied that you played a leading role in

411

this joint enterprise. As the independent evidence of the taxi driver confirmed, the others looked to you as the leader. You were steeped in the gang culture of B3 to the point of obsession, preoccupied with violence and knives. You were one of those who entered the house. If you did not yourself, take part in the stabbing of Ben Gilham-Rice you must have been very close to it and encouraging it. By your own admission in your diary, you stabbed Ryan Brown and Tom Honhold and I am quite sure you played an active physical leading role in stabbing Dom Ansah outside the house.

43. I have read the impressive letters from your uncle and your grandmother, and the letter which you have written yourself. I accept that you had a very troubled and deprived upbringing, born to a 14-year-old mother who was never able or willing to look after you properly. Your grandmother brought you up and there remains a strong bond between you as there is with your uncle, too. Your childhood was blighted by tragedy. Your father committed suicide when you were only seven or eight years old. It was you who found him hanging. Such events have scarred you emotionally. I accept that you looked to B3 almost as your substitute family. The writings in your diary do not, in my judgement, suggest a lack of maturity or intelligence. You knew perfectly well what you were doing that night when you led B3 into this fatal confrontation.

44. I accept that, as you say in your letter, you are genuinely remorseful and you understand the pain and grief of the families of your victims. The clearest expression of remorse would have been a guilty plea. I accept that the period you have already spent in custody has provided the stability which your life has lacked for so long.

45. The strongest mitigation in your case is your comparative youth, coupled with your troubled upbringing. You were still only 19 years old when these offences were committed, and that requires me to make a significant reduction from the starting point which would otherwise be appropriate after an increase to reflect the aggravating factors.

46. The minimum term in your case will be 28 years. There will be concurrent sentences of six years custody for each of the offences of wounding with intent.

47. Stand up please. Clayton Barker: For the offences of murder, counts 1 and 2, I sentence you to custody for life, with a minimum term

of 28 years from today, less 411 days already served. On counts 3 and 4 there will be concurrent sentences of six years detention in a young offender institution.

Charlie Chandler

48. I turn to you, Charlie Chandler.

49. You are now just 23 years old. You were aged 21 years nine months at the time of these offences. You have no previous convictions. For the reasons I have already explained I am satisfied that you played a full part in encouraging these attacks; your role was to remain outside the house to lend assistance if required. You did not take part physically in the stabbings inside the house. Nor can I be sure that you physically took part in the stabbing of Dom Ansah outside the house. Nevertheless, you were close by when that stabbing took place and you encouraged all the stabbings.

50. In your case too, the strongest mitigation is your comparative youth, coupled with the secondary role which you played, albeit a very serious role. I also have to ensure, in sentencing all of you, that there is no unfair disparity between the minimum terms you are required to serve beyond the disparity which necessarily flows from the different starting points for each of you under schedule 21.

51. The minimum term in your case will be 27 years. There will be concurrent sentences of six years imprisonment for each of the two offences of wounding with intent.

52. Stand up please. Charlie Chandler: For each of the offences of murder, counts 1 and 2, I sentence you to imprisonment for life, with a minimum term of 27 years from today, less 439 days already served. On counts 3 and 4 there will be concurrent sentences of six years' imprisonment.

Earl Bevans

53. I deal next with you, Earl Bevans. You are now 23 years old. At the time of these offences, you were aged 22 years six months, the oldest of all the defendants. You had previous convictions for battery in the context of domestic violence and resisting the police, for which you were made the subject of a community order in 2018 at the age of 21. However,

413

I do not treat those convictions as an aggravating factor.

54. You had no direct affiliation to the B3 gang, save your friendship with Ben Potter and Jamie Chandler, who were several years your junior, and your acquaintance with Clayton Barker. Nevertheless, you willingly went along with this criminal venture, seemingly to avenge the previous stabbing of Jamie Chandler and the humiliating assault and degradation of Ben Potter. I am quite sure that you went armed with a knife which was later disposed of in the drain near Furzton Lake. You are one of the four who entered the house. You admitted in your second defence statement that you had stabbed both Ben Gilham-Rice and Dom Ansah, although at that stage you were falsely suggesting you were in some way acting in self-defence. Nothing could have been further from the truth. By your participation in the stabbings, you were strongly encouraging those who inflicted the fatal injuries.

55. The greatest mitigation in your case is that you pleaded guilty to all these offences, albeit only on the first day of the trial. In accordance with the Sentencing Council guideline on reduction in sentence for a guilty plea, the maximum credit I should afford you is one-twentieth. As I observed at the time you entered those guilty pleas, to do so required some courage and is the best demonstration of your genuine remorse. However, in addition to allowing you the prescribed one-twentieth credit for plea, it is appropriate also to reflect to a modest extent, as part of your general personal mitigation, the remorse exemplified by your pleas. Although you denied these offences throughout your police interviews, there was a creeping acceptance of your guilt over the months leading up to the trial: first in your admission to the psychiatrist in November 2019 of taking some part in the stabbings, echoed in your revised defence statement in January 2020. Then in the week before the trial you made it plain to those representing you that you wished to plead guilty to all counts without prevarication. It was necessary for counsel to see you and confirm your instructions, and that process could not be completed until the day before your pleas were entered.

56. The other mitigation advanced in your case derives from the psychiatric report dated March 23 2020. Whilst not affording you any partial defence to murder, it is clear that you were suffering from an emotionally unstable personality disorder associated with traits of

414

antisocial personality disorder. This is likely to have led to some impairment of your judgement and actions at the material time. Although I take it into account, it does not, in my view, reduce your culpability to any significant extent. You knew perfectly well what you were doing and how serious it was.

57. Had you been convicted after a trial your minimum term would have been 29 years. To reflect your guilty plea and the additional mitigation of your genuine remorse, the minimum term in your case will be 27 years. There will be concurrent sentences of six years imprisonment for the offences of wounding with intent.

58. Stand up please. Earl Bevans: For each of the offences of murder, counts 1 and 2, I sentence you to imprisonment for life with a minimum term of 27 years from today, less 438 days already served. On counts 3 and 4 there will be concurrent terms of six years imprisonment.

Ben Potter

59. I deal next with you, Ben Potter. You are now 17 years old. At the time of the offences, you were aged 16 years two months. You have only one previous finding of guilt, possessing a knife in a public place, for which you were made the subject of a 12-month referral order in February 2019. These offences were committed during the currency of that order.

60. You were an enthusiastic member of B3. For reasons already explained, I am quite sure that you were one of the four who went into the house, and sure that you were armed with a large knife. I am sure, on the evidence, that you were physically involved in at least one of the fatal stabbings. You were boasting of it in the rap you recorded a month later when you were on the run and you were boasting of it to Katie Dart only hours after the murders. By your participation in the attacks, you were encouraging all the stabbings, with the intention that really serious harm should be inflicted. I have no doubt that your motivation related to the traumatic experience of the assault you had suffered yourself at the hands of M4 two years earlier. But that did not begin to justify your participation in these murders.

61. Your culpability has to be judged in the light of the fact that you were only just 16 at the time of the offences. You were in the company

of three much older defendants. I have considered carefully the psychology assessment report dated January 31 2020, and the insight it gives into your troubled upbringing and early involvement in gang culture. That report was prepared principally for the purpose of establishing whether you required an intermediary for the trial. You did not. In her written and oral submissions your counsel outlined in detail the background set out in the report. As a very young child you witnessed domestic violence and you never had the consistent support of a male father figure. You suffered from anxiety and depression from an early age. You first joined a gang at the age of 12, at a time when you were particularly vulnerable. When you joined the rival B3 gang, you suffered the humiliating and traumatic assault soon after your 14th birthday to which I have already referred. That led to further anxiety and depression, and panic attacks. You twice made some attempt at suicide. You did not engage fully with the mental health service to which you were referred by the youth offending team in 2019. All this sad background reduces to some extent your culpability for these very serious offences, but I am quite satisfied that your culpability remains high despite this and despite your young age. You had become streetwise and the picture of your involvement in the offences which was painted in the evidence does not suggest that you were particularly immature. You knew perfectly well what you were doing, and how serious it was.

62. The starting point of 12 years must be very substantially increased to reflect the fact that you have been convicted of two murders and two offences of wounding with intent. I have already identified the aggravating factors common to all of you. I accept in your case, as in the case of the others, that there may not have been an intention to kill, but the ferocity of the two fatal attacks was so great that the mitigation of that point is limited. Whilst in custody you have behaved well and made good progress with your studies which is to your credit. I take fully into account your young age and your troubled background.

63. The minimum term in your case will be 22 years. There will be concurrent sentences of four years detention for the two offences of wounding with intent.

64. Stand up please. Ben Potter: For each of the offences of murder, counts 1 and 2, I sentence you to be detained during Her Majesty's

pleasure, with a minimum term of 22 years from today less 432 days already served. On counts 3 and 4 there will be concurrent sentences of four years detention, pursuant to s.250 of the Sentencing Act 2020.

Jamie Chandler

65. I turn finally to you, Jamie Chandler. You are just 17 years old. At the time of the offences, you were aged 15 years nine months. You are therefore the youngest of all the defendants. You have no previous convictions. However, despite your young age and good character you took a particularly prominent part in these stabbings. You were an enthusiastic member of B3 and subscribed to all it stood for. You ordered the taxi which took the five of you to Archford Croft. That phone call was played during the trial. You sounded calm and self-assured, although you knew perfectly well what was planned. As I have already explained, I am quite sure that you were male 3 in the dash cam footage, chasing Dom Ansah in company with Clayton Barker. You were armed with a large knife. I am sure on all the evidence that you were one of the three who were taking part physically in the horrific sustained attack on Dom Ansah outside the house when he was finally cornered. You admitted to Chloe Congdon only hours later that you had been involved in the killings.

66. Your culpability has to be assessed in the light of the fact that you were only 15 years nine months old at the time of the offences. I bear in mind the Sentencing Council guideline: overarching principles for sentencing children and young people. I note in particular the sound general advice that children and young people are unlikely to have the same experience and capacity as an adult to understand the effect of their actions on other people, or to appreciate the pain and distress caused, and a child or young person may be less able to resist temptation, especially where peer pressure is exerted. It is said on your behalf that the fact that you yourself had been stabbed but survived effectively unscathed may have lessened your appreciation of the potentially fatal consequences of such stabbings. I find that impossible to accept. You are clearly an intelligent young man. You must have known that multiple stabbings of a victim were likely to risk not merely really serious injury but death. I am quite sure that the fact that you yourself had been stabbed was a

417

powerful motivating factor in your willingness and enthusiasm to take part in these very serious offences. I am sure that you believed Dom Ansah to have been involved in your stabbing, as was generally the word on the street on social media.

67. Following your own stabbing, your mother warned you of the consequences of continuing to involve yourself in this gang culture, as the extracts from text messages between the two of you clearly show. You chose to ignore that advice and continued to embrace the gang culture wholeheartedly. You had done well at school until 2018, excelling in film and media studies, which no doubt accounts in part for the professionalism of the B3 gang video. I accept that you had lost your way, dropping out of school, but I cannot accept that you were immature for your age. Like Ben Potter you had become streetwise. I am satisfied that your culpability remains high despite your young age and troubled background.

68. The starting point of 12 years must be very substantially increased in your case as well, to reflect the fact that you have been convicted of two murders and two offences of wounding with intent. I have already identified the aggravating factors common to you all. I accept that the time you have already spent in custody, and the experience of this trial, has altered your view of the gang culture in which you had become immersed. That cannot alter the seriousness of your culpability.

69. The starting point of 12 years must be very substantially increased in your case as well, to reflect the fact that you have been convicted of two murders and two offences of wounding with intent. I have already identified the aggravating factors common to you all. I accept that the time you have already spent in custody, and the experience of this trial, has altered your view of the gang culture in which you had become immersed. That cannot alter the seriousness of your culpability.

70. The minimum term in your case will be 22 years. For the two offences of wounding with intent there will be concurrent sentences of four years detention.

71. Stand up please. Jamie Chandler: For each of the two offences murder, counts 1 and 2, I sentence you to be detained during Her Majesty's pleasure, with a minimum term of 22 years from today, less 418 days you have already served. On counts 3 and 4 there will be

concurrent terms of four years detention, pursuant to s.250 of the Sentencing Act 2020.

SO THE B3 gang members will effectively be imprisoned for their 20's, 30's and 40's. No freedom, no girlfriends, no holidays, no visits to pubs or restaurants. Nothing that 20-Somethings and more can enjoy. An occasional visit by a friend or family member, but that's about it. Home will be a cell. Room service not available and for the next almost 30 years the infamous five will not enjoy the relative luxury of McDonald's, Domino's or KFC.

The Ministry of Justice says all meals served to prisoners must meet nutritional guidelines. At an average of £2 per head for food those guidelines are stretched to the limit.

Breakfast, is not, despite popular belief and the name of a prison comedy series, not porridge. Prisoners typically receive a pack containing cereal, milk and tea and coffee sachets. Lunch is a sandwich, wrap, or portion of pasta, served with fruit, crisps or biscuits, followed by dinner of curry, pie, or baked fish.

Will they care about their sentences? Initially, probably not. They sought revenge in gangland and in their perverted minds it had to be done. They did what they felt they had to do. Turf wars take no prisoners. Mission accomplished. They became instant heroes within B3, but such "fame" is likely to fade and as 10 years becomes 20, they are forgotten so-called heroes. Names from the long distant past.

Some may claim that the defendants were also victims, experiencing broken childhoods with love and parental guidance in short supply. Clayton Barker was born to a 14-year-old mother and brought up by his grandmother. Aged seven or eight, Barker found his father who had committed suicide by hanging. B3 became almost a surrogate family to him. Ben Potter started gang life aged 12.

But any sympathy vote only goes so far and few would use it as mitigation. Many people have awful childhoods, but do not go on to be violent criminals or even murderers. It is no excuse that those who are killed in gang warfare may not be fine upstanding citizens. Despite the revenge law of the gang, the law of the land does not allow any life to be taken.

As the judge said when he handed out life sentences to the B3 murderers, the real, life sentence is with the families of the two deceased.

SOME FINAL THOUGHTS
NO SUITS… NO SUNDAY BEST…
AND KEEP YOUR ROLEX
AT HOME

WHAT can sway a jury to its verdict, apart from the evidence it hears? Well, nothing else, of course, according to the oath or affirmation the jurors take when being sworn in. The jury will reach its verdict only on the evidence it hears in court from those involved in the trial.

Seriously?

It would be naive to think most of us do not have a bias to some degree, even if the subconscious operates without our awareness and over which we have no active control. It is something that is difficult to manage and is like a memory bank that stores our beliefs, life experiences and memories, all stored away somewhere in the back of our mind.

For starters, first impressions matter whoever you are and wherever you are. While the appearance of a witness should not influence a jury as it decides its verdict, it is difficult to think how anyone looks when giving evidence does not play a role in the way they are perceived.

The general public, which of course is what jurors are, tends to react, perhaps subconsciously, to what it sees and often makes judgments based on first sightings. Whether intentional or not, it can reveal an underlying bias.

A claimant who is the alleged victim of rape should not wear a low-cut dress (and yes, some do). Females should use minimal make-up because they are not on a Saturday night date. If they have been battered by an ex-partner they need to appear like a victim, not someone who would have Tinder on meltdown.

In a domestic violence case, the defence barrister would not want their client to have a mullet or Mohawk, a T-shirt with a dubious slogan, too much jewellery or tattoos covering their arms. The defendant who wore a baggy T-shirt with BAD on the front may as well have had

GUILTY on it.

Stereotypes tend to have an element of truth to them, so defending someone who does not look the part can add to their barrister's task.

Similarly, over-dressing can send out a negative message. Why is he wearing a suit, collar and tie? The tie usually with a knot too large. Is he trying to impress the jury? That is what it could look like. "I'm not really a violent thug. OK, yes, I am a violent thug, but I hope I don't look like one." Apart from the occasional police officer or expert witness, it is very unusual for anyone in a courtroom to appear wearing his best bib and tucker, especially a juror.

If you are on trial for burglary, money laundering or fraud then best to keep the Rolex (real or fake) at home. No winter tans (real or fake).

The dress code for court, whether you are a claimant, witness or defendant, should be simple and conservative with no expensive jewellery (see Rolex and winter tans) on display. Never dress to distract. The jury should look at you, not what you are wearing. As one barrister said: "Make your appearance anonymous and let your voice do the talking. Dress as if you were meeting your future in-laws for the first time."

One defendant took the detail of his dress code to pedantic levels. A police officer was giving evidence about the incident and said the defendant was wearing a Burberry baseball cap. The defendant tapped on the glass of the dock and beckoned his barrister, who, after consultation, told the jury: "My client is adamant it was Boss."

Advising a dress code for court may sound like the blindingly obvious, but too many witnesses are unaware of how they should be seen — and therefore perceived — by the jury.

Men — dark trousers (no jeans and trainers, even if you look like David Beckham or think you do), a dark jacket and a white shirt open (only one button) at the neck.

Ladies — nothing too tight, similar colour scheme to men, minimal jewellery (perhaps a wedding ring and anything of a religious meaning). No bright red lipstick or nail varnish. Display minimal leg if wearing a skirt and do not exaggerate how kind Mother Nature may have been to you.

For both — no T-shirts, especially with a slogan which could easily be misinterpreted however obvious or personal it may be to you. Do not even think about wearing a track-suit.

Respect the court and the chances are it will respect you.

SOME USA states' web sites advise on court attire. Massachusetts says females should not wear a see-through top, while both sexes must avoid clothes that "show or promote violence, sex acts, illegal drug use or profanity."

Louisiana tells females not to expose "any part of the breast, midriff, backside or undergarments."

Of course, when celebrities appear in court what they wear can almost be as important to some news outlets as what they say. The *Daily Mirror* reported: "TV Goddess Nigella Lawson's all black outfit and stern make-up said she was ready for battle. Gone is the homely domestic Goddess and in her place, a stern and serious woman ready to fight for her reputation.

"Nigella ditched her trademark bright clinging dresses for a sharp black trouser suit with serious power make-up — you don't want to mess with those eyebrows."

The message she was giving, according to the *Daily Mirror*, was: "I am ready for you."

Glamour could not hide its admiration (and some) for one English actor, not needing to answer its own question. The magazine said: "How utterly gorgeous did Jude Law look arriving at the Old Bailey? Jude kept it simple with a grey suit and a spotty tie."

It was less flattering about Britney Spears, saying: "We know that style in LA is laid-back, but we're pretty sure it's still *de rigeur* to dress up — at least a bit — for court. The sartorially hapless Britney Spears fell short of the mark when she wore a patterned dress with brown knee-high boots and a mismatching white handbag."

Ms Spears might have pointed out *Glamour's* spelling also fell short of the mark — it is *de rigueur*, not *de rigeur*.

It would normally not be newsworthy if a defendant went to court wearing a blouse and skirt... if they were female. The *Daily Mail* reported a new slant on this attire: "David Jeffries-Tipton was turned away from court for wearing shorts during this week's sweltering temperatures and stunned magistrates by strolling back for his hearing dressed in a blouse and skirt."

It is important that mobile phones are switched off. Not on silent as even that can interfere with the court's Wi-Fi. Switch it off, however unnatural that may be to many. While all witnesses are reminded of this, some either forget or can't be bothered. Even professionals in the witness box can make this mistake. A police officer from the Flying Squad was a few minutes into his evidence when his phone went off. The ring tone was the theme from the TV series The Sweeney.

The most blatant breach of phone security I saw was by a member of the family of a teenager who had been murdered and all seven defendants were found guilty on the joint-enterprise doctrine. Sitting in the public gallery for the sentencing, she took out her phone and started to film those in the dock. She was subsequently handed a three-month prison sentence for contempt of court.

NAMES may also raise a few jury eyebrows. One defendant changed his surname to Supercalifragilisticexpialidocious — no doubt a huge Mary Poppins fan.

The importance of asking how a name should be pronounced was underlined by the name of a young girl which was listed as "La-La." She initially was called "LaLa" but corrected the advocate by saying it was pronounced "La-dash-La."

Determining whether a witness is single, married or divorced can be a minefield. The witness was Belinda Ippi and the court was told Mrs Ippi would be next to give evidence. No doubt it flowed.

A defendant, no stranger to Her Majesty's pleasure, changed his surname to "Sir". It ensured this exchange with prison officers: "Sir." "Yes Sir…"

MOST CLAIMANTS have never been to court before unlike defendants, some of whom would qualify for frequent flyer cards. It can be a terrifying experience for a first-time claimant, even though they are the innocent party and not on trial. They will be made to feel as if they are, though, when cross-examined by a defence barrister who is probably university educated and has risen up the legal ladder to the top of their profession — a Crown Court advocate.

A courtroom rookie against a legal expert.

The defence barrister's job is to win the case for their client and discredit the evidence of someone who has allegedly been raped, beaten up or robbed. Despite a popular belief they are defending the guilty, only a jury can find someone guilty at a Crown Court. Until then, defendants remain innocent, in the eye of the law if not the claimant.

Claimants do not meet the prosecutor until the day of the trial. To ensure there is no coaching, the Crown advocate is accompanied by a member of the court staff when they speak to the claimant. Prosecutors should not provide the detail of or speculate upon the sort of questions a witness is likely to face or discuss with them how to answer the questions.

Police advise claimants not to start therapy before a trial as it may have an effect on the evidence they will give in court. There should be no pre-trial therapy.

Volunteers from the Witness Service, which was launched in 1994 and has a presence at all Crown and magistrates' courts in England and Wales, meet claimants and prosecution witnesses as they arrive at court. They will run through the court procedures in a private room. Claimants may have had a pre-trial visit to familiarise themselves with a courtroom, but WS volunteers should stop short of telling witnesses how to answer specific questions, apart from advising them of three of the most important words when giving evidence: "Less is more."

Keep replies to a minimum. Just answer the question, maybe with a simple yes or no… not true… incorrect. For example…

"Where were you on the night of the 12th?"

"I was with my mate Tony. We were in the King's Head watching England play Croatia."

No. Just say: "In the King's Head." If the advocate wants to know who you were with, or what you were doing, they will ask. Do not give any extra information.

Defence barristers are looking for their next question to come from a claimant's answer, so the less said the better.

"I suggest you are making this up…" is a popular point to put to a claimant. A natural response would be: "I'm not a liar" (that cannot be proven) or "why would I make it up?" (witnesses should only answer questions, not ask them).

So the reply should be: "I'm not." The question has been answered and leaves no scope for a follow up. Move on.

WS volunteers are not allowed to discuss the intricacies of claimants' evidence or even what the charge the defendant faces may be. Their role is to support prosecution witnesses by putting them at ease and most are grateful to have their mind taken away from what awaits them in court.

In contrast, defendants have been in regular contact with their legal team since pleading not guilty, which means there will be a trial. Can a defendant have legal tutoring? Officially no. Unofficially yes.

The Bar's Code of Conduct states: "A barrister must not... rehearse, practise or coach a witness in relation to his evidence." However, the Solicitors' Code of Conduct is less clear: "Witness coaching may amount to attempting to influence a witness and so misleading of a court" but stops short of saying it is prohibited.

Lord Justice Judge (who went on to be Lord Chief Justice, the Head of the Judiciary of England and Wales) said: "The witness should give his or her own evidence, so far as practicable, uninfluenced by what anyone else has said, whether in formal discussions or informal conversations. The rule reduces, indeed hopefully avoids, any possibility that one witness may tailor his evidence in the light of what anyone else said and equally avoids any unfounded perception that he may have done so.

"These risks are inherent in witness training. Even if the training takes place one-to-one with someone completely remote from the facts of the case itself, the witness may come, even subconsciously, to appreciate which aspects of his evidence are perhaps not quite consistent with what others are saying, or indeed not quite what is required of him. An honest witness may alter the emphasis of his evidence to accommodate what he thinks may be a different, more accurate, or simply better remembered perception of events."

Fine in theory, but different in practice. Every defendant is innocent until proven otherwise and their legal team, whose duty is to defend their client and do all it can for the jury to return a not guilty verdict, is likely to stage a mock trial with someone assuming the role of the prosecutor.

Crown Court advocates are masters at casting doubt on what might have initially appeared a seemingly black and white issue but which can soon have various shades of legal grey. Jurors do not like to see witnesses badgered or harassed and the judge would stop an advocate if it is felt they have crossed the line. The most effective method of cross-examination is to be controlled, meticulous and methodical.

Barristers are aware that if a juror takes a dislike to them for whatever reason it could have a negative knock-on effect on how they view their client, whether it is the claimant or defendant. Grandstanding must be avoided. While the courtroom is, to some extent, a legal stage, barristers are there to act on behalf of their client, not auditioning for a movie.

One barrister said: "Your audience — the jurors — are watching you from the moment they walk in, long before you say anything. Their only entertainment in the courtroom is watching you. They can't check their phones, talk to one another or do anything but look and listen. They'll notice everything you do and draw conclusions about who you are.

"We'll never know how much we can affect a verdict on a personal level. It's often hard to separate the messenger from the message. If we like somebody who's delivering a message, we're more likely to accept their message.

"At the same time, it would be an oversimplification to say that just because a jury doesn't like an advocate, that's why it ruled against their client. We can make too much of that."

Barristers prepare their arguments meticulously, often rehearsing what they will say and how they say it in front of a mirror. In court, you get one hit, one chance, one take so an important part of their cross-examination will be to find the arguments that the other side would think of and contradict them. Be prepared for that. Leave any surprises out of court.

And however well the defence barrister believes they have done to put their case, the prosecution usually wins. The conviction rate at Crown Court is 80 per cent.

Yet when all is said and done, how the 12 most important people in the courtroom reach their verdict remains one of life's great secrets.

Because only the jurors know how they decide the verdict.

Printed in Great Britain
by Amazon